"Information through Innovation"

Local Area Networking
with
Novell® Software

Second Edition

Alvin L. Rains
Casper College

Michael J. Palmer
University of Wyoming

bf

boyd & fraser publishing company

Dedication
To Sally, Shawn, and Kristy — MJP
To Deborah, Jennifer, and Greta — ALR

Senior Acquisitions Editor: James H. Edwards
Associate Production Editor: Jean Castro
Compositor: Octal Publishing, Inc.
Interior Design: Octal Publishing, Inc.
Cover Design: Hannus Design Associates
Cover Photo: Paul Steele, The Stock Market
Manufacturing Coordinator: Tracy Megison
Marketing Manager: Eileen Pfeffer

© 1994 by boyd & fraser publishing company
A Division of South-Western Publishing Co.
One Corporate Place • Ferncroft Village
Danvers, Massachusetts 01923

International Thomson Publishing
boyd & fraser publishing company is an ITP company.
The ITP trademark is used under license.

This book is printed on recycled, acid-free paper that meets
Environmental Protection Agency standards.

Manufactured in the United States of America

Library of Congress Cataloging-in-Publication Data
Rains, Alvin L., 1948–
     Local area networking with Novell software / Alvin L. Rains,
Michael J. Palmer. —2nd ed.
    p.   cm.
    Palmer's name appears first on the earlier edition.
    Includes index.
    ISBN 0-87709-041-6
    1. Local area networks (Computer networks)   2. NetWare (Computer
file) I. Palmer, Michael J., 1948–   . II. Title.
TK5105.7.R35   1993
004.6'8—dc20

93-8136
CIP

3 4 5 6 7 8 9 10 M 7 6 5 4

Brief Contents

Contents

CHAPTER 5   **The LAN Workstation**   **87**

CHAPTER 9   **NetWare and Windows Integration**   **215**

CHAPTER 10   **Network Management**   **249**

Preface

Novell's NetWare has not remained static since the first edition of this book. Novell continues to introduce new products and capabilities. Novell's standing as the leading source of network operating systems has grown with each new product.

About This Book

As NetWare has evolved, so has the second edition of this book. The book still targets students and NetWare system managers. In the process, the book is changed to reflect new features of NetWare, such as NetWare version 4. There is still a strong introduction to networking components that is linked with use of NetWare. But new advances in networking are included to parallel enhancements in NetWare.

The practical side of the book has evolved to provide start-to-finish information on setting up a file server, from selecting the CPU to setting-up network printers. There is also more on file server management, application software installation, memory management, hardware selection, and problem solving.

Every chapter has been revised or rewritten. Several new chapters have been added to broaden the scope of the text. There are new chapters on operating systems, network printing, NetWare and Microsoft Windows, and future directions of technology.

Five appendices have been added to the book for general reference. They provide information on NetWare commands and utilities, hardware diagnostics, menu design, login scripts, the capture utility, and Microsoft Windows.

Organization

Chapter 1 introduces networking basics and describes why LANs have become an important part of computing. Chapter 2 presents more complex networking concepts such as network topologies, standards, media, and protocols. Chapter 3 compares non-network operating systems with network operating systems, using NetWare as the networking standard. Chapter 4 shows how to configure the file server hardware and install NetWare. Chapter 5 focuses on workstation selections and connecting the workstation to the network. Chapter 6 shows how to set up a file server, including creating users, establishing directories, and assigning security access. Chapter 7 describes how to install application software such as word processors and databases on a file server. Chapter 8 explains how to establish network printing for users. Chapter 9 shows how Microsoft Windows can be integrated into NetWare. Chapter 10 describes how to successfully manage all aspects of a network. Chapter 11 explains the details of interconnecting networks across town and around the world. Chapter 12 introduces new technologies such as wireless networking.

Each chapter begins with a statement of chapter objectives. A list of key terms is provided at the end of each chapter. The key terms are highlighted in bold when first introduced in the chapter. The chapter questions and exercises are new to this edition, and they reflect changes in NetWare and networking.

Novell NetWare is a major force in today's computer industry and this book is intended to give you a strong start in mastering this powerful networking tool.

Acknowledgements

The authors especially thank Jim Edwards for making this book possible. We also appreciate the dedicated assistance of the boyd & fraser staff. Jean Castro in particular was invaluable in coordinating and shepherding the production of this book. Casper College was instrumental in supporting all the efforts that made this book possible. Finally, and very importantly, we thank our families for their profound support.

Local Area Networking: The Basics

Chapter Objectives

The objectives of this chapter are the following:

- To define computer networking.
- To provide an introduction to local, metropolitan, and wide area networks.
- To explain the popularity and growth of networking.
- To explain network components and terms.

Introduction

The use of local area networking (LAN) technology has grown phenomenally in businesses, public schools, industry, and higher education. LAN technology has proven to be very effective in making microcomputer applications available to many users. Also, new LAN software applications are rapidly emerging. More and more people now depend on LANs for processing and sharing information. LANs have taken over what were once firm minicomputer strongholds, and they are now challenging the mainframe computer.

At the forefront of this technological upheaval is the Novell Corporation and its NetWare operating system for LANs. Novell has been very successful with LANs, in both industry and education. Novell

LANs have become popular for a variety of reasons. First, they enable a range of microcomputers or workstations to be linked together for information sharing. IBM, IBM-compatible, Apple Macintosh, Unix workstations, and other computers can be networked together to share messaging capabilities, common software, documents, reports, data, and desktop publications. Networks of these computers can be as small as three or as large as 250 units. These networks can operate as independent units, or they can be linked to other networks or to many popular mini and mainframe computers.

Another attractive option of Novell networks is that they can host nearly all commercially available microcomputer software. The options include word processors, spreadsheets, databases, desktop-publishing software, computer-language compilers, office-automation software, electronic mail, and computer-aided design (CAD) software.

Novell file servers, the heart of Novell LANs, can be made by any of a number of manufacturers. File servers can contain a host of add-on equipment such as disk drives, disk controllers, memory expansion, and tape-backup equipment. Novell tests equipment for compatibility and provides that information to prospective buyers. Novell is not unique in offering these advantages, but it brings together one of the most effective software and hardware environments available.

This book is designed to explore that environment, along with specific ways to establish and enhance the Novell networking system. In this chapter, we begin the networking story with an introduction to networks.

Definition of a Network

A **network** is a communication system that links together people and their computing resources. The link may extend across a room, throughout a building, or to the other side of the world. You may have a computer and printer on your desk at work. If your computer is not connected to any other resources, it is a "stand-alone" system. If you can access other computers through cable or telephone hookups, then you are part of a network.

Each network has two main components. The first is **hardware,** which consists of computers, printers, cable, and communication equipment (see Figure 1.1). The computers can be mainframes, minicomputers, or microcomputers. Printers range from simple dot matrix printers to complex laser printers. Cable is used to physically link computers and printers. Communication equipment also connects to the cable and serves many purposes. Some communication devices extend the distances

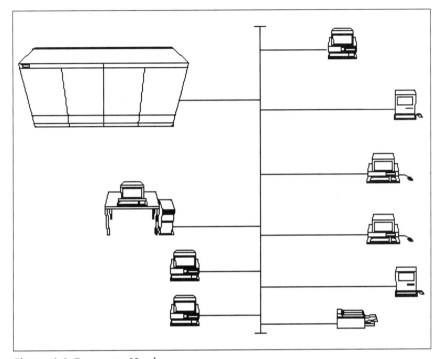

Figure 1.1 *Computer Hardware*

reached by cable, and some may link networks in different cities or countries. Other devices join different networks, such as a Novell network with Digital's Pathworks network.

The second component of a network is **software,** as shown in Figure 1.2. Software is a set of computer programs that enable people to accomplish their work. Examples of software include word processors, spreadsheets, scientific computation routines, and information databases. There is also software that enables one computer to communicate with another on a network. The NetWare software made by Novell performs communication tasks between computers, as well as more complex tasks.

Local Area Network

A **local area network** is a system that permits computing devices such as micro, mini, and mainframe computers to communicate with one another over distances from a few feet to six miles.

Devices on the LAN coexist in a **decentralized computing** relationship, which means that the network gives each device the same priority.

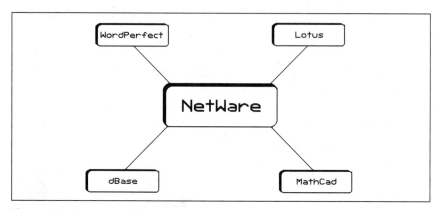

Figure 1.2 *Computer Software*

No single device has more access to the network than any other device. By comparison, a mainframe computer exerts **centralized computing** control, where some devices have higher priority than others.

Communication distances on a LAN are defined as "moderate" by the Institute of Electrical and Electronic Engineers (IEEE). (This group consists of committees that work to establish standards for LANs.) LANs link computer devices within a single building, or among several adjacent buildings within a range of up to six miles.

Communication speeds on a LAN are also defined as moderate by the IEEE. Speeds are rated in terms of the number of data bits per second (bps), which are transmitted over a communication medium, such as a cable. Transmission speeds for LANs without fiber-optic cable range from 1 Mbps (million bits per second) to 20 Mbps. LANs that use fiber-optic cable can attain data transmission rates of 100 Mbps. (The transmission rate section in this chapter presents more information about data transmission speeds.)

Several LANs can be connected to one another, which means that a user on one LAN can access information on a different LAN. One or more LANs connected together form an **internetwork**.

Metropolitan Area Network

A LAN grows into a **metropolitan area network (MAN)** as it spans the geographic limits of a city. Four colleges networked within the same city limits would form a MAN. MANs extend up to about ten miles.

Wide Area Network

A **wide area network (WAN)** links computer users who are separated over a wide geographic area. WANs use public and private telecommunications facilities to access computers all over the world. For example, BITNET and Internet are wide area networks that connect educational computer users in the United States and in several foreign countries. NSFNET is a wide area network started by the National Science Foundation to provide access to supercomputer sites throughout the United States.

LANs, or an internetwork of LANs, can be connected to a wide area network. Thus a scientist in Colorado can use a microcomputer to log onto a LAN in his or her building and reach a supercomputer in Illinois by connecting to a WAN.

Why a Lan?

Computing is an evolving technology. Twenty years ago most computing was done on mainframes or minicomputers. Today LANs are competing in areas once dominated by mainframes and minicomputers.

Why is the LAN such a popular technology? There are several reasons. First, *the success of the LAN is linked to the success of the microcomputer.* The microcomputer has introduced large numbers of people to computing—from business people, secretaries, and teachers to students and factory workers. The LAN offers a way for people in a small geographic area to communicate with one another and share microcomputer resources. The LAN also provides a way for microcomputer users to communicate through electronic mail. Electronic mail enables users to send messages to one another and to establish bulletin boards of common information.

Resources such as programs and files can be made available for common use. It is no longer necessary to have 20 separate copies of a word processing application for 20 microcomputers. One LAN version with 20 licenses can be installed instead. And two users can share the same word processing file without walking from desk to desk with a diskette.

Devices are also shared on a LAN. For example, it is unnecessary for every microcomputer user to have his or her own printer. Twenty microcomputer users can share two or three printers, or they can share one modem.

Cost is a second reason LANs are popular. Because resources are shared, the cost of equipment goes down. Fewer printers are needed, as compared to stand-alone microcomputer installations. Also, the cost of software is reduced on a LAN.

Maintenance is a third advantage of the LAN. With stand-alone computers, 20 users may have 20 copies of a word-processing application. When an upgrade to that application becomes available, it is necessary to install the upgrade 20 times. On a LAN with 20 word-processing users, only one copy of the upgrade needs to be installed.

Mainframes and Minis Versus LANs

Mainframes and minicomputers are based on a central CPU (central processing unit) design. The system consists of terminals or workstations connected directly to the mainframe or mini. Access to these computers is controlled by the CPU. Each connection gets a "timeslice" of the CPU or is assigned a priority level. The timeslice is the amount of CPU time the connection shares with all other connections. If the timeslice is small for a particular connection, that user has less access to the computer's resources than another user with a higher timeslice. Or, if the connection's priority is low, the user has less access than users with connections assigned a higher priority.

Programs and data files are also centralized on mainframes and mini-computers. They do not reside on individual terminals or workstations.

LANs are not based on centralized computing; they are *decentralized*. Each user has the same access to the LAN. Also, because the LAN is decentralized, programs and data files can be distributed over the LAN. Programs and files may be stored on individual workstations or on the LAN.

Programs stored on the LAN file server are not run from the file server. Instead, when a workstation requests the use of a program, the server loads that program into the workstation's memory. The program is then run from the workstation. Mainframe and minicomputer programs are not transferred to the workstation or terminal. They are run on the host computer.

Mainframe and minicomputer software is written for specific brands and models of computers. Thus software that runs on one computer may not be available on another model, even when both computers are made by the same company. Data files, too, are often not compatible between different models.

Because LAN technology is based on the microcomputer, there is a large volume of applications software available. The software will work on most LAN equipment without compatibility problems. For example, the Lotus 1-2-3 spreadsheet program will run on IBM, Zenith, Compaq,

Gateway, CompuAdd, and many other computers. A data file created on a Zenith computer can be ported to a Compaq computer.

Software costs are higher for mainframes and minicomputers than for microcomputer-based LANs. Electronic mail packages, spreadsheets, and databases for mainframes and minis are more expensive than the equivalent software for microcomputers. Maintenance costs are also higher for mainframes and minicomputers than for LANs consisting of microcomputers. This is true for hardware and for software maintenance. Figure 1.3 lists the differences between mainframes and minicomputers versus LANs.

Mainframes and Minicomputers Compared to LANs	
Mainframes and Minicomputers	**LANs**
Centralized processing	Decentralized processing
Programs run on the host	Programs run on the workstation
Limited range of software	Wide range of software
More expensive software	Less expensive software
Costly maintenance	Less costly maintenance

Figure 1.3 *Mainframes and Minicomputers Compared to LANs*

Growth of Networks

Networking is a technology that has grown rapidly. There are four reasons for this growth (see Figure 1.4). *First, many organizations are downsizing their computing from mini and mainframe computers to microcomputer networks.* **Downsizing** is a process that enables organizations to replace their traditional mini and mainframe operations with a network of microcomputers. These organizations can save millions of dollars per year by replacing a large IBM mainframe with a microcomputer-based network. The hardware and software costs are normally less for the microcomputer network than for an IBM mainframe. Maintenance costs are also lower for the network. Not only is money saved but the network is more robust since it provides access to more application software.

The second reason for network growth is the ability to access databases of information and for people to communicate electronically over vast distances. We are rapidly approaching a time when nearly all

---

Reasons for the Growth of Networks

- Organizations are downsizing
- Access to databases and electronic mail
- Computer resource sharing
- Evolution of communication standards

Figure 1.4 *Reasons for the Growth of Networks*

information entered into computers can be accessed from your home or office using **modems**. Already, networked computer users can search library holdings in other states or find databases of medical research. The Library of Congress is working on a project to digitize some of its information for network access. For example, a researcher interested in President Kennedy would be able to retrieve text about the Kennedy administration, as well as pictures and sound clips.

CompuServe and Prodigy are two other examples of information databases available through wide area networks. Both publish online news and weather updates, enable people to make plane reservations, and offer a large array of shopping alternatives. They also provide electronic mail communication and access to databases on topics such as investments.

The third reason for network growth is the ability to share resources. People on networks can share application software such as WordPerfect. They can share WordPerfect text files for common editing, and they can share devices such as a laser printer to print their WordPerfect files.

The fourth reason for network growth is movement toward standards. Standards enable communication between different types of networks and computers. For example, the Federal Government is working on a standard called **Government Open Systems Interconnection Profile (GOSIP),** which would allow different networks to communicate.

There are also several defacto standards. Defacto standards are those that have become widely used by vendors and users without formal acknowledgment from any one group. One example is Novell's network communication protocol, Internetwork Packet Exchange (IPX). IPX is a format for sending data between computers. It has become a defacto standard because of Novell's popularity. IPX is discussed in more detail in Chapter 2.

Types of Networks

A network can also be classified by the hardware used. For example, some networks use only microcomputers. These are *microcomputer-based* networks (see Figure 1.5). Other networks consist of a mainframe accessed by terminals. These are *host-based*, where the mainframe is the host that makes software applications accessible to terminals. Figure 1.6 illustrates a host-based network. *Workstation-based* networks use large computer workstations such as Sun or IBM workstations. These are typically Unix workstations with computing power greater than micro-computers. There are also combination networks that are host- as well as microcomputer-based.

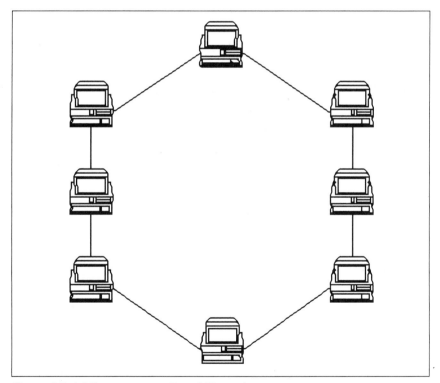

Figure 1.5 *A Microcomputer-Based Network*

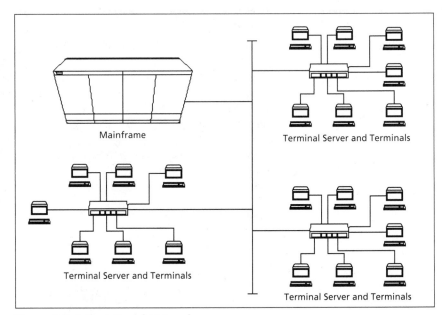

Figure 1.6 *A Host-Based Network*

Novell Network Components

File servers and workstations   NetWare LANs consist of one or more file servers and workstations. The **file server** is a microcomputer that allows other microcomputers to share its resources. Novell's NetWare is installed on the file server, and this **operating system** makes the server's resources available to the microcomputers that log on to it. In one sense, the file server is a large hard disk that stores programs and files for other microcomputers. The file server also connects to printers that are made available to logged-on microcomputers.

The NetWare operating system is an administrator of resources, similar to DOS (disk operating system). They both control input/output activities, access to the CPU, and the commands that are available to the computer user. However, NetWare permits more than one user to access programs and files. DOS is a single-user system.

Because DOS is a popular operating system, NetWare provides a way to use DOS commands. NetWare is loaded onto the file server, and DOS can be made available from the server to the workstation, like any other software provided by the NetWare host.

Microcomputers that log-on to a file server are called **workstations**. Workstations may be as small as a microcomputer with an 8088 CPU, or as large as an 80486 microcomputer or Macintosh. They can also vary in brand and model. Some workstations have no disk drives and rely entirely on the file server's network drive.

Network Shell   The **network shell** is software that is loaded onto the workstation. In the Novell operating system, the shell consists of IPx.COM and NETx.COM. The NETx.COM file was specific to a DOS version so that NET3.COM was used with workstations using DOS 3. NETx.COM is now used for all DOS versions.

Node   Any device that is connected to the network is called a **node**. Nodes consist of file servers, workstations, communication devices, and printer devices. Nodes have access to network and communication services. All nodes have a unique network address.

Protocol   Workstations communicate with each other and the file server through a **protocol**. A protocol is a set of rules that determine the formatting, timing, sequencing, and error checking in communications. NetWare uses the **Internetwork Packet Exchange** (IPX) and **Sequenced Packet Exchange** (SPX) protocols.

Cabling   Nodes are connected to the LAN through *cabling*. The cable provides a medium for transmission of electronic signals. The physical layout of cable connections is the LAN **topology**. Nodes can be connected in several different ways—for example, in a star layout or a ring pattern.

Packets   Data travels from one node to another in **packets**. A packet is a discrete unit of data bits. Each packet contains the following information:

- The address of the node that sent the packet
- The address of the node that is to receive the packet
- The data to be transmitted
- Error-control information

Transmission Rate   The speed at which data packets travel on a LAN is called the *transmission rate*. The transmission rate is measured in **bits per second** (bps). Each LAN cabling method has a bps rating from 1 Mbps to 100 Mbps. The rating applies to ideal transmission conditions only.

In a typical LAN installation, there are many factors that increase the time it takes for information to go from one node to another. For example, some LANs have a high number of *packet collisions*. When packets collide they have to be retransmitted, which slows the rate of communication. Another example of slower communication is the network where cabling runs exceed the maximum lengths as specified by the vendor. These networks will experience low transmission rates and a high number of lost packets.

Communication rates are also affected by the characteristics of file servers and workstations. A file server with a slow CPU clock speed, such as 16 MHz, will slow the exchange of information more than a server with a higher clock speed, such as 33 MHz. And communications will be slow to a workstation having low memory access and low disk drive access ratings.

Summary

LAN implementations are a vital part of computing. Many LANs use Novell NetWare file servers to create access to popular microcomputer software, such as word processors and spreadsheets. LANs can make computing cost effective and versatile when compared with traditional mainframe and minicomputer installations.

There are two main components of LANs. The first is hardware that consists of computers, printers, cable, and communication devices. The second is software such as NetWare, WordPerfect, and Lotus.

NetWare LANs use file servers to make a variety of software available to workstations. The network shell enables workstations to communicate with NetWare. Novell's network shell uses the IPX protocol to transfer packets of data to and from a NetWare file server.

Key Terms

Bits Per Second (bps)   The transmission speed of data on a network. Depending on the type of cabling and the LAN topology, transmission speeds range from 1 Mbps to 100 Mbps.

Centralized Computing   A system of control used by mainframe and minicomputers that assigns a priority on communications with the CPU.

For example, some terminals have more access (higher priority) to computer functions than other terminals. Mainframes and minicomputers also are centralized, in that software is run on the computer, not on the terminal or workstation.

Decentralized Computing   A system of control on a LAN where all devices have equal priority when communicating with the LAN. Also, software is distributed so it is run on the workstation and not on the file server.

Downsizing   The process of replacing large expensive computers, such as mainframes and minicomputers, with less expensive computers and networks.

File Server   A computer system that runs a network operating system such as NetWare. The file server also has disk storage shared by network users and makes software applications available to other computers. The file server can be a micro, mini, or mainframe computer.

GOSIP (Government Open Systems Interconnection Profile)   A standard used by computer vendors when manufacturing their products. GOSIP is designed to enable government agencies to use multivendor hardware systems and networks for joint communication.

Hardware   Computer equipment, such as computers, printers, communication devices, and cable.

Internetwork   Two or more physical networks connected through communication devices to one another.

IPX (Internetwork Packet Exchange)   Software that is used by NetWare to enable communication between workstations and file servers on a network.

LAN   (Local Area Network)   A system that consists of file server(s), workstations, printers, and communications devices linked together by cable. LANs operate within a small geographic area, such as within a building or throughout a college campus.

MAN (Metropolitan Area Network)   A network of computer devices that operates within an extended geographic area, such as a city.

Modem   A device that transmits electronic signals over telephone lines permitting one computer to communicate with another. Modems send and receive signals that are translated for the host computer. A modem can be external to the computer or a circuit board installed inside a computer.

Network   A system of interconnected hardware and software components. Through interconnection, these components link people and permit the sharing of computing resources.

Networked Computer   A computer that can communicate with other computers by modem or by cable hook-up.

Network Shell   Software used on a workstation to enable it to communicate with NetWare. The workstation's shell directs command requests to DOS or NetWare. The shell is loaded into a workstation's memory. It stays in memory while a user is logged into NetWare. The shell files are IPX.COM and NETX.COM.

Node   A device connected to a network such as a workstation, file server, printer, or communication device.

Operating System (OS)   Software that provides the interface between the user and the computer system. For example, NetWare is a network operating system that enables multiuser access to one computer, the file server. DOS (Disk Operating System) is a system designed to allow a user to control the activities of a single computer.

Packet   A discrete unit of data bits transmitted over a network. The unit includes addressing information, error control information, and data.

Protocol   A set of rules that establish how computers communicate with one another. IPX is a protocol used by NetWare.

Software   Computer programs that enable people to accomplish work tasks on a computer. Word processors, spreadsheets, operating systems, and information databases are examples of computer software.

SPX (Sequenced Packet Exchange)   A communication protocol used by NetWare.

Stand-alone Computer   A computer system that is not connected to a network.

Topology   The way nodes are physically connected—for example, in a star or ring configuration.

Transmission Rate   The speed at which data travels on a network. The rate is measured in bits per second.

WAN (Wide Area Network)   A system that connects computers located in different cites, countries, or continents. Most WANs use some public communications access, such as the Internet.

Workstation   A computer system connected to a network for the purpose of accessing applications software, such as a spreadsheet. Workstations are also referred to as nodes and clients.

Questions and Exercises

1. (a) Compute the cost of a computer lab that has 20 stand-alone computers, each with its own dot matrix printer. Assume that the computers cost $2,500 each, the printers cost $350 each, and printer cables cost $15 each. Every computer will have WordPerfect at $100 per computer.

   (b) Compute the cost of a computer lab with 20 networked computers. The computers are $2,500 each and network interface cards are $135 for each computer. The cabling is $300 for the lab. One lab printer is purchased for $2,000 with a $15 printer cable. The file server with operating system costs $10,000. A network copy of WordPerfect is $99 plus $35 each for 20 licenses.

   (c) Which alternative appears the most favorable if you are looking only at the costs of both approaches? Which alternative is the most attractive if you are examining the time to set up the hardware and install the software for the workstations and the file server? Would the furniture and space requirements be different? Please explain.

2. Provide three reasons why a network is a better solution for a given business. State the type of business and any of your assumptions such as use of application software, type of business, experience of the users, etc.

3. Is the growth of networks primarily driven by the network vendors "selling" users on buying networks or is the growth of networks driven by the users demanding a better solution to stand-alone computers? Provide an adequate explanation.

4. You are at home and have a modem to dial into your organization's network. Is your workstation now part of a LAN or a WAN, or is it not part of either? Explain why.

5. Obtain an article that describes the growth of microcomputer-based networks at the cost of mini or mainframe computers. Using the article, describe why microcomputer-based networks are growing. Comment on whether microcomputer-based networks will completely replace mini and mainframe computers.

Network Topology, Standards, Protocols, and Media

Chapter Objectives

The objectives of this chapter are the following:

- To explain the three common network topologies: bus, ring, and star.
- To explain the OSI seven-layer model for networking.
- To describe network protocols and access methods.
- To illustrate cabling technologies and options.

Introduction

A local area network connects nodes in a building, or it connects a series of buildings together, with cable. Two important local area networking considerations are the layout of the network nodes, such as computers, and the **media**, or cable connecting the nodes. The typical node is a desktop computer. Connecting the nodes with cable or linking computers is like drawing lines from desk to desk. The lines take the shape of a geometric figure, which is referred to as the **topology**.

The choice of topology and cable has a significant impact on the success or failure of a network. Each topology and cable has characteristics that determine cost, performance, and manageability. Designing a network topology requires answering the following questions:

- **Segmentation:** Does the network have the capability to be divided into smaller sections, which improve network support and reliability?
- **Diagnostics and troubleshooting:** Is the network accompanied by diagnostic software and hardware to facilitate the analysis of network problems? An important consideration is whether the network diagnostics can be used without shutting down the network.
- **Bandwidth:** This refers to the network-cable transmission qualities. Does the transmission design enable smooth and fast flow of data along the cabling, without bottlenecks or excessive data collisions?
- **Manageability:** Does the network topology support management control systems? Is there sufficient ability to control access, security, and user applications?
- **Bridging:** Will the topology allow additional LANs or mini and mainframe computers to be connected for future growth?
- **Expansion:** Does the network topology provide for expansion? Relative considerations are whether new nodes can be added and moved easily.

This chapter explains network topologies and discusses LAN standards, protocols, and media. The topologies covered here include bus, ring, and star. Also, LAN standards and protocols are described along with media types such as twisted pair, coaxial, and fiber-optic cable.

Network Topology

Network topology is the geometric or physical layout of the nodes on a network. The nodes are connected together with sections of cable, which are often called **links**. At its simplest, a network can be considered a series of nodes and links. The resulting layout of the network is then largely determined by the building containing the network.

When nodes are linked one after another down a hallway, the layout is a straight line or **bus topology**. Another topology may connect each node with a separate cable. In a roughly drawn layout, this arrangement resembles, and is named, a **star**. A third common topology is the **ring**, which is like a bus with the two end links coming together at the same node.

The three topologies are considered below in terms of comparative cost, support, and performance. All of these factors are important and have an impact on the decision of which type of network to install.

BUS TOPOLOGY

The bus is the most common topology. As an observer might determine by examining the physical layout of offices and the links connecting the offices, this topology generally results in the shortest network links or amount of cable. Cable length is certainly a cost factor when evaluating topology alternatives. Figure 2.1 illustrates a bus topology. Each node is connected to another node, and the file servers can be connected at any location on the cable, as can workstations. The bus topology has two distinct ends, which are fitted with terminating devices so the signal is properly managed.

The digital signal is sent from one node to all the other nodes on the cable, much in the same way that a city bus picks up passengers and goes to all stops on its route, with passengers getting off at their designated stops. Just as the city bus goes from one stop to the next, the network bus topology goes from one point to the next on the network. The obvious problem occurs when the city bus stops running. All the passengers on the route are affected. On the electronic route, if one link is broken, the entire network goes down.

The bus topology uses the least amount of cable to link the nodes and also closely fits the physical layout of most offices. The cost advantage of using less cable is more than offset by the higher support costs of keeping the network operational. If one link is faulty, communication is broken to all of the nodes on the network. Further, adding nodes to the bus requires that the cable be broken and the network be shut down. Troubleshooting cable problems requires investigating the entire cable from one terminator node to the other.

RING TOPOLOGY

As the name "ring" implies, a ring topology is a network where the nodes are physically connected to two adjacent nodes to form a closed loop. In the standard design, the signal travels around the loop in a

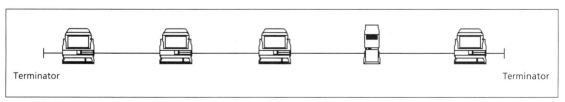

Terminator   Terminator

Figure 2.1 *Bus Topology for a LAN*

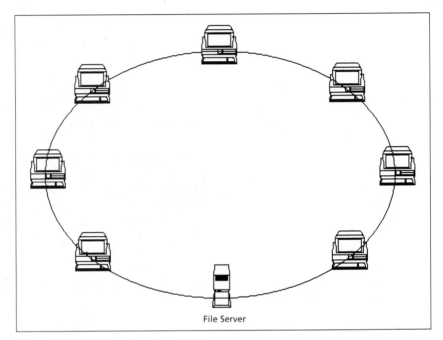

File Server

Figure 2.2 *Ring Topology for a LAN*

single direction, usually clockwise. The data are sent around the ring until the desired node is reached, at which time the next node takes its turn to send data around the ring. Figure 2.2 illustrates the standard ring design topology.

A variation on the single ring topology is the two-ring topology. With two rings, each unit of data is put on both rings simultaneously. This provides data redundancy so that if one ring is damaged, data continue to reach the destination on the other ring. The FDDI protocol discussed later in this chapter uses two rings.

The classic ring topology is characterized by permitting only one packet of data to be active on the ring at any given moment. More efficient versions of this topology permit several packets of data to be active at the same time. Another characteristic of the ring topology is that nodes will see some traffic that is not intended for them.

STAR TOPOLOGY

In the typical star topology each node sends data through a central hub, much like telephone lines connected to a central switching office. The

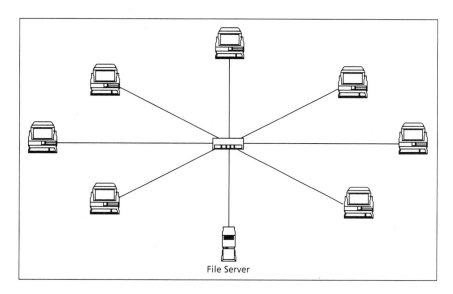

File Server

Figure 2.3 *Star Topology for a LAN*

hub can be an intelligent device like a data PBX switch, which takes data from one node and sends them to another designated node. Passive hubs do not switch signals but simply split the signal to all branches in the star. Each node is responsible for receiving the data. Figure 2.3 shows the typical star topology.

Nodes are added at the hub and do not require the network to be disrupted. A node can also be removed from the hub without affecting the network. A star topology is therefore easier to support than other topologies because troubleshooting and wiring changes are isolated within the hub. The prime disadvantage of this topology is that if the hub goes down, the entire network also goes down. Table 2.1 provides a comparison of the common topologies.

Table 2.1 Comparative Analysis of Topologies

Bus	Ring	Star
Adding or removing nodes requires breaking the bus, causing down time.	Nodes are added and removed without causing down time.	Nodes are added and removed without causing down time.

Network Standards

Network standards are guidelines that vendors follow to enable a variety of computers and devices to communicate on a LAN. An IBM AS/400 minicomputer, a DEC Unix workstation, and a Novell file server can be networked together because there are network standards. When different computers are able to communicate on a network, they are **interoperating**. Any one of the computers can be accessed from the network. Exchange of files and electronic mail is possible. Shared use of printers, faxes, modems, and other network equipment is also possible because equipment can interoperate.

To have interoperability of hundreds of network devices requires that vendors build equipment to recognized world standards. For LANs, there are three important organizations that establish standards. One organization is the International Standards Organization (ISO) based in Geneva, Switzerland. The ISO works on LAN communication standards. Also based in Geneva is the Consultative Committee on International Telegraphy and Telephony (CCITT), which sets standards for telephone and data transmission. A third group, the Institute of Electrical and Electronic Engineers (IEEE), has a set of LAN standards known as IEEE Project 802.

OSI Seven-Layer Model

The ISO has developed a seven-layer model so that network devices can interoperate. The model is known as *The Reference Model of Open Systems Interconnection* (OSI). The OSI model addresses the way different systems exchange information. It is concerned not with how individual systems function but how they communicate. For example, sharing files, handling communication errors, conversion of data formats, and routing of data are functions addressed by the OSI model.

The seven layers of the OSI model are defined as follows:

1. **Physical Layer** The layer governing areas of physical medium connectivity. One area is the mechanical nature of how communication devices are connected together. A second area is the signaling characteristics for the medium. Signaling characteristics are different for each medium.

2. **Data Link Layer** The layer providing error detection and correction for data **packets** or frames. The data link layer makes packets that are sent to the physical layer. The data link layer checks for errors that may have occurred in sending data. If an error is detected, it requests a retransmission.

3. **Network Layer** The layer establishing addresses for the packets sent to the data link layer. Packets can be addressed to devices on the same network or to devices on connected networks. The network layer is the highest layer of the OSI model supported by some networks.

4. **Transport Layer** The layer having the responsibility for data transfer between two users. This layer controls the flow of traffic and provides error notification.

5. **Session Layer** The layer controlling synchronization of transmissions between users. It determines when users can send and receive.

6. **Presentation Layer** The layer enabling data to be put into a meaningful format for users. If necessary, the presentation layer converts data so it can be read by the receiving user, and it also controls the screen display of information.

7. **Application Layer** The layer providing a way for software applications to function across a network. It permits the function of various applications—from electronic mail and file transfers to operating systems such as DOS.

All seven layers of the model are accepted by the CCITT. The physical and data link layers are implemented in IEEE standards.

Each layer in the model communicates with the adjacent layer. Think of each layer as part of an assembly line where one layer assists in moving information to the next.

The physical layer is the lowest layer (see Figure 2.4). It is associated with cable and other physical media for transporting information. Data are transported along the cable by electronic signals. The OSI model addresses how devices connect to the cable. It also addresses the characteristics of signals such as transmission speeds on the cable.

The data link layer communicates with the physical layer. It makes packets of data to be transmitted onto the network cable. The data link layer contains error detection and error correction capability to ensure that packets sent from one user to another user arrive with the right information.

Packets are able to find the right destination on a network due to the network layer. The network layer provides for addressing of packets so the address of the receiving user is known, along with the address of the sender.

The coordination and quality of data transport are the responsibility of the transport layer. Like a police officer, this layer controls the flow

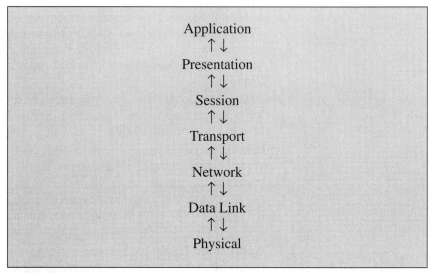

Figure 2.4 *The OSI Seven-Layer Model*

of packet traffic on a network. The layer also monitors the service quality of transmissions and provides notification when there are problems.

The session layer establishes when users can send and receive packets. On some networks, packets are sent as soon as there is no network traffic. On other networks, packets are sent in a given order.

In some instances, data from one user must be converted in order to be used by another user. This is the responsibility of the presentation layer. For example, a NetWare file server uses the ASCII format for data. An IBM mainframe uses the EBCDIC format. The presentation layer enables conversion from ASCII to EBCDIC and back. Screen displays such as graphical presentations are also handled by this layer.

The highest layer is the application layer. It enables file transfers from user to user and from network to network. The application layer permits electronic mail to be sent from different systems. Connection and disconnection of services such as file transfers are also handled by this layer.

Protocol

The selection of a protocol influences how well the network interoperates. This is because protocols control how a network device, such as a workstation, gains access to the cable. The protocol also controls the flow of data on a network.

A node gains access to the network for the purpose of sending a data packet through **access methods**. There are two types: **Carrier Sense Multiple Access with Collision Detection (CSMA/CD)** and **token passing**. Each access method is associated with specific protocols.

Carrier Sense Multiple Access with Collision Detection

A protocol using CSMA/CD monitors, or listens to, the media for traffic. Traffic is the presence of packets sent from one user to another. If no traffic is sensed, a device, such as a microcomputer, can send packets onto the media. A network packet is like a letter mailed to a friend. Your letter is put in an envelope that has your return address and the address of your friend. Data are like your letter and a packet is like the envelope. The data is placed in the packet and the packet has the addressing information and error-checking code. Each protocol puts the data into a distinctive packet. The device continues sending until it finishes or until a collision occurs.

A collision happens when more than one device transmits at the same time and their packets collide. The transmitting devices are able to detect collisions. When a collision occurs, the devices wait a specified amount of time before trying to retransmit. The collision detection and packet retransmission are part of the protocol.

Devices that are CSMA/CD–based can access the media at any time unless another device is transmitting. For those familiar with telephone party lines, CSMA/CD is a similar access method. There might be as many as 15 houses on a party line. The only way you know if the party line is busy is to pick up the telephone receiver and listen. If no one is on the line you can dial your number.

Ethernet Protocol

Ethernet is the protocol associated with the CSMA/CD access method. Ethernet comes in two flavors, XNS and IEEE 802.3. The XNS (Xerox Network System) protocol was developed by Xerox in the 1970s. Xerox issues all Ethernet addresses to vendors who manufacture Ethernet **network interface cards** (NICs). Network interface cards are circuit boards placed inside a computer or other network device. The network cable connects to the NIC so the computer is able to send packets onto a network. Xerox ensures no two Ethernet addresses are the same. The address is "burnt" into a chip on the NIC.

XNS is used by Xerox, Intel, and Digital Equipment Corporation (DEC) as network standards. Most minicomputer and mainframe vendors offer this Ethernet protocol. A modified form of the XNS protocol, IPX, is used by Novell. Due to wide use, Ethernet provides the highest degree of interoperability of all LAN protocols.

The XNS version of Ethernet has been modified by a committee of the IEEE 802.3 organization. The difference between XNS and 802.3 protocols is slight, but a device using XNS cannot communicate with a device using the 802.3 protocol. More discussion of these protocols is provided later in the text.

The maximum Ethernet transmission rate is 10 **Mbps** (ten million bits per second) on all cable media. This transmission rate is based on ideal conditions. The actual transmission rate depends on how well the network is installed and the particular usage pattern. Network performance is degraded by not following IEEE standards for installing cable.

Ethernet Media

Many types of Ethernet media are available. Coaxial, twisted pair, and fiber-optic cabling are all used on LANs. Coaxial cable is frequently referred to as coax. There are two types of coax used for Ethernet: thick and thin. For many years, coax was the medium of choice for LAN cabling.

The use of twisted pair and fiber-optic cable has grown with the development of network equipment that takes advantage of their features. Twisted pair has replaced coax as the most popular cabling medium. Coax, twisted pair, and fiber-optic are all explained in the sections that follow.

Thick Coax

Thick coax is referred to as 10 BASE 5 in the IEEE 802.3 standard. It is used for building-to-building cable runs and for long cable runs inside a building. These types of connections form the network **backbone**.

The maximum length of a cable segment is 500 meters. Up to 100 devices can be connected per cable-run segment. Thick coax is 50 ohm wire and uses a communication device called a **repeater** to regenerate the signal for added distance. Repeaters are network devices frequently used with thick coax. A repeater picks up the signals, regenerates them, and sends the signals onto all the segments attached to the repeater. Repeaters typically have ports or connections for eight LAN segments. Six of the ports connect to thin coax and two ports connect to AUI (Attachment Unit Interface) ports. AUI ports have 15 pin connections that allow for connecting to thick coax or fiber-optic cable.

Table 2.2 802.3 Physical Layer Specifications of Ethernet

Characteristics	10 BASE 5	10 BASE 2	10 BASE T	Fiber Optic
Cable level	Coax 50 ohm	Coax 50 ohm	Unshielded twisted pair	Optic fiber
Maximum segment length (meters)	500	185	100	1000
Topology	Bus	Bus	Star	Bus
Devices per segment	100	30	1	N/A
Signal regeneration	Repeater	Repeater	Concentrator	Repeater

Thick coax is used for bus type topologies. Table 2.2 lists the guidelines for all media types that support Ethernet.

Thin Coax

Thin coax or 10 BASE 2 is used to connect microcomputers to each other on a LAN. Table 2.2 lists its characteristics. Thin coax is installed from device-to-device in a bus topology. Each device on the LAN is connected to the cable with a T-connector (see Figure 2.5). A disadvantage of thin coax is that one user can shut down others on the network, through a bad NIC connection or defective T-connector.

Each thin coax segment can run up to 185 meters. The segments can also have a repeater (see Figure 2.6), which further expands the length

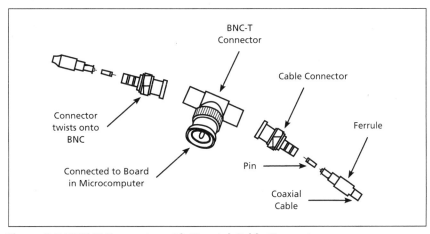

Figure 2.5 *BNC-T Connector with Coaxial Cable Connectors*

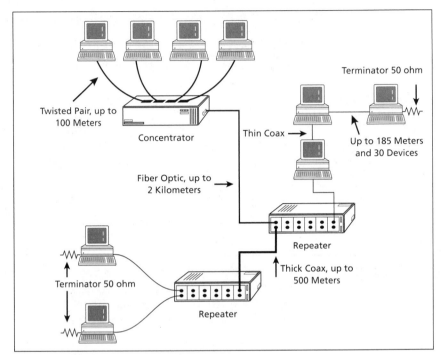

Figure 2.6 *Ethernet LAN with Thick and Thin Coax, Twisted Pair, and Fiber-Optic Cable*

of the LAN. An important rule for the Ethernet protocol is that devices cannot be separated by more than two repeaters. This restriction is necessary due to the time needed to send a packet over two repeaters and to send an acknowledgment back indicating that the packet did not collide with another packet.

Twisted Pair

Twisted pair or 10 BASE T is the newest IEEE standard for Ethernet. Refer to Table 2.2 for its characteristics. Twisted pair cable is the medium of choice for LANs. Unlike thin and thick coax, twisted pair allows for point-to-point connections. This type of configuration is a star topology. As mentioned earlier, the star topology is easier to manage and is more reliable. The tradeoff is a LAN that initially costs more to install. Additional costs are incurred because the network interface boards are more costly and there is the requirement for a concentrator (see Figure 2.7).

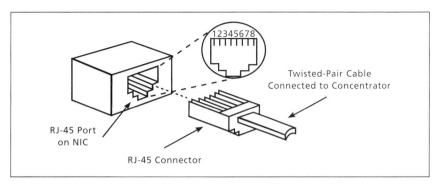

Figure 2.7 *Twisted Pair Cable with RJ-45 Connector*

The concentrator is the hub or center point of the star topology and provides for network isolation. Each network node is isolated on its own cable segment. By isolating segments of the LAN, problems are easier to troubleshoot. Users can be added to the LAN without shutting down the LAN.

One reason for the popularity of twisted pair cable is that it is also used for telephone systems. Although there are several kinds of twisted pair cable, most new installations of twisted pair are suited to telephone and data transmission.

Fiber Optic

An IEEE 802.3 standard has not yet been established for Ethernet on fiber-optic cable. However, a task force has been assigned the task of developing such a standard. The new standard will be called 10 BASE F.

Fiber is used for LAN backbones and is replacing the use of thick coax. Table 2.2 illustrates the superior qualities of fiber cable. While it is possible to connect microcomputers directly to fiber, it is not cost effective. The fiber network interface cards are two to three times more expensive than twisted pair network interface cards. Figure 2.8 shows the construction of a fiber-optic cable.

Unlike coax and twisted pair, fiber-optic cable transmits light, rather than electronic signals. The outer jacket of fiber-optic cable is plastic. The next layer is reinforcing material. This material serves to maintain the integrity of the cable during installation. Next, there is a buffer material called "cladding" that surrounds the optical fiber and aids in signal carrying. The optical fibers are glass or plastic strands that use light to transmit signals. Multiple strands are required, because light moves in

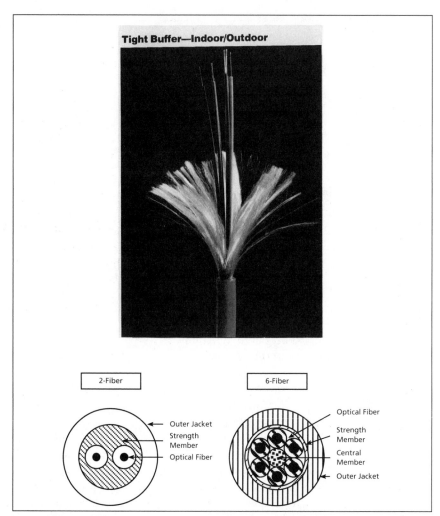

Figure 2.8 *Two Views of Fiber-Optic Cable, Showing Actual Cable and an Illustrated End View*

only one direction. Fiber-optic cable comes in multistrands for sending and receiving signals, with some of the strands reserved for backup and growth.

The size of a fiber-optic cable is referred to by the outer diameter of its core, cladding, and coating. Diameters like 50/125/250 refer to an optical fiber with a core of 50 microns, a cladding of 125 microns, and a coating of 250 microns. One micron is one-millionth of a meter. Twenty-five microns equal approximately one-thousandth of an inch. The lightweight materials used to make fiber-optic cable mean it is ten times lighter than metal conductor cable. Since the core of the cable is glass or plastic, the core can break when the cable is bent. Fiber requires a greater bending radius that restricts where it can be installed.

Token Passing

A token-passing protocol controls access to the media by allowing only the device with the token to transmit. The token is a non-data packet or string of bits. When the device finishes transmitting the token is passed to the next device on the network. If a device does not have anything to transmit, the token is passed to the next device.

Each device on a LAN has an address. The token is passed from the device with the lowest address to the device with the next highest address. Each time the token is received by a device, the device regenerates the token so that the signal quality is maintained. Token passing is more complex than CSMA/CD access but provides each user with equal access to the media. There are three protocols that use token passing: token ring, ARCNET, and FDDI.

Token-Ring Protocol

The token-ring protocol was developed by IBM and has become the IEEE 802.5 standard. This protocol supports 4 Mbps transmission using a token-passing access method. Token ring uses a star topology that is supported by the IBM Cabling System. Figure 2.9 illustrates a token-ringpassing network.

On a token-ring LAN, up to eight devices can attach to a Multistation Access Unit (MAU), which is the hub of the star topology. The ring part

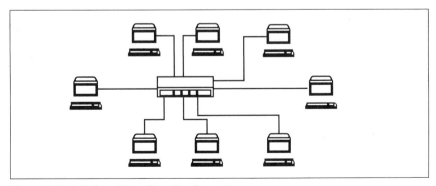

Figure 2.9 *A Token-Ring Star Configuration*

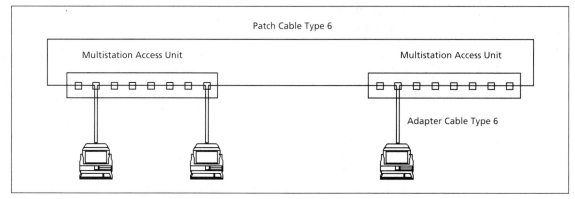

Figure 2.10 *A Token-Ring LAN with MAUs*

of the network is created within the MAU. MAUs, using shielded twisted pair, can be linked creating a LAN with up to 260 devices. Figure 2.10 shows how MAUs are used to create a token-ring network.

Unlike the CSMA/CD access method, which does not establish a token for network access, the token-ring access method generates and circulates a token packet around the network. Devices wanting to transmit wait for the token to pass. When the token is taken by a device, the device changes the token to start-of-frame sequence by changing one bit in the token. The device then appends and transmits the remaining fields of the data frame.

Once the device has removed the token by changing the bit pattern, no other device can transmit. This ensures that only one device can transmit at a time. The device that changed the token has control of the LAN until a new token is generated. The node generates a new token when both of the following conditions are met:

- The station has completed transmission of its frame.
- The leading edge of the transmitted frame has returned (after a complete circulation of the ring) to the station.

Once a new token is on the ring, the next device can take it and transmit data. The token-ring protocol gives each device equal access to the network. Networks with heavy traffic benefit from a token-ring protocol because there are no collisions, as there are with the CSMA/CD protocol.

When a device sends a packet to another device, the sending device detects one of three outcomes:

- The receiving device is nonexistent or not active.

- The receiving device exists, but the contents of the packet are not copied.
- The contents of the packet are copied.

A packet contains the data to be transmitted and information that helps test for transmission errors.

The token-ring eight-foot adaptor cable has an NIC adaptor on one end and an IBM Cabling System device that connects to either a patch cable or to an MAU. Patch cables are IBM type 6 cables with an IBM Cabling System connector on each end. Patch cables are available in 8-, 30-, 75-, and 150-foot lengths. Patch cables can be connected to each other, to adapter cables, or to an MAU. Token-ring network specifications are listed in Figure 2.11.

Although the IEEE 802.5 standard supports 4 Mbps transmission, IBM also supports a token-ring network that uses a 16 Mbps transmission rate via shielded twisted pair or fiber-optic cable. There are other vendors besides IBM offering both the 4 and 16 Mbps token-ring network products.

- Maximum number of stations is 96.
- Maximum number of MAU units is 12.
- Maximum patch cable distance between an MAU and a station is 150 feet.
- Maximum patch cable distance between two MAUs is 150 feet.
- Maximum patch cable distance connecting all MAUs is 400 feet.
- The total length of the main ring must not exceed 1200 feet.
- One eight-station hub counts as 16 feet of cable.
- One nonbridged main ring will support up to 33 eight-station hubs.
- The maximim number of nodes one main ring can support is 260.

Figure 2.11 *Token-Ring Specifications*

ARCNET Protocol

The ARCNET protocol is not an officially recognized standard, although it has been used since 1977. ARCNET, developed by Datapoint Corporation, is a combination of two acronyms, ARC, attached resource computer, and NET, network. Even though ARCNET does not fall under IEEE standards, there are nearly one million users.

ARCNET is a token-passing protocol. It uses active hubs in a star topology. An active hub is a signal regenerator that splits the signal onto other segments connected to the active hub. The cabling medium is 93 ohm coax, twisted pair, and fiber optic.

The ARCNET network interface card has a set of eight switches that are used to set the device address from 1 to 255. An ARCNET network is therefore limited to 255 devices. The address 0 is used by ARCNET to send broadcast messages on the network (see Figure 2.12).

Since ARCNET is a token-passing protocol, each device has equal access to the network. The token is passed to the device that has the next highest address. After the token reaches the highest active device, that device sends the token to the lowest active device address. Figure 2.13 shows an ARCNET LAN.

ARCNET has a slow transmission rate of 2.5 Mbps. There are vendors working on ARCNET protocols that will support a transmission rate of 20 Mbps (see Figure 2.14).

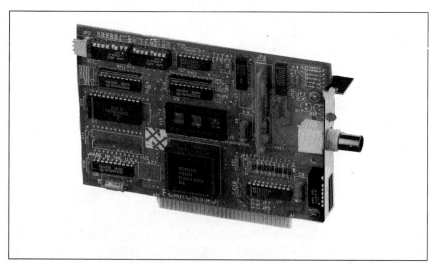

Figure 2.12 *An ARCNET NIC*
Courtesy of Interface Corporation

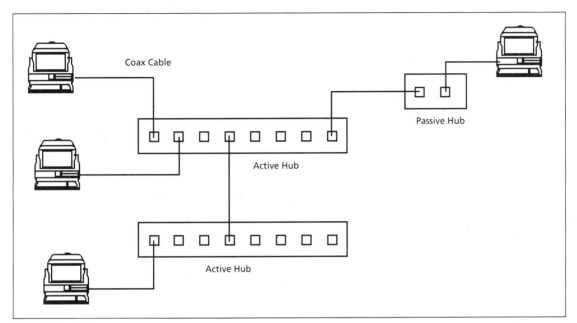

Figure 2.13 *An ARCNET LAN*

- Maximum cable distance from one end of the network to another is 20,000 feet.
- Maximum distance between active hubs is 2,000 feet.
- Maximum distance between an active hub and a network node is 2,000 feet.
- Maximum distance between an active hub and a passive hub is 100 feet.
- Maximum distance between a passive hub and a station is 100 feet.

Figure 2.14 *ARCNET Specifications*

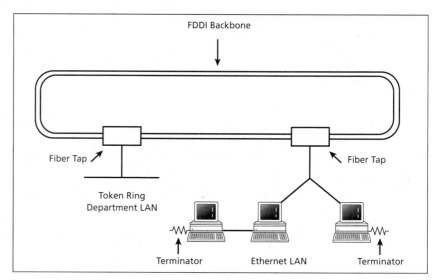

Figure 2.15 *FDDI Network*

FDDI Protocol

Fiber Distributed Data Interface (FDDI) is an emerging LAN protocol that uses a modified form of the token-passing access method. Figure 2.15 illustrates an FDDI LAN. The standards for FDDI are being developed by the American National Standards Institute (ANSI).

FDDI uses fiber-optic cable and supports transmission rates of 100 Mbps for distances up to 100 kilometers. FDDI is a super highway for network traffic. Some of its features are as follows:

- Its token-passing access provides different priorities for devices.
- It has large packet sizes and low error rates, and it can support more than one packet at a time on the network.
- It uses dual rings for backup and fault tolerance.

Summary

This chapter begins by explaining the bus, ring, and star topologies. The advantages and disadvantages of each are compared as an aid in network planning. The selection of topology is also influenced by network standards. Network standards determine the interoperability of networks and of devices connected to networks. The seven-layer OSI model is a standard developed to promote more complete interoperability.

Standardization of network access is achieved through two access methods: CSMA/CD and token passing. CSMA/CD uses protocols that function by monitoring for packet collisions. Ethernet LANs use the CSMA/CD access method. Token passing involves protocols that pass information by using a token that goes from network node to network node. Token ring, ARCNET, and FDDI all use a form of token-passing access.

Several media or cable types are used to build a network. These include coax, twisted pair, and fiber-optic cabling. Twisted pair is currently the most popular cable type in use.

Access Method   The means by which a node gains access to the network for the purpose of sending a data packet. Two access methods are CSMA/CD and token passing.

Backbone   A large cable segment that joins two or more LANs in the same building or across several buildings.

Bus Topology   A physical layout of a LAN, in which all nodes are connected to a single cable. The ends of the cable are fitted with terminating devices.

CSMA/CD (Carrier Sense Multiple Access with Collision Detection)   A network access method. Devices on this type of network monitor for packet collisions. If there are no collisions, network access is available for packet transmission.

Ethernet   A network protocol that uses the CSMA/CD access method.

Interoperate   A network characteristic that permits different devices on a network, or different networks, to communicate with one another.

Links   A segment of cable with connectors which provides the physical connection between network nodes.

Media   The cable connecting the nodes in a network. There are several cable or media types. These include coax, twisted pair, and fiber-optic cable.

Network Interface Card (NIC)   A circuit board installed in the file server and in each workstation. It works with the Novell operating system to send and receive data on the network.

Packet   This is a discrete unit of data bits transmitted over a network. Each packet contains addressing information, error control information, and data.

Repeater   A network communication device that amplifies and retransmits a network signal. Repeaters enable cable runs to be extended over greater distances.

Ring Topology   A topology in which all network nodes are connected in a logical ring-like pattern.

Star Topology   A topology in which each node is connected by a single cable link to a central point called a hub.

Token Passing   A network access method that involves using a token to transmit data. The token is passed from network node to network node.

Topology   The way that the nodes on a LAN are physically connected. The three LAN topologies are bus, ring, and star.

Questions and Exercises

1. Identify a computer protocol other than those used in this chapter. Describe how using the standards of this protocol has promoted the use of the protocol. Identify two limitations of the protocol.

2. Explain the access methods for contention and token-passing protocols. Which access methods would be recommended if there were 300 devices transmitting large files among each other? Explain your selection.

3. Thin coax networks often use a repeater. What functions does a repeater provide a LAN?

4. Define the relationship between Ethernet, twisted pair cable, and star topology. For example, how does selecting Ethernet determine the type of cable that can be used?

5. Find a building code reference for installing either telephone cable, electrical cable, or network cable. One example is the NEC or National Electrical Code. Identify three codes that a cable installer must follow.

Operating Systems

Chapter Objectives

The objectives of this chapter are the following:

- To explain the function of operating systems.
- To provide an overview of the DOS, Windows, OS/2, Unix, and Macintosh systems.
- To explain how network operating systems work.
- To explain network operating system services.

Introduction

The modern computer relies on an **operating system** (OS) to run. The operating system is software that permits you to interact with your computer so you can accomplish your work. When you first power on your microcomputer, the computer "boots up" because the operating system contains software to enable this process. Copying a file as well as printing it is made possible because of the operating system. You are able to run your favorite programs such as WordPerfect and Lotus because the operating system provides a way for them to run on your computer and tie into your operating system.

The operating system determines to what extent a computer will be able to address your work needs. The basic services of the computer and the programs that the computer will run depend on the operating system.

Host and Desktop Computers

In the 1950s and 1960s all computing was performed by mainframe computers. In the late 1960s, minicomputers became available. Mini and mainframe computers were mainly accessed through punch cards, paper tape, and terminals (a keyboard and monitor with no processing capability). Because programs and processing are centralized on the mainframe and minicomputers, they are now called **host** computers. Their operating systems are host operating systems.

From the late 1970s and to the present, the microcomputer has exploded onto the computing scene. Today, computing power has been placed on the desktop. For our discussion, microcomputers will be referred to as desktop computers and their operating system as a desktop operating system. The term desktop tells us not only that this is a microcomputer but also its location.

In many locations, more computing takes place at the desktop than in the computer rooms housing minicomputers and mainframes. Computing has thus been distributed to individual desktops. What is distributed computing? Why has it happened? What are the roles of operating systems in distributed computing? This chapter will address these questions and provide information on modern operating systems.

Distributed Computing

When the computer age began, all computing took place on host computers. Users first communicated with the host by means of electrical switches, punch cards, and paper tapes. The introduction of terminals permitted the user to attach directly to the host. Terminals had no CPU (central processing unit) or ability to run programs. The CPU was located in the computer room on the host.

The arrival of the microcomputer, each with its own CPU, has made it possible to do computing at the desktop. **Distributed computing** is simply the process of moving the CPU and processing to the desktop. Desktop computers become even more useful when they are connected to a network of other computers.

In the sections that follow, we will examine the desktop, network, and host operating systems. Why be concerned with host operating systems? There are thousands of installed mainframes and minicomputers. Many are connected to networks so data can be accessed by desktops. File servers that use NetWare also share data with mainframe and minicomputer hosts.

Conceptual Operating System Model

Figure 3.1 shows the most popular operating systems and the relationships between them. The upper part of the model illustrates the desktop operating systems. Most networks support more than one desktop operating system. For example, a microcomputer running DOS and a Macintosh can run on the same network.

Figure 3.1 also shows that a network can be used by a desktop to connect to a host operating system. For example, a desktop computer can use Windows software to first access a network and then attach to a host computer. Figure 3.1 will be referred to often in this chapter as the operating systems shown in the figure are discussed.

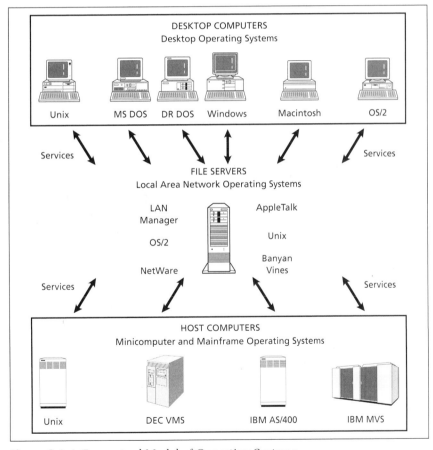

Figure 3.1 *A Conceptual Model of Operating Systems*

Desktop Operating Systems

DISK OPERATING SYSTEM (DOS)

The most widely used desktop operating system is the Disk Operating System (DOS). MS-DOS, developed by Microsoft, is the most popular. PC-DOS is another version of DOS used by IBM microcomputers. The newest DOS is DR DOS, developed by Digital Research, owned by Novell.

DOS is software that provides a user interface between the user and the computer hardware. As most users know, the interface requires that commands be entered from the keyboard. You use DOS either through commands or the DOS Shell (available in DOS 4.0 and above). The DOS Shell is used with either a mouse or with function keys.

DOS is a single user OS, meaning it is only able to process input on a single desktop computer. Important characteristics of DOS are as follows:

- It runs on 8088 generation computers, such as 8086, 8088, 80286, 80386, and 80486 computers.
- It supports a wide variety of application software.
- It supports only file names up to eight characters in length and a three-character extension.
- It boasts the largest installed base of operating systems.
- Programs must run within a limited 640 KB of memory.
- It has limited network support and awareness.
- It supports many peripheral devices such as printers, disk drives, and monitors.

These characteristics show why DOS is popular, functional, and a challenge to support. Why is DOS a challenge to support? Imagine a network of DOS computers ranging from 8088 CPUs to 80486 CPUs, all using monochrome to SVGA (super video graphics adapter) monitors. Printers might range from dot matrix to expensive laser printers.

As Figure 3.1 shows, DOS is able to communicate with a network operating system. This is made possible through **network shell** software, such as Novell's NETX.COM shell. If DOS were more network aware, these shells would not be needed. It is likely that future versions of DOS will incorporate software programs to make them more network aware.

WINDOWS

Windows was developed to overcome some of the limitations of DOS and to improve the user interface. Windows is not an operating system but a program that runs on top of DOS like a shell.

Windows requires much memory, processing, and disk space to support its user friendliness. Compared to DOS, it offers improved memory management and switching between applications, and it supports more sophisticated application software and a graphical user interface (GUI). Windows has become very popular, and many applications are now tailored to take advantage of its features.

Windows is a desktop environment that enables you to connect to a network operating system. Since Windows requires DOS, extra memory, and network shells, it works best on a 80386 or larger computer with at least 4 MB of memory.

OS/2

OS/2 is an operating system also available for 80386 or larger desktop computers. OS/2 appears similar to Windows because it presents the user with a GUI. Unlike Windows, OS/2 does not require DOS. It is a 32-bit operating system, while DOS is a 16-bit system. The benefit is that more memory and disk space can be addressed with a 32-bit system than with a 16-bit system.

OS/2 has the ability to create one or more virtual computers through memory management (the virtual computer exists only in memory). With this feature, OS/2 can be used as a single user OS and a network OS.

OS/2 requires a large amount of memory and disk space to support the virtual computer capabilities. IBM recommends a minimum of 8 MB of RAM and suggests 16 MB for desktops using OS/2. At least 30 MB of disk storage are also recommended.

OS/2 can run DOS, Windows, and OS/2 applications at the same time. Also, desktop computers running OS/2 can log into a network. To log into NetWare requires a network shell called OS/2 Requester.

Another feature of OS/2 is the ability to have file names with up to 254 characters. Uppercase and lowercase letters can also be used for file names.

FUTURE 80xxx OPERATING SYSTEMS

Operating systems for 80xxx desktop computers are constantly improving. Some of these improvements are represented in DR DOS 7. This operating system has all the features of DOS 6 plus the ability to access other computers on a peer-to-peer network (see peer-to-peer later in the chapter).

It is inevitable that future desktop operating systems will include a wide range of utilities that are currently sold separately. Companies such as Novell and Microsoft will develop their desktop operating systems with increased network awareness.

Unix

Unix is unique in that it can operate as a single-user desktop OS, a network OS, or minicomputer OS. Unix is also available in several different versions. Two popular versions are Berkeley and AT&T. The Berkeley version is referred to as BSD (Berkeley Standard Distribution) with a numeric version, for example 4.3. AT&T currently supports Unix System Five.

Unix was developed in the late 1960s for the DEC PDP-7 minicomputer. Unix is a multiuser and multitasking OS. Like OS/2, Unix requires significant amounts of RAM and disk storage.

As Figure 3.1 shows, desktop systems with Unix can be connected to a Unix network and to a minicomputer running Unix. Unix is one of the most versatile operating systems because it is the most network aware.

Unix is popular in the educational computing environment because it is network aware and enables the sharing of data. One limitation of Unix is that it requires a high level of computing experience.

Macintosh

The current operating system for Macintosh is System 7. Macintosh sports a GUI operating system that has built-in network support. AppleTalk, which is the protocol, supports connecting Macintoshes and printers. LocalTalk, a network system provided under AppleTalk, is completely supported with hardware and software that comes with the Macintosh. An EtherTalk network interface card is used for connection to Ethernet networks.

Macintosh is unique in the computer industry because only Apple makes these computers, including the hardware and OS. Its uniqueness means that Macintosh offers a desktop environment that is much more consistent than any of the others. Software installation is standardized as are hardware peripherals such as printers and disk drives.

Network Operating Systems

There are nearly as many network operating systems as there are desktop operating systems. A network operating system, such as Novell's NetWare, enables desktop computers to access a file server for programs and data files.

Figure 3.1 shows many of the available network operating systems. These include Banyan Vines, Lan Manager, AppleTalk, and others. Of the network operating systems listed, NetWare is one of the most powerful. This is why NetWare represents about 60 percent of all network operating system installations.

NETWARE

NetWare provides a range of services to desktop computers. Figure 3.2 presents a list of services offered by NetWare.

NetWare file servers support a wide range of desktop applications including word processors, spreadsheets, databases, and electronic mail. When the application requests a file from the file server, the NetWare network operating system locates and transfers the file from the server disk to the user's desktop computer. Figure 3.3 shows the relationship between the network operating system and a desktop application.

As a network operating system, NetWare makes application software and data files available to desktop computers. Application software, such as a word processor, is not run on the NetWare server. It is loaded from the server into the desktop's memory. *The application is run on the desktop computer, not on the file server.* The limitations of the desktop computer, such as memory or CPU speed, will affect how the application runs on that computer.

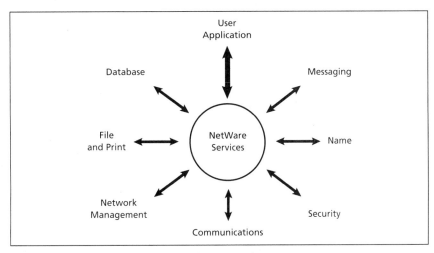

Figure 3.2 *NetWare Services Provided to Desktop Computers*

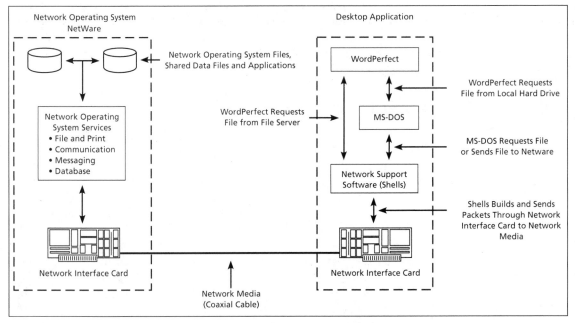

Figure 3.3 *Network Operating System Interacting with Desktop Application*

The network operating system performs memory management, scheduling of operations, and file processing for the file server only. The operating system activities determine the speed at which the file server can find the requested files and transmit them to the workstation for processing.

There is specific network terminology used to explain the relationship between desktop and network operating systems. The desktop OS is referred to as a **client** on a network. The network OS is referred to as a **server**. In combination, they form a *client-server network*. The client makes requests for services from the server. Since each server will have more than one client, the server schedules the requests so it can provide services to the client as quickly as possible.

PEER-TO-PEER NETWORKS

There are also *peer-to-peer* network operating systems. NetWare Lite and Lantastic are two examples of peer-to-peer networks. Peer-to-peer networks can have all users functioning as clients, or one computer can be configured as a server. In a peer-to-peer network, each desktop OS can access another desktop for files or to share printing. These networks, compared to client-server networks, provide limited network services, but they are easy to set up and are inexpensive.

FILE SERVICES

File services, such as sharing files, are at the core of local area networking with Novell NetWare. Before LANs, the best way to share a Microsoft Word file with coworkers was to give them a diskette. This is fine if a coworker is in an office next to you. It is more work if he or she is on another floor, in another building, or in another town.

Sharing files on a LAN saves time and money. You and your coworkers can be more productive because file services are offered on a LAN.

Sharing application software is also an advantage of file services offered by a network operating system. Why purchase 25 copies of a word processor if one can be purchased with 25 licenses and installed on a network? It's easier to install and support one copy in one place than it is to install and support 25 copies in 25 different desktop locations.

NetWare file services for versions 3.11 and above are especially powerful because NetWare will support a very large "disk farm" on a single server. Up to 32 terabytes of disk space can be made available on a NetWare server. A terabyte is 1,000 gigabytes or a million megabytes. Imagine being able to sit at your desktop computer and access this much disk space. NetWare is also powerful because several file servers can be accessed on a single network. The disk storage available to users is immense when four, five, or more servers are on a single network.

The time needed to access a file on a NetWare server is another important aspect of file services. When high-quality disk drives are purchased for a Novell server, a request for data from a file can be completed very quickly.

PRINT SERVICES

Just as files can be shared through a network operating system, so can printers be shared. Network **print services** save dollars in printer expense. Instead of providing each person in a workgroup with an inexpensive printer, why not purchase one good laser printer and still save money? LAN print services make this possible.

Print services are available in two ways. Novell offers print service utilities. You can also purchase print services from third-party vendors. NetWare print service utilities enable printing from the file server or the desktop. Printers can be connected directly to the file server. The limitation with file server printing is that it is convenient only if you are located near the file server.

Printing can also be distributed across the network to *print servers*. A print server is a desktop computer on the network that has one or more printers connected to it. Or it can manage print queues and direct printouts to printers that are directly connected to the network with special communication boxes. The print server can handle any print request from a desktop on the network. With NetWare utilities, the print server can be *dedicated* or *nondedicated*. A dedicated print server handles only print requests. A nondedicated print server handles print requests, and it functions as a desktop computer for a user.

An innovative solution to network printing is offered by Hewlett-Packard laser printers. For Ethernet networks, Ethernet network interface boards are installed in the printer and the printer is directly connected to the network. With the proper software configuration, the printer is accessed by file servers for shared printing.

APPLICATION INTERFACE SERVICE

Let's assume you have a health food store and you want to install a local area network to assist in running the business. One of your employees took a COBOL programming course in college and wants to write the program to keep track of inventory. This employee knows NetWare has a database language called Btrieve that performs database processing. She is also aware that Btrieve programming statements can be coded into her COBOL program. These Btrieve statements will create the inventory database and update the inventory records. This is one example of a network operating system supporting a database application interface.

There are other applications developers that use **Application Program Interfaces (APIs)**. NetBIOS is one API that is used for DOS, OS/2, and NetWare. Because Novell publishes the technical information on its APIs and sells developer kits, there are third-party developers writing applications that use these APIs to manage network printing, monitor network performance, add network security, perform resource accounting, and so on. In the case of networking printing, NetWare's APIs would specify how to access the operating system to get printing information. With the printing information a vendor is able to write a printer application. APIs are how the operating system communicates with the application.

SECURITY SERVICES

Network operating systems provide more services for data security than do desktop operating systems. Since files and programs are shared in a LAN setting, there is a greater need for security in a network operating system. For example, NetWare security begins by assigning file and directory protection rights to users. Users may also be required to log-on with a password to a file server.

Every new NetWare user is given a security profile. The security profile contains a password, trustee rights, and file and directory rights. The password controls access to the network. Passwords on NetWare 3.11 are encrypted so no one can read them. When a user forgets his or her password, the network manager must assign a new password.

Users are not allowed to access files unless granted trustee rights to the directory where the files are located. Before users can copy or create files on a Novell file server, they must have rights to the directory. Directory and file security is discussed further in later chapters.

NetWare security enables the network manager to control log-on times and days. For example, some users' access may be restricted to Monday through Friday from 8 A.M. to 5 P.M. Some users may be further restricted to a specific desktop computer. John's access to his NetWare account may be restricted to 8 to 5 working hours and only from the computer on his desk. His boss Mary may have unrestricted access in terms of time. But her access may be limited to the computer in her office and the computer in her secretary's office.

Another source of network security is through disk integrity. NetWare achieves disk integrity through several means. One is by maintaining two copies of directories and files. This is part of NetWare's **System Fault Tolerance (SFT)** feature. Directory and file redundancy is accomplished by enabling disk mirroring or disk duplexing. Mirroring means a second disk drive is installed, and it becomes a mirror image of the primary disk drive. All read and write operations are performed on both drives. Mirroring ensures there is a copy of all directories and files.

Disk duplexing goes one step further by using a separate disk controller board for the mirrored disk drive. Duplexed drives have their own disk channel. If the disk controller should fail on the primary drive, the duplexed drive remains in service.

A new disk integrity technology is called RAID or Redundant Array of Inexpensive Disks. RAID is several disks working as one. RAID systems are becoming available on network operating systems, such as

NetWare, that support critical applications software. These applications involve large cash transactions or large databases such as cash register transactions, banking transactions, hospital patient databases, and other applications that require constant access to information.

A RAID system segments large files into "logical blocks" using a process called "striping." By striping the file into blocks and putting the blocks on more than one disk drive, several drives are used at one time. Performance is improved and data can be redundantly kept on the drives. No data are lost should one of the drives fail.

Using RAID, the system can "hot swap" a bad disk without shutting down the file server. The bad disk is removed from service and the data remain intact on a functioning network ready drive. Figure 3.4 illustrates disk mirroring, disk duplexing, and RAID.

COMMUNICATION SERVICES

Turn back to Figure 3.1. Notice that the network OS can communicate with the desktop OS and a host OS. This interaction of operating systems occurs because of the communication services provided by the network operating system.

Communication services support LAN-to-LAN, LAN-to-host, and remote-to-LAN connectivity. An example of a LAN-to-host network would be in a hospital where each department is networked over a LAN and the LAN is connected to an IBM mainframe. LAN-to-host networks require a network OS like NetWare but need added communication hardware and software (see Figure 3.5).

A LAN-to-LAN network is simply more than one local area network connected together. An organization may have this configuration because there is a need to have specialized networks. An engineering company might have a network configured to support engineering applications and another network to support the business operations. By connecting the two networks, all employees can access electronic mail on the business network and the accounting department can access engineering data on the engineering network.

A remote-to-LAN network provides off-site access. For the engineering company described above, this might involve a group of consulting engineers who need to access their company network while traveling. Remote access equipment with communication software makes this possible.

Communication services also support different network protocols and topologies. For example, NetWare can support Ethernet, token ring,

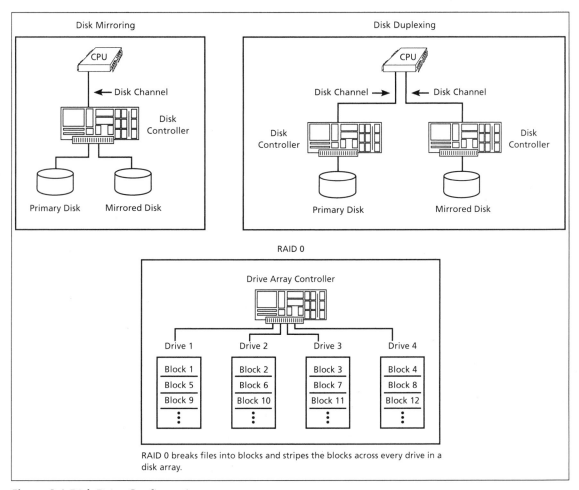

Figure 3.4 *Disk Drive Configurations*

and ARCNET from a single file server. An Ethernet user can send a message to the token ring and ARCNET users on the network.

Through *NetWare Loadable Modules* (NLMs) and additional software and hardware, AppleTalk can be connected directly to a NetWare file server. An NLM is a separate software program that is loaded to run alongside the NetWare operating system. Each NLM performs a specific task, such as the AppleTalk NLM that enables communication services between NetWare and AppleTalk. Macintosh users can have their familiar icons to

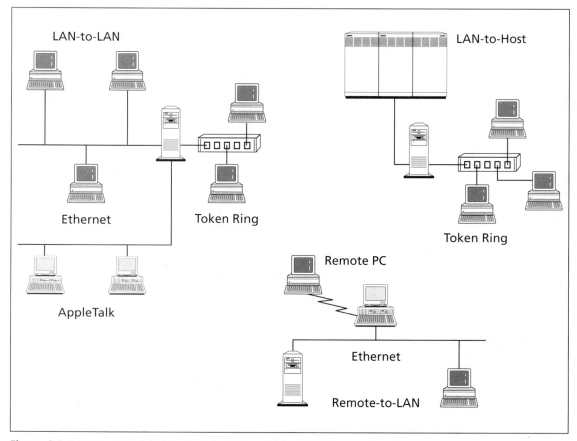

Figure 3.5 *LAN-to-LAN, LAN-to-Host, and Remote-to-LAN Communication*

select file and print services on the NetWare network. Non-Macintosh users are able to print to Apple PostScript printers.

TCP/IP (Transmission Control Protocol/Internet Procotol) is a communication protocol made popular by Unix and education networks. TCP/IP is a protocol that enables desktop users to connect to a network OS and a host OS at the same time. NetWare supports TCP/IP and its related file and print services.

Desktop Operating Services

Refer again to Figure 3.1. It illustrates that you can access the network OS using DOS, Unix, OS/2, Windows, or Macintosh operating systems. A network can consist of only DOS users or any combination of the above OS users. This is possible because of the ability to support all of the respective file naming conventions and also to provide printer support.

NetWare supports DOS file naming by default. Unix, OS/2, and Macintosh file naming is supported by installing NetWare NLMs. Here the NLM takes file names from the desktop operating systems and processes them so they can be stored on the NetWare file server.

Messaging Services

Electronic mail (e-mail) and applications called groupware are popular on networks. Groupware applications contain in a single suite of programs e-mail, calendaring, appointment book, and other applications. This software links people and resources. For example, the calendar might enable several people to review one another's schedules to find a common opening for a meeting.

Many network operating systems support the X.400 and X.500 electronic messaging standards. This enables software developers to write e-mail applications that work with many network and desktop operating systems.

Novell has developed the Message Handling System (MHS) that has become an industry standard electronic messaging protocol. Developers such as Lotus have interfaced this standard with their e-mail product, cc:Mail.

Host Computer Services

Mainframes and minicomputers now have networking services through Ethernet access. Modern IBM mainframes that use the MVS operating system connect to Ethernet "front end" communication equipment. The IBM 3745 communication controller is an example of this kind of equipment. The IBM 3745 acts as an intermediary between the network and IBM mainframes. An Ethernet network interface card can be purchased for the 3745. With the interface card installed, the Network Control Program (NCP) on the 3745 is configured for compatibility with Ethernet protocols, such as TCP/IP.

DEC computers are also Ethernet compatible, with an option to install an Ethernet card directly into the computer. The DEC VMS and DEC Ultrix (Unix) operating systems have extensive network capabilities.

Software programs such as Telnet can be run from a NetWare server using the TCP/IP protocol. With TCP/IP you can access an IBM or DEC computer from a NetWare server. With the TCP/IP based File Transfer Utility (FTP), you can upload or download a file from an IBM or DEC computer.

Summary

The operating system gives every computer and computer network a foundation on which to build. The services any computer can provide to the user depend on the capabilities of the operating system.

Many computer networks interface to several operating systems. The Unix, DOS, and NetWare operating systems may coexist on the same network, with each operating system running on a different computer.

This chapter has reviewed many different kinds of operating systems for desktop computers and for network operating systems. Desktop operating systems include DOS, Unix, Macintosh, and OS/2. Windows also is discussed with desktop operating systems, since it provides the user with a popular graphical interface between the user and their desktop.

Novell's NetWare is presented as an example of a network operating system. As such, it provides a wealth of system services. These include print, file, security, application interface, communication, and host access services. These services illustrate why NetWare has been adopted by so many network sites.

Key Terms

Application Program Interface   A service that incorporates flexibility into an operating system so that specialized and third-party programs can be written to interface with the system. NetWare has API capability for developers to add print server, communication, and other extended capabilities to the operating system environment.

Client   A desktop computer on a network that uses services, files, and applications made available by the network operating system. For example, a desktop computer that requests WordPerfect from a NetWare file server is a client.

Distributed Computing   The process of moving computing applications away from host-based systems. Programs and CPU activities are moved to smaller desktop computers. Data files are also distributed to the desktop. Networks make distributed computing very appealing due to the ability to share data.

File Service   A networked file server offers file services to desktop clients. Data, application, and other files are shared with clients that request access to these files.

Host   A mainframe, minicomputer, or other computer accessed by multiple users for the purpose of running software. A terminal or desktop computer connects to the host to run software, such as an accounts receivable program.

Network Shell   The software used on a desktop computer to enable it to communicate with other computers on a network. The shell is loaded into the desktop's memory and controls the communication of the desktop with the network.

Print Service   A network operating system service that can enable desktop clients to share printers, direct printing to specific printers, and control printers on the network.

Server   A computer on a network that enables other computers to share its resources. For example, a file server makes files and applications available to client computers. A print server enables client computers to share printing services on a network.

System Fault Tolerance   A set of procedures in software and hardware that enables a system to recover after a power or computer failure. The procedures prevent or minimize lost and corrupt data. They also minimize downtime.

Questions and
Exercises

1. Compare mainframes, minicomputers, and desktop computers in terms of how they might be used on a college campus.

2. What are the benefits and problems faced by a medium-sized business that is downsizing from a mainframe to a LAN?

3. Why do businesses need mainframe computers?

4. Of the desktop operating systems—DOS and Windows, OS/2, and Macintosh—which one would you recommend to a fellow college student who wants to buy his first computer? Use at least four criteria to make your recommendation.

5. Using recent literature, find the current prices for the latest versions of MS-DOS, Windows, OS/2, and Macintosh. Also include the version of the OS and the recommended minimum hardware configuration.

6. Obtain a Unix and DOS reference and find at least two commands that have the same syntax. Is it possible to use Unix syntax for more DOS commands? For example, to list your files on a Unix system, you would enter "ls" and in DOS you enter "dir." Can "ls" be made to list files on a DOS computer?

7. DOS compatible computers require the 8088 or 80xxx microprocessor. What family of processors is used in the Macintosh? Which Macintosh processor would equate to the processing power of an 80386?

8. Other than electronic mail and groupware that require a network to function, name other types of application software that require a network.

9. A word processor can be installed on a local hard drive or a file server hard drive. If your company has a 100-user network, explain the benefits of installing the word processor on the network hard disk. Identify two reasons why you would install the word processor on the local hard drives and not on the network.

10. Password protection is available on network and host operating systems. How would a password protection system be installed on a desktop OS? What would passwording access to the files on a desktop computer accomplish?

75 feet

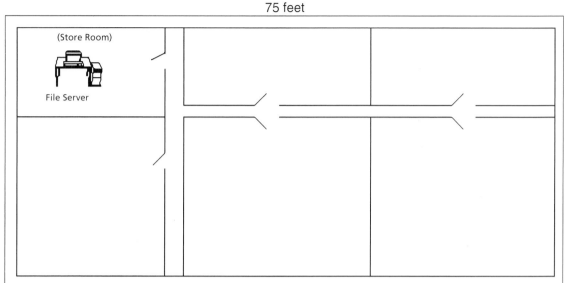

Figure 3.6 *Floor Plan for Network Cable Installation*

11. Using your knowledge of network topology and network OS services, draw a diagram that illustrates a network that meets the following requirements. An office building of five offices is to be networked. Each office will have three PCs and one dot matrix printer. There will be one laser printer attached to the file server. You should be aware of the distance limitations of printer cables.

Using Figure 3.6, draw in the network cable and lines indicating how the computers and printers will be wired. There is ceiling space to run all the cable. What type of network topology did you use?

The File Server: Hardware and Operating System

Chapter Objectives

The objectives of this chapter are the following:

- To learn how to select and configure the file server hardware.

- To determine how much memory is needed for a file server.

- To explain how to install the NetWare operating system on the file server.

Introduction   An IBM mainframe using the MVS operating system weighs more than a ton and occupies a significant amount of floor space in a computer machine room. At any given moment, it may have 100, 200, or more connected users. The typical Novell NetWare file server can be lifted by a single individual and placed on a desk. It, too, may have 100, 200, or more connected users.

The Novell file server is lightweight because it is simply a microcomputer. Novell operating systems will run on 80286 microcomputers, although an 80386 or larger microcomputer is often the best choice. The 80386 computer allows for network growth in size and complexity. There are hundreds of microcomputers with different configurations that will run the different versions of NetWare. Fortunately, Novell helps make the selection process a little easier by certifying NetWare compatible computers and computer equipment.

Table 4.1 Comparison of SFT 2.2 and NetWare 386

Feature	SFT 2.2	NetWare 386
Operating System Support		
MS-DOS 3, 4, 5; DR DOS 6	Yes	Yes
Windows	Yes	Yes
OS/2	Yes	Yes
Macintosh	Yes	Yes
Unix Network File System	No	Yes
OSI FTAM	No	Yes
TCP/IP	No	Yes
AppleTalk	Yes	Yes
Management Support		
Dynamic Memory Configuration	No	Yes
Workgroup Management	Yes	Yes
Password Encryption	Yes	Yes
Resource Accounting	Yes	Yes
UPS Monitoring	Yes	Yes
Remote Management	No	Yes
Disk Mirroring, Duplexing, Hot fix	Yes	Yes
Capacity		
User Configuration	5, 10, 50, 100	5, 10, 20, 50, 100, 250, 1000
Internetworking	Yes	Yes
Maximum Disk Storage	2 GB	32 TB
Maximum File Size	256 MB	4 GB
Maximum Number of Open Files	1,000	100,000

The decision about which version of NetWare to select is easier than the decision on a microcomputer. NetWare comes in several levels supporting from 5 to 1,000 users. Table 4.1 outlines the features of the two basic operating system versions. As the table indicates, *SFT 2.2* (System Fault Tolerant version 2.2) supports up to 100 users and minicomputers and mainframes networked on the LAN. The SFT version introduces features that permit recovery from power and hardware related problems. *NetWare 386* supports up to 1,000 users and provides the greatest degree of connectivity and network management. NetWare 386 requires an 80386 or larger CPU while NetWare Lite and SFT 2.2 can run on an 80286.

This chapter offers guidelines for the selection and installation of the network file server. NetWare 386 is used as an example of how the installation process works. Figure 4.1 provides an overview of the steps used to install a NetWare file server.

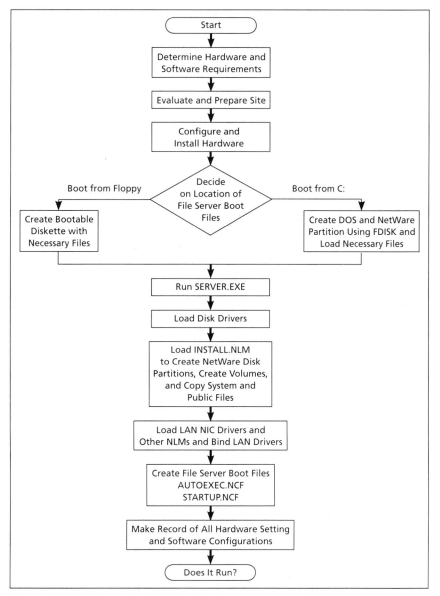

Figure 4.1 *File Server Installation Chart*

File Server Hardware

The first step in selecting a file server is to find a reliable vendor with a solid reputation for proven hardware quality and prompt support.

Many vendors opt to have their hardware certified by Novell. The certification process is extensive and is performed in Novell's laboratories using NetWare. You can contact Novell for their published certification results. The results provide assurance that the microcomputer, disk drives, and other hardware you select are compatible with NetWare.

There are three options when buying a file server. The first is to buy the file server completely configured with hardware and operating system installed. This is the easiest method and the most expensive.

The second option is to buy the file server with all hardware installed and to install the operating system yourself. You will save several hundred dollars by following this option.

The third option is to buy the file server components and install them yourself. The components might include memory, disk drives, and the network interface card. Once the hardware is installed, you then install NetWare. This option will save money, but requires that you have some hardware and software knowledge. Configuring the hardware and software is more complex for a file server than for a basic DOS desktop computer; the hardware is not certified by Novell.

The option you select depends on your time, money, and computer expertise. In many situations, option two is preferred. Vendors can often configure the hardware at a lower price than the user. This is particularly true for Novell certified equipment.

Regardless of the option you select, you will need to make a determination of appropriate hardware needs, such as memory and disk storage.

AN OVERVIEW OF THE FILE SERVER COMPONENTS AND ARCHITECTURE

A basic configuration for a file server includes CPU, disk drives, memory, NICs, floppy disk, and monitor. The CPU consists of the CPU motherboard, computer channel architecture, memory capacity, number of open circuit board slots, and parallel and serial ports. These are housed in the CPU chassis.

There are three computer architectures to consider. They are ISA, EISA, and MCA. The architecture is important because it dictates the type of components you can select for the file server.

Industry Standard Architecture (ISA) has been around the longest. It offers the lowest cost solution and the greatest selection of compatible hardware. The ISA architecture does not have the performance potential of either EISA or MCA.

Extended Industry Standard Architecture (EISA) offers a computer with a bus that has twice the data throughput of an ISA computer. The EISA expansion slots support bus mastering, a technology that allows the computer to distribute some of the processing away from the CPU.

Microchannel Architecture (MCA) offers many of the same features as EISA. MCA has fast data throughput and bus mastering. MCA is available on computers made by IBM. EISA and MCA computers are more expensive than ISA computers. EISA and MCA compatible components, such as NICs and disk controllers, are also more expensive than ISA components.

Architecture selection depends on cost considerations and the network requirements. A small network with under 100 users will work fine with an ISA file server. Networks with 100 users or more should have an EISA or MCA computer as the file server.

HARD DISK DRIVES

Disk drive selection is the most difficult because of the many options. Figure 4.2 illustrates some typical disk drive components and how they interact with the file server.

There are several important criteria to consider in disk drive selection:

- Selection of the drive technology such as ESDI, SCSI, or IDE
- Selection of the drive controller board or adapter
- Determination of disk capacity
- Determination of whether to mirror or duplex the disks
- Determination of which drive to use to boot the server
- Determination of how to configure the drives into volumes

The **disk controller** is a circuit board that controls how data are written onto or read from a disk drive. The controller may be a separate board that fits in a slot in the computer or it can be built into the disk drive. There are three disk controller technologies best suited for a file server. *Integrated Device Electronics* (IDE) is the latest disk technology. The drive capacity of IDE is limited to 425 MB. This is an important limitation to consider before selecting an IDE drive for a file server.

Enhanced Small Device Interface (ESDI) drives are installed in many file servers. Data transfer rates of 5 to 15 megabits per second are common with ESDI technology. ESDI incorporates defect-mapping information on the disk drive. Defective or bad disk track information is stored on the disk like other data.

Small Computer System Interface (SCSI) technology is the most versatile. Many disks can be daisy-chained together to make large disk

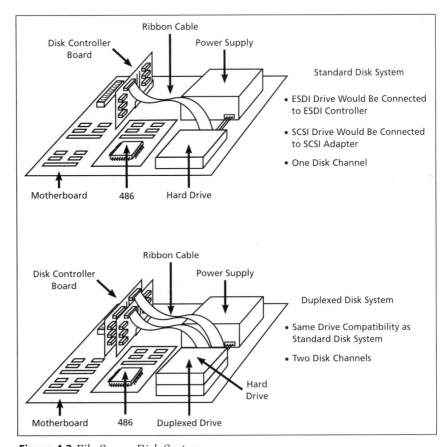

Figure 4.2 *File Server Disk Systems*

capacities (gigabytes) available to the file server. Unlike the ESDI controllers, IDE and SCSI controllers are built into the disk drive.

SCSI drives provide the best solution for a file server because of performance, proven reliability, and compatibility. ESDI drives are the next best alternative. IDE drives rate third due to the capacity limitation.

The performance of a file server disk drive will help with overall file server response. Performance is measured in terms of average **disk access time** and the **data transfer rate**. Access time is the time required to move the read/write heads to the data. The transfer rate is determined by how fast the data moves to memory once the heads have been positioned over the data. A high transfer rate of 5 to 15 Mbps is most desirable. Average access time should be low, such as under 20 milliseconds.

The time required to access data is helped by the design of NetWare. NetWare uses disk-seeking utilities that improve file server disk performance.

The reliability of a file server disk drive is as important as speed. Obtain the manufacturer's specification sheet for information about reliability. Many manufacturers publish the **mean time between failure** statistic of a disk. This statistic shows how long the average disk made by that manufacturer performs before experiencing a disk failure. Some disk drives have a mean time between failure of ten years or more.

If you choose to install your own disk drives, controllers, and adapters, take adequate precautions. First, be certain the controller is compatible with the disk drives you install. Second, some disk drives are formatted by the manufacturer and should not be formatted again when you install the drive. Reformatting can make the drive unusable. Third, some disk adapters used for SCSI disks are "bus mastering" and should be installed in a bus mastering slot in the computer. Bus mastering distributes some of the input and output processing to the bus mastering adapter and away from the CPU.

Let's consider two file servers and determine a suitable disk system configuration for each server. One file server has less than 100 users and the network administrator has selected a 300 MB disk drive. Another file server has 200 users and a 1.2 GB disk drive. The 100-user file server will function well with an ISA computer and ESDI or IDE disk technology. The 200-user network should have an EISA or MCA computer with SCSI disk technology.

FLOPPY DISK DRIVES

Your file server also needs a floppy disk drive for loading files. Select a 5 1/4 inch or a 3 1/2 inch high-density drive.

NETWORK INTERFACE CARD

A network interface card is available for each type of network protocol (Ethernet, token ring, ARCNET, etc.) used on a LAN. The network cable will reflect what type of protocol and connector is used. For example, if the cable is thin wire coax, the NIC must be an Ethernet board with a BNC type of connection. The file server architecture also dictates a particular type of NIC. An ISA computer takes only an ISA compatible NIC. EISA and MCA computers require EISA or MCA compatible NICs.

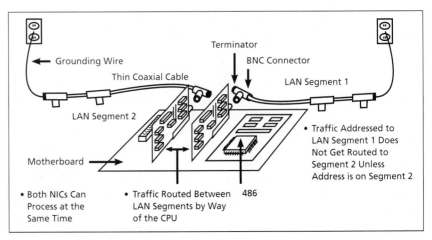

Figure 4.3 *File Server with Two NICs*

NICs must be configured for the characteristics of the file server and software. Some NICs are configured by setting dip switches or jumpers on the circuit board. Other NICs are configured by a software program.

The selection of an NIC is nearly as complex as disk drive selection. There are many NIC vendors, and each offers unique features. Most importantly, look for NIC memory features and diagnostic software. These features give you more flexibility as NIC software drivers and other network options become more complex.

A file server can support more than one NIC. The NIC is one source of bottlenecks on a file server. Installation of two or more NICs can improve file server performance. Figure 4.3 illustrates how a file server with two NICs provides better performance than a file server with one NIC.

FILE SERVER MEMORY

Decisions are easier to make for memory. NetWare 386 requires a minimum of 4 MB, and each file server has an upper limit that is supported on the motherboard. When using NetWare 386, purchase a file server that will support 32 MB of memory on the motherboard. This provides for expansion as your network grows.

Since user programs are not run on the file server, why is memory needed? The memory is used to load the operating system, to cache the disk directory information, to load NLMs, and to cache application software.

DISK DIRECTORY CACHING

Caching the disk directory increases disk performance. When the directory is cached, the CPU can find the location of a file by looking in the file server's memory. This is significantly faster than reading directory information from disk, as is done on desktop computers. The performance increase results because memory operations are much faster than disk operations. Each time the file server is booted, it loads or caches all the directory information into memory. The larger the disk storage, the more memory required.

Disk storage also influences memory requirements in terms of how the storage is allocated in **volumes**. NetWare manages disks by creating volumes. A volume is a logical unit of disk space. Each volume can reside on one or more disks, or an individual disk can be divided into more than one volume. For example, the NetWare operating system and printer files reside on a volume called SYS:. (Note that the colon is part of the volume name.)

By default, NetWare supports DOS volumes for DOS files. It also supports non-DOS volumes for Macintosh, OS/2, and Unix files. The type of volume influences calculations for determining how much memory is needed for caching. To determine the memory requirement for volumes, use the following steps:

1. Calculate the memory for each DOS volume.

   ```
   Memory₁ = .023 * volume size (MB) / Block size
   ```

2. Calculate the memory for each non-DOS volume.

   ```
   Memory₂ = .032 * volume size (MB) / Block size
   ```

3. Add the calculations from steps 1 and 2 to determine the amount of cache memory.

   ```
   Memory₁ + Memory₂
   ```

The block size used in these formulas can be 4, 8, 16, 32, or 64 KB. The default block size is 4 KB. File server data are stored in segments or blocks. Smaller block sizes are used when it is determined the average file is relatively small. The small block sizes enable more files to be created. They also mean more memory is needed for caching. Large block sizes are used when the average file in the server is relatively large. Although large block sizes require less memory, they also result in more inefficient handling of small files. The block size is configured when the file server is set up.

AN EXAMPLE OF MEMORY CALCULATION

Let's perform an example calculation. The file server in our example has three volumes, SYS:, USR:, and UNIX:. The block size is 4 KB (the default). We want to determine the amount of memory needed to cache the volume directories.

Volume	Type of Volume	Size
SYS:	Required DOS volume	50 MB
USR:	DOS volume	500 MB
UNIX:	Non-DOS volume	300 MB

Results

SYS:	= .023 * 50/4 =	.2875
USR:	= .023 * 500/4 =	2.8750
UNIX:	= .032 * 300/4 =	2.4000

6 MB (to the nearest MB)

NLM MEMORY REQUIREMENT

An NLM is an operating system add-on, so there must be memory available for each NLM that is loaded. Some NLMs require other NLMs to be loaded along with them. For example, CLIB.NLM is a C language NLM required by some other NLMs.

Novell and third-party NLM vendors will provide information about how much memory their product requires. For example, Brightwork sells a SiteLock NLM for software license monitoring and virus checking. This NLM requires 160 KB of server memory.

Determine the NLMs you will need on your file server. Total the memory requirements of these NLMs to determine how much memory you will need for NLM add-ons.

MEMORY FOR APPLICATION SOFTWARE

Memory not used for the operating system, disk caching, and NLMs is available to cache applications. Applications are moved in and out of memory as users make requests. Just as caching benefits directories, it also has benefits for applications. Access to a software application is fastest when the application is loaded in the file server's memory.

Let's look at an example. In a classroom setting, 20 students may be told by their instructor to load WordPerfect. The first student request causes the file server to check the cached directory memory for the location of WordPerfect. WordPerfect is then copied into memory from the file server's disk and sent to the desktop. The next 19 students will get their copy of WordPerfect from cache memory.

Caching applications offer a performance improvement that makes users more productive. Over a period of months, the extra expense for memory is far outweighed by the benefit of increased user productivity.

TESTING THE HARDWARE

If you select to configure all or part of the hardware, test it at each stage of configuration. The system should be fully checked out before NetWare is loaded.

First test the basic CPU unit before adding memory, disk drives, or other equipment. Power it on to be certain all original parts are functioning. Note the results of built-in memory tests and any other tests that come with the system. Try writing to the internal disk drive and the floppy drive. Perform a DOS disk check on the hard drive. Format a diskette in the floppy drive and check to ensure it can format at high density. Run the computer system for one or two days.

Once the basic system is verified, install any additional memory. Test the system again with the memory installed. Next add other components, such as extra hard drives, and test them.

When the initial testing is completed, install the NICs. Each board that is installed must be configured so it does not conflict with any other component. For example, an improperly configured NIC can cause the monitor or a disk drive not to function. EISA, ISA, and MCA computers differ in how they are configured with a NIC. Consult the NIC and computer vendors' instructions for proper installation.

CONFIGURING HARDWARE COMPONENTS

Many hardware components require special configuration steps, such as setting dip switches, setting jumpers, or running software configuration programs. Figure 4.4 illustrates an Ether Express NIC. In many cases the current or default jumper settings will work for your configuration. Record configuration settings for later reference. The settings will influence how software drivers are configured.

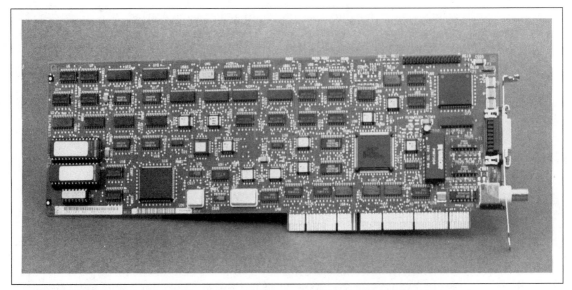

Figure 4.4 *The Major Components of the Intel Ether Express 32 EISA NIC.*

Many SCSI hard drive adapters are configured using software provided by the vendor of the computer. In these cases, each SCSI adaptor comes with its own software configuration drivers. You begin by copying the drivers to the configuration disk and then running the configuration utility. When the utility loads, it searches out all the SCSI adapters installed in the computer and sets the addressing, hardware interrupts, and other necessary information. The configuration information is then written to the EPROM of the respective adapter. (The EPROM or Erasable Programmable Read Only Memory is a chip on the SCSI adapter.) When the computer is rebooted, each SCSI drive will use the new EPROM information.

SITE PREPARATION

Your file server requires a safe and controlled environment. Clean power, constant temperature and humidity, and protection from intruders are all important. Power problems are a major cause of file server interruptions. Erratic power can cause loss of data, damage to components such as disk drives, and service interruptions.

Inconsistent temperature and humidity can also cause problems for file server components. High temperatures cause wear and damage to components. Security is important to prevent intentional or accidental tampering with the file server. You will have a significant hardware, software, and time investment in your file server. A controlled environment reduces problems and headaches. For example, consider an office with 100 users connected to a file server that is on a power strip with a desktop computer. If someone accidently turns off the power strip, all 100 users will lose their connection (and possibly their work).

Your file server should have dedicated power lines, properly grounded outlets, power conditioning equipment, and humidity control to reduce static. The server also needs to be in a location protected from general access, such as a closet or computer room.

POWER CONDITIONING

Clean power is a must for your file server. The file server needs protection from fluctuations in power, from power outages, and from sources of interference on the power line.

Power interference can be solved by bringing isolated power to the file server. Wire the power so it is not on the same line as heavy equipment such as an air conditioner or other appliance. A line filter that smoothes out power sags and surges will also help condition the power to the server. A good ground is another step toward ensuring safe, clean power to the server.

Many organizations install an **uninterruptible power source** (UPS) to condition power and protect against power failures. There are two types of UPS: on-line and off-line. The off-line UPS does not supply power to the file server until AC power is lost. There is a brief switching time when no power is supplied to the server while the UPS switches to back-up battery power. The server may go down during the switching time, causing file errors.

An on-line UPS is the best alternative. The on-line UPS supplies power to the file server through a battery. The battery is charged when the AC power is working. When the AC power is lost, the battery continues to supply power without a switch-over delay or power fluctuations. Depending on the load the file server is drawing and the size of the UPS, the file server will continue to function 10 to 30 minutes without AC power. This is enough time to shut down the file server.

Power sags and surges are other power problems addressed by a UPS. (Sags occur when power on the line drops well below 120 volts. Surges occur when power exceeds the normal 120 volt level.) A good UPS will condition the line to eliminate dramatic sags or surges.

Every UPS is rated by calculating the volt and amperage (VA) capacity. Multiply the voltage of a file server times the amperage to determine the minimum VA tolerance needed in a UPS.

If your file server is installed where there must never be downtime due to a power outage, you may want to add a generator for extra insurance. Some organizations have a diesel or natural gas powered generator. During an extended power outage, the generator supplies electricity to the UPS. The UPS and generator combination can provide uninterrupted power for many hours.

Installing the Network Operating System

CREATING A DOS PARTITION

NetWare boots from a DOS formatted disk. You have two choices about where to boot NetWare: from a floppy diskette or from a hard drive. Booting from a hard drive is the best choice. The server will boot faster from a hard drive than from a floppy. The hard drive method is also more convenient and reliable.

The DOS partition on the hard drive should be up to 5 MB in size. The partition must be large enough to hold system and utility files such as SERVER.EXE (which starts the operating system), INSTALL.EXE (for system configuration), and VREPAIR (a utility to fix disk problems).

Some disk drive vendors send the disk already formatted. Others require that you format the disk. If the disk requires formatting, use the DOS FORMAT command. (Be sure this agrees with the manufacturer's instructions before you use FORMAT.)

Partition the disk by using the DOS FDISK or PART utility, depending on your version of DOS. Follow the instructions in your DOS manual when using FDISK or PART. If you plan to use disk mirroring, create partitions of equal size on the primary disk and the disk to be used for mirroring.

Most disk vendors provide **disk drivers** for use with NetWare. Novell also supplies drivers for some disks. The disk drivers are software programs that enable NetWare to recognize and use the disk. The drivers come on a floppy diskette and are files with the extension .DSK. Copy the drivers onto the DOS partition.

GENERAL INSTALLATION STEPS FOR NETWARE

Once the DOS boot area is created, you should follow the following general steps to install NetWare:

1. Run SERVER.EXE.
2. Mount the disk drives.
3. Load INSTALL.NLM.
4. Use the INSTALL menus to configure the OS.
5. Load the NIC drivers.
6. Load other NLMs.
7. Create the boot files.

SERVER.EXE is the core of NetWare 386. This program is loaded from the DOS formatted hard drive or floppy diskette. You will see a colon (:) prompt after loading SERVER. The disk drivers, one for each drive, are then loaded.

After the disk drivers are loaded, you load INSTALL.NLM, an NLM that is a menu driven configuration program. Once the OS is configured, the NIC drivers are loaded. The NIC drivers are provided by Novell or the NIC vendor, depending on the kind of NIC you select to use.

Next, the add-on NLMs you have chosen, such as the PSERVER print server NLM, are loaded. The last step is to create two boot files that are used to boot the file server.

RUNNING **SERVER.EXE**

After your DOS partition is created, copy the NetWare SERVER.EXE program onto the DOS partition of the hard drive. Type SERVER to start the program. SERVER prompts you for the file server name. The name must be unique to the network and contain between 2 and 47 characters. Spaces and periods are not allowed.

Next, SERVER prompts for a unique internal network number. The number can be a hexadecimal number (0-F) with one to eight digits. An acceptable number would be BEEF. The internal network number is used by the IPX protocol for addressing.

If your file server has more than 16 MB of memory, you must enter the statement, REGISTER MEMORY 1000000 1000000. Make certain you type only zeros, not the letter "O."

When you run SERVER, there is a prompt to load the disk drivers. Use the name of the driver software file to load drivers for each disk installed in your file server. For example, on an ISA computer, the driver file may be ISADISK.DSK. In this example you would load the driver by typing LOAD C:ISADISK.

Your file server may have external disk drives that use Novell's Disk Coprocessor Board (DCB) adaptor. The DCB is configured using the NetWare DISKSET utility.

THE INSTALL PROGRAM

The next step is to run the INSTALL program. INSTALL is used to format drives for NetWare, specify mirrored drives, and to create NetWare partitions, volumes, and file server boot files. INSTALL also loads the SYSTEM and PUBLIC files onto the file server. These files are used to manage the NetWare system and provide NetWare users with utilities to accomplish their work. The Installation Options menu in INSTALL is shown in Figure 4.5.

CREATING NETWARE PARTITIONS

Make sure the NetWare INSTALL.EXE program is copied to the drive C: DOS partition. To begin INSTALL, enter LOAD C:INSTALL. Select "Disk Options." Choose *Select Partition Tables* from the Available Disk Options menu. This selection partitions the file server drive for NetWare. If there is more than one drive on the server, INSTALL will prompt you to partition it as well as the main drive.

The next step is to select *Create NetWare Partition* from the Partition Options menu (see Figure 4.6).

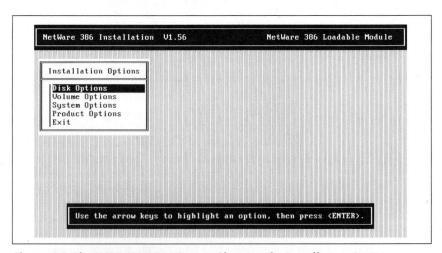

Figure 4.5 *The INSTALL.NLM Screen Showing the Installation Options*

```
NetWare 386 Installation  V1.56              NetWare 386 Loadable Module

 ┌─────────────────────┐
 │ Installation Options │
 ├─────────────────────┘
 │Disk Options
 │Vo┌─────────────────────────────┐
 │Sy│ Available Disk Options       │
 │Pr├─────────────────────────────┘
 │Ex│ Format (optional)
   │ │ Partition Tables
   │ │ Mirroring
   │ │ Surface Test (optional)
   │ │ Return To Main Menu
   └─┴──────────────────────────


  ┌────────────────────────────────────────────────────┐
  │ Use the arrow keys to highlight an option, then press <ENTER>. │
  └────────────────────────────────────────────────────┘
```

Figure 4.6 *The INSTALL.NLM Available Disk Options Menu Used for Creating Partitions*

Novell allows one NetWare partition per disk. The disk space not used for the DOS partition is allocated to the NetWare partition. Two percent of the NetWare partition on each disk is automatically reserved for the **hot fix redirection area**. The hot fix function is used when a portion of the disk is found to be defective after the file server operation begins. Data on the defective area are rewritten to a hot fix area of disk.

Figure 4.7 illustrates how a disk can be partitioned. In this example, the DOS partition is 5.9 MB and the NetWare partition is 636.0 MB. The free space is allocated for hot fix activity and is not determined by the installer.

MIRRORED DISK DRIVES

When you use a mirrored disk, you duplicate the partitioning process for that disk so that it matches the primary disk. After partitioning, you indicate which drive is the primary drive and which one is the mirrored drive.

The primary and mirrored drives are designated from the Available Disk Options menu using the *Mirroring* selection (see again Figure 4.6). Select the primary partition on the Partition Mirroring Status screen by using the INSERT key to select the partition. Figure 4.8 shows the screen after the partition has been selected.

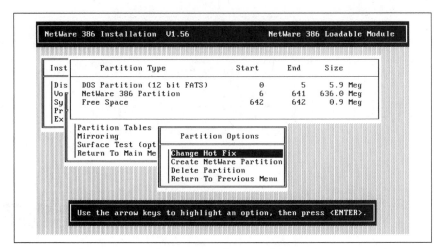

Figure 4.7 *The INSTALL.NLM Screen Showing the Partition Type and Size*

From the screen in Figure 4.8, use the ENTER key to select the partition. The screen shown in Figure 4.9 will appear, indicating that there are two partitions in synchronization (Sync). Sync means that the drives are mirrored.

There are times when the drives are not in Sync. For example, the mirroring can be turned off for a period of time so the drives are not in Sync. Mirroring can be restarted, causing the mirroring process to begin by first making a mirror image of the primary drive.

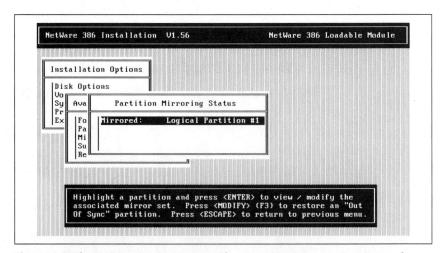

Figure 4.8 *The INSTALL.NLM Screen Showing a Partition to Be Mirrored*

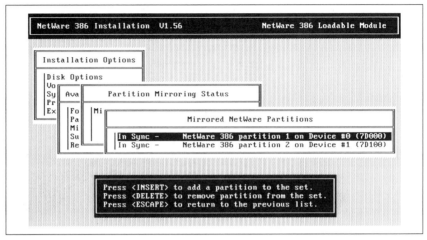

Figure 4.9 *The INSTALL.NLM Screen Showing that the Partitions Are Mirrored and in Sync*

The installation process to duplex drives is the same as for mirroring drives. The only difference between mirroring and duplexing is that a separate controller is used for a duplexed drive.

CREATING VOLUMES

NetWare 386 supports up to 64 volumes. A volume is a logical unit of disk space that can be on one or more disk drives. If a volume spans more than one drive, the drives should be duplexed. Even though only one drive might fail, the total volume of several drives is lost with a disk failure. Duplexing ensures that data will not be lost in the event of a single drive failure.

Creating more than one volume is a way to isolate problems on a hard drive and provide options for recovering the drive. It is possible to lose one volume but still have other volumes function.

All NetWare file servers need a SYS: volume for NetWare files. The operating system requires creation of a SYS: volume. The size of SYS: depends on what is loaded into the volume. The SYS: volume should be allocated at least 25 to 50 MB, depending on the disk capacity of the file server. The SYS: volume contains the operating system files, system maintenance files, print queues, and software utilities.

A volume called VOL1:, USR:, or a similar descriptive name is designated for users. Application software may be placed on the VOL1: volume or on a separate volume, such as APPS:. Spreading files out

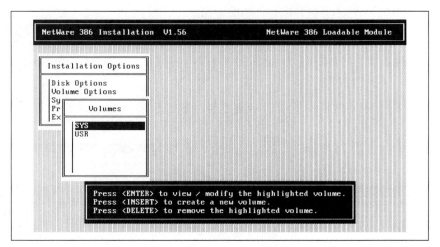

Figure 4.10 *The INSTALL.NLM Volumes Screen Listing the Two Volumes*

based on volume not only is useful for times when there are disk problems, but it also makes security easier to establish on the file server.

Figure 4.10 shows an example where the server has two volumes, SYS: and USR:.

Using the screen in Figure 4.10, type ENTER to select a volume. The next screen, Volume Information, is used to set parameters on the volume (see Figure 4.11). From this screen you can establish the volume name, block size, volume segment, volume size, and volume status. Unless you anticipate mostly large files on the file server, the block size is set at the default of 4 KB. The volume segment enables you to link more than one disk to the volume. The volume size is used to show the amount of disk space associated with the volume. The volume status indicates that the disk is to be mounted for use when the file server is booted.

Once the volumes are created, use the MOUNT volume command to mount the volumes that will be available for use. SYS: must be mounted or else the file server will not boot. To mount all of the volumes, enter MOUNT ALL.

SYSTEM AND PUBLIC FILES

Now return to the first menu, Installation Options, of the INSTALL program (see again Figure 4.5). Select *System Options* from the menu. Next select *Copy System and Public Files* from the Available System Options menu as shown in Figure 4.12. This option copies the system and utility files to the SYS:SYSTEM and SYS:PUBLIC directories.

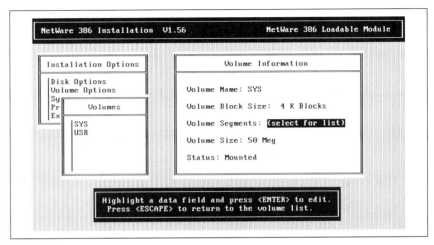

Figure 4.11 *The INSTALL.NLM Volume Information Screen for Volume SYS:*

Once the files are copied, leave the INSTALL program by using the ESC key to exit through each menu.

LOADING THE LAN DRIVERS

The LAN drivers are loaded next. These drivers enable the NIC to communicate with the network. Many NIC vendors provide the NIC LAN drivers on a floppy disk. Drivers for popular NICs, such as Novell's NE3200, are loaded by the INSTALL program into the SYS: volume.

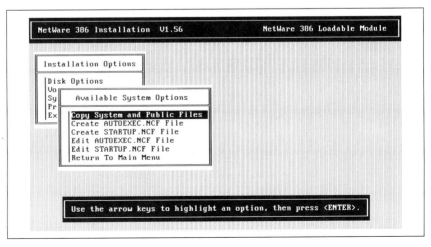

Figure 4.12 *The INSTALL.NLM Available System Options Menu*

To load an NIC driver, enter LOAD (drivername) if the driver was copied to the file server by INSTALL. If the driver is supplied by the vendor, copy it to the DOS C: partition and type LOAD C:(drivername).

Once the driver is loaded, bind it to IPX. The bind process assigns the NIC to a network number that identifies the cabling system and also assigns other protocol information to the NIC. To bind the NE3200 NIC, you enter BIND IPX to NE3200. Use the LOAD and BIND commands for each NIC.

CREATING THE FILE SERVER BOOT FILES

The LOAD, MOUNT, and BIND commands can be automated so they do not have to be entered each time the file server is booted. They are automated through the creation of two NetWare boot files, AUTOEXEC.NCF and STARTUP.NCF. AUTOEXEC.NCF is located in the SYS:SYSTEM directory. STARTUP.NCF is placed on the DOS boot partition, C:.

AUTOEXEC.NCF provides the same function for a NetWare server as the AUTOEXEC.BAT file does for a DOS desktop computer. AUTOEXEC.NCF is run when the server is booted. Each line of AUTOEXEC.NCF is a command such as a LOAD command that you would otherwise have to type manually. Figure 4.13 shows an example AUTOEXEC.NCF file.

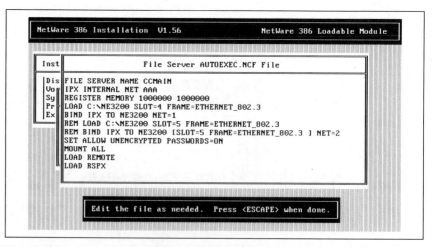

Figure 4.13 *The INSTALL.NLM Screen Showing the Contents of the File AUTOEXEC.NCF*

```
NetWare 386 Installation  V1.56          NetWare 386 Loadable Module

    Inst        File Server STARTUP.NCF File

    Dis  load RFDRVR mem=D8000 int=C
    Vo   load RFDRVR mem=DC000 int=B
    Sy   set minimum packet receive buffers=100
    Pr   set maximum physical receive packet size=4202
    Ex




       Edit the file as needed.  Press <ESCAPE> when done.
```

Figure 4.14 *The INSTALL.NLM Screen Showing the Contents of the File STARTUP.NCF*

To edit the AUTOEXEC.NCF file, load the INSTALL program (LOAD INSTALL) and select *System Options* from the menu shown in Figure 4.5. Next select *Create AUTOEXEC.NCF File* from the Available System Options menu. The create option pulls in the commands which were entered during the configuration process. You also can edit the file to automatically load NLMs, such as PSERVER. Figure 4.13 shows a file that loads NLMs and that sets unencrypted passwords to *on*. Setting unencrypted passwords to "on" permits older versions of NetWare 286, without password encryption, to run on the same network as NetWare 386 servers, which have encryption.

The STARTUP.NCF file has commands that load disk drivers and named space support for non-DOS files, such as Macintosh. This file is run after SERVER is executed. Figure 4.14 shows the commands to load two disk drivers.

Summary

This chapter focuses on selecting and installing a file server. Selection of the server begins with choosing a reliable vendor. Not all vendors are equal, so you want to choose one whose equipment is dependable and who can provide prompt service. Novell publishes information on which vendors manufacture computers that are compatible with NetWare.

The selection process also includes choosing disk drive technology, the network interface card, and additional equipment such as memory for the server. IDE, ESDI, and SCSI are disk technologies from which to choose. The network interface card is the server's connection to the network. You may decide to purchase more than one interface card to increase throughput on the network. Memory also influences the performance of your file server. Calculate the amount of memory you need and purchase it when you purchase the file server.

The location of the file server and power for the file server are part of the site preparation. The server should be in a secure area with conditioned power. Purchase of a UPS will help provide insurance against power problems.

The installation of NetWare begins with creation of a DOS partition on the file server. Once the partition is created, run the SERVER program, mount each disk, perform the INSTALL program functions, load the NIC drivers and the NLMs, and create the system boot files. Loading NetWare is not much more difficult than loading an application program such as WordPerfect. Allow yourself a margin of time to perform the installation, so you can become familiar with NetWare and handle any installation problems that might arise.

Key Terms

Data Transfer Rate   The time required to read data into memory once the read/write heads are located over the data on a disk.

Disk Access Time   The time required to move the read/write heads to the location of the data on the disk.

Disk Controller   A circuit board that is placed inside the computer and that controls the functioning of one or more disk drives. This circuit board oversees the read and write activity on the disk drive.

Disk Driver   A software program that enables a disk drive to communicate with the software or operating system on a computer so that disk functions can be performed.

Hot Fix Redirection Area   An area used by NetWare to partition a disk. When NetWare finds a bad area on the disk, it writes the data to the hot fix area instead of to the bad area.

Mean Time Between Failure   The average time a piece of computer equipment, such as a disk drive, will run until it is likely to fail.

Uninterruptible Power Source (UPS)   A device containing batteries that supply power to a computer device when there is a power failure.

Volume   A logical unit of disk space as recognized by NetWare. A NetWare volume can span more than one physical disk.

Questions and Exercises

1. Explain why site preparation is important for a file server.
2. If you suspect that your file server is experiencing power-related problems, what steps should you take to determine the source of the problems?
3. What type of room provides an ideal environment for the file server? Why?
4. What type of testing is required on all new computers? What specific test(s) would you perform?
5. If the file server hardware costs $7,000 and the operating system costs $3,000, how would you justify to management paying $15,000 to a vendor for a file server with the operating system installed?
6. Of the three architectures—ISA, EISA, and MCA—which would you recommend for a desktop computer? Why? Which would you recommend for a file server? Why? Begin by stating your assumptions of how the computers will be used.
7. Determine the disk drive and controller in your computer or one you have access to. What is the capacity of the disk?
8. Obtain an NIC. Determine the amount of memory, the memory addressing, and the IRQ setting on the NIC. What protocol does the NIC use? What type of cable will the NIC connect to?

9. Determine the amount of memory in a computer you use. How much memory is supported by the motherboard? What process would you use to add more memory?

10. A file server has the following hard disk configuration. Determine how much memory is required to cache the disk directories. How much memory should you install to operate NetWare?

    ```
    SYS:    50 MB
    APPL:  600 MB DOS Volume
    MAC:   1.2 GB Non-DOS Volume
    ```

11. Calculate how much total server memory to install by using the volume information from question 10. Besides the volumes from question 10, you also want to load 2.5 MB of NLMs. The operating system takes 2 MB. You also plan to have 7.5 MB to cache for application software.

12. What is the function of the INSTALL.NLM?

13. When the disk drives are loaded after SERVER.EXE is run, where are the driver files located? What is the syntax to load a disk driver called RFM5500.DSK?

14. What is the purpose of AUTOEXEC.NCF and where does this file reside?

15. Your file server has just arrived. You test it and everything looks fine. You then install an NIC and now the file server will not boot. The monitor is blank with no error messages. What is the problem? What steps will you follow so that the file server will boot with the NIC?

The LAN Workstation

Chapter Objectives

The objectives of this chapter are the following:

- To explain workstations and desktop computers.
- To show how workstations are configured for use with NetWare.
- To explain workstation memory requirements.

- To show how the workstation network interface card is installed.
- To explain the NetWare software needed for a workstation.

Introduction

The term **workstation** has several meanings. If your company has a mainframe or minicomputer, you may access the host by using a microcomputer. If your college has a campus-wide network, you may use a microcomputer to access a NetWare file server. If you work for an electronics company, you may design electrical equipment by using a powerful Unix desktop computer with computer-aided design software. In the first two examples, the microcomputers are workstations. An IBM, Dell, or Gateway computer with an 8088 or larger CPU would be a workstation in these examples. In the third example, the Unix computer is also a workstation. This workstation might be a SUN, IBM RISC, or DECstation computer with significant processing power.

In this chapter, our main interest is in the example of the microcomputer or other workstation connected to a file server. It is a workstation because it has its own CPU and has the added capability to interface with a file server for more work options.

A desktop computer is transformed into a workstation with the installation of a network interface card. The NIC is attached to the network cable and enables the desktop computer to communicate by means of network software.

The Workstation Processor

Any DOS compatible or Macintosh microcomputer can be used as a LAN workstation. The SUN, IBM RISC, and DECstation computers can also be used with NetWare.

In a single office area there might be 8088, 80286, 80386, and 80486 computers. These computers will use different versions of DOS including DOS 3, DOS 4, DOS 5, and DR DOS 6. Some of these desktops will also use Windows or OS/2. Another office might have Macintosh and Unix users. These computers will also have different operating systems and software interfaces.

A successful network provides users with the workstations and capability they need to accomplish their work. All users will have the functionality they had before the network implementation, plus the added function of access to file servers.

This chapter explains the setup of DOS desktop computers for network access. In later chapters we cover the installation of desktop computers that use Windows. Figure 5.1 presents an overview of the steps used to transform a DOS desktop computer into a networked workstation.

Workstation Computing Environment

The process of networking a workstation starts by determining the computing requirements of the user. There may be requirements for word processing, desktop publishing, computer-aided design (CAD), or programming in C. Each requirement involves a certain level of hardware and software.

Two important considerations are memory and the DOS version. Desktop publishing and CAD applications require more memory than word processing. Because some users may have workstations with higher versions of DOS, they can use advanced features of the operating system or they can use Windows. Memory and DOS issues are discussed in the sections that follow.

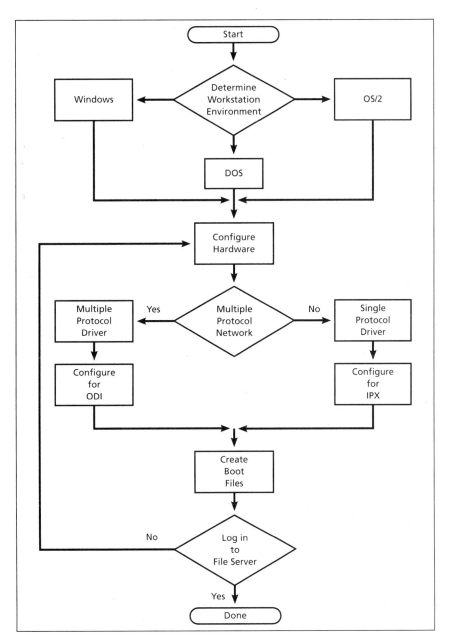

Figure 5.1 *Installation Process Chart Showing the Steps for Configuring a Workstation*

Workstation Memory

Sufficient DOS workstation memory must be available to run software applications, to run network software, and to run DOS functions. If you load AutoCad from the file server, your workstation will need enough memory to run AutoCad, along with memory for the network shell programs and the DOS COMMAND.COM utility.

In the DOS environment, memory management has evolved from nil to more advanced memory management features. MS DOS 5.0 and DR DOS 6 both introduce memory management to the desktop. Memory management is useful because in the DOS operating environment all applications run in **conventional memory**, which is the first 640 KB of memory. Memory management provides the ability to load network software, DOS, and other programs into memory above 640 KB. The memory between 640 KB and 1 MB is called **expanded memory** and memory above 1 MB is called **extended memory**.

Memory managers are used to load software into expanded or extended memory. Prior to advanced versions of DOS, memory managers were available only from third-party vendors. Now DOS and DR DOS provide memory management.

Let's use some approximate memory requirements to get an idea of how memory becomes scarce in an 8088 or 80286 computer without memory management. As the following chart shows, you plan to load the necessary DOS files, your network shell software, WordPerfect, and a terminate and stay resident (TSR) dictionary program. (A TSR is a utility program that stays in memory until you unload it.)

Workstation Memory

Boot with DOS 3.1	25 KB
Network software	77 KB
WordPerfect	380 KB
Dictionary TSR	55 KB
Mouse drivers	30 KB
Mouse menu TSR	70 KB
Cache software	20 KB
Total	657 KB

An 8088 computer can have up to 640 KB of conventional memory. An 80286 has the 640 KB and perhaps 384 KB of expanded memory. Without a memory manager, only the 640 KB is usable on the 80286. Since the software you want to load exceeds 640 KB, one of the programs such as the dictionary TSR cannot be loaded.

A memory manager would solve the problem. Some versions of DOS come with a memory manager. Third-party vendors also offer memory mangers, such as QEMM from Quarterdeck. A memory manager on the 80286 computer would enable you to load the network software and the dictionary TSR into expanded memory, leaving 155 KB of conventional memory free.

Configuring the Hardware

The first step in configuring workstations is to "burn in" each new workstation before placing it on the network. Run each workstation for one or two days to ensure all components are functioning. Test the floppy and hard drives by writing to files and reading from files on each drive.

Follow the manufacturer's setup guide as you prepare the workstation for use. Many vendors include diagnostics to test memory, video functions, disk drives, and other components. Use these diagnostics to thoroughly test a workstation before you connect it to your network.

Installing the Network Interface Card

After you have tested a workstation, install the NIC in an open slot on the computer. The procedures to follow for installing any card in a computer are documented in the computer operations manual and in the manual that comes with the card.

The installation procedure for a NIC depends on the protocol (ARCNET, Ethernet, token ring), the cable (thin coax, thick coax, twisted pair), the type of computer (desktop, notebook, Macintosh), and the computer's architecture (ISA, EISA, MCA).

Figure 5.2 shows an Ethernet NIC. This NIC has several jumper settings, which establish the interrupt request level (IRQ), the memory base address, and I/O base address. All three settings are used to coordinate the exchange of information between the NIC and the computer.

The network address on an Ethernet card is built into the NIC by the manufacturer. The same address on an ARCNET or token-ring card is set by changing jumper switches on the card. The Ethernet NIC in Figure 5.2 can be cabled to either thick or thin coaxial cable. Thin wire would be connected to a BNC connector while the thick wire would be connected to an external transceiver connector. The network selection jumper is set to indicate thick or thin coaxial.

Not shown on this NIC but available on some is a socket for a remote boot PROM. This chip allows the computer to boot without having a disk drive on the workstation. Boot PROMS are required in diskless computers.

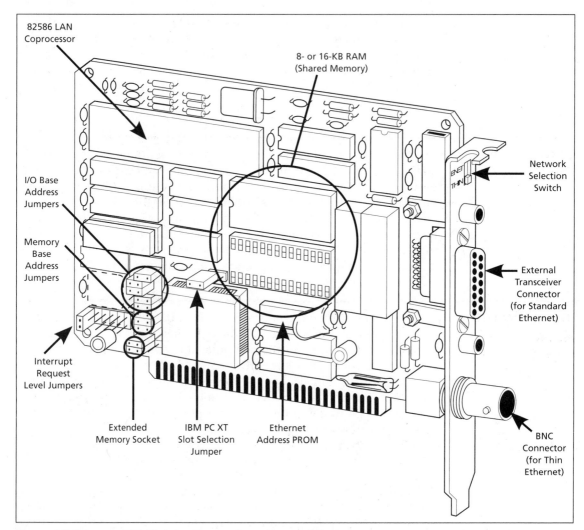

Figure 5.2 *Ethernet NIC Showing Jumper Locations and Settings*

The configuration process also depends on the type of computer. ISA computers use jumpers on the NIC while EISA and MCA computers use configuration software. ISA computers are the most prone to hardware conflicts because of the use of jumpers. For example, the COM1 port frequently used for a modem uses interrupt (IRQ) 4. If you set the NIC to use IRQ 4, then the COM1 port will not work.

All NICs are set at the factory with default configurations. The factory default settings will work in many computers. Consult the manual that comes with your NIC to determine if the default settings will work with your computer.

Write down how the switches are set on your NIC before closing up the computer. You will need this information later as you install the network software for the NIC. Many computers now come with the NIC installed. This saves you time and is often cost effective. It is a particularly useful feature for notebook computers because they have few available slots for expansion. If you do install the NIC, be certain the slot inside the computer is free of dust and obstructions. Also, ground yourself on the computer chassis to prevent static discharge. The NIC should be firmly installed in the slot to make good contact.

The Network Software

The history of network software is much like the history of DOS. Both have evolved to meet the functional needs of users and to take advantage of the developments of workstations. It is important to stay up-to-date with current versions and releases of network software, just as it is with DOS. Each new release is intended to fix problems or to add features.

As a network administrator, you should test each new release before you make it available to your users. It may not be fully compatible with your workstations, or it may introduce new problems that are unknown to the vendor.

The network software consists of the **network driver** and **network shell**. The driver enables the workstation to communicate with the network—for example, by sending data to or receiving data from the file server. The shell coordinates work so that DOS and network commands are properly interpreted and acted on.

NetWare relies on a driver called IPX and its shell is called the NETx software. Both are explained in the next sections.

The IPX Driver

Internetwork Packet Exchange (IPX) is a NetWare protocol that manages packet routing and packet flow. To understand how IPX works, let's examine a typical network with ARCNET and Ethernet workstations connected to a single file server (see Figure 5.3). In that figure, IPX is loaded in each workstation and at the file server. The IPX loaded at the file server has the ability to route packets between networks—for example, between ARCNET and Ethernet. When the file server in our example was

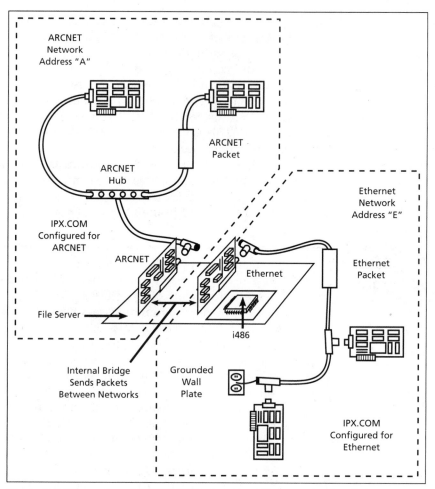

Figure 5.3 *Ethernet and ARCNET Workstations Communicating Using IPX.COM Protocol*

installed, the Ethernet and ARCNET segments were assigned unique network addresses. The Ethernet network was assigned address *E* and the ARCNET network was assigned *A*.

Each workstation has as part of its address the network address as well as its own unique address. When a workstation on network E sends a packet addressed to a workstation on network A, the packet goes to the Ethernet NIC in the file server. IPX determines that the packet is addressed to another network. The file server looks in its routing table to determine where to send the packet. IPX then routes the packet to the file server ARCNET NIC, and that NIC sends the packet to the ARCNET workstation. In this example, sending packets between networks is called **internal routing.**

Networks can use multiple versions of protocols, such as in our Ethernet and ARCNET example. Ethernet uses a version of IPX that is different from the one ARCNET uses.

When a DOS workstation must communicate with an AppleTalk or Unix network, then more versions of IPX are created and supported. One solution to having multiple versions of IPX is to create a *logical network interface card*, as discussed in the next section.

IPXODI

A logical NIC allows more than one protocol at a time to use one NIC. Novell's solution for a logical NIC is the *Open Data-link Interface* or ODI driver. With a NIC that supports ODI and that uses IPX, a workstation can load a protocol for each type of network with which it needs to communicate. A DOS workstation can attach to a Novell file server using IPX and at the same time connect to a TCP/IP network. Figure 5.4 illustrates how this works.

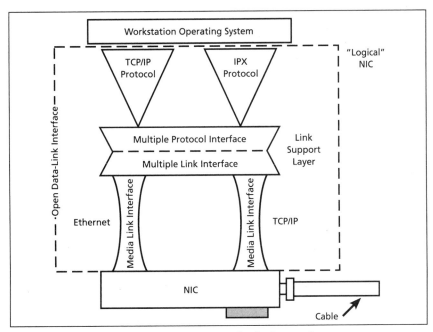

Figure 5.4 *A "Logical" NIC Supporting Multiple Protocols*

The illustration shows that two protocols are loaded on the workstation: IPX, and TCP/IP. The logical NIC that makes multiple protocol access possible is several layers of software. The software operates between the hardware NIC and the protocols and is known as *Link Support Layer* (LSL) (see Figure 5.4).

SPX and NCP

Besides IPX and associated utilities like ODI, NetWare uses two other protocols, **SPX** and **NCP**. SPX or Sequenced Packet Exchange is used by applications programs for support functions. SPX can establish program-to-program communication. Database applications developers use SPX to assist with sending data between applications and recovering from data errors in the event of a network disconnection.

NCP or NetWare Core Protocols are responsible for processing packets the file server receives. NCP uses the services of IPX for packet delivery. NCP provides access to file server data, file printing, security, and other basic operations.

During the login process, NCP verifies the user name and the password, and then it creates a connection to the server. The server assigns a connection number to each user that is viewed by using the NetWare USERLIST command.

The NETX Shell

NETX.COM is the network shell program. It is customized to work with specific versions of DOS. For example, NET3.COM works with DOS version 3 and NET4.COM works with DOS 4. NETX.EXE is another network shell that works with all versions of DOS. Since it is an executable file (.EXE), it is easily loaded into high memory. The NETX.COM and NETX.EXE programs intercept each request from the workstation and route DOS commands to DOS and NetWare commands to the file server. For example, the DOS command to copy files, *copy c:letter.txt a:*, would be routed to DOS for action. The NetWare command to list a directory, *ndir h:*, would be routed to NetWare for processing.

Figure 5.5 illustrates what happens when a DOS workstation application makes a request using the network software, IPX.COM and NETX.COM. When the workstation establishes a connection with the file server, it makes requests for services from the file server. The most common service requests are for file and print services.

The NETX.COM and IPX.COM programs are loaded into the workstation's memory. Both programs are provided by Novell. Some NIC manufacturers provide their own version of the IPX program for specialized interface with NetWare.

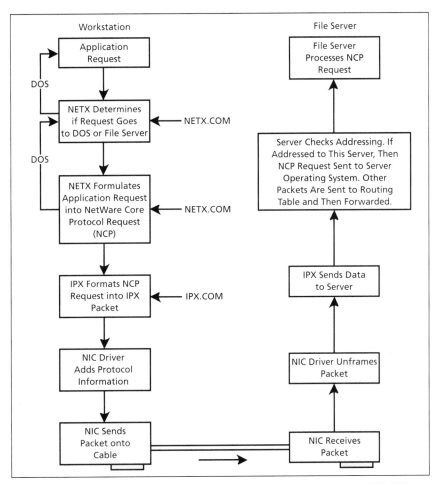

Figure 5.5 *The Process of an Application Making a Request Using IPX.COM and NETX.COM*

EMSNETX and XMSNETX

The NETX.COM network shell requires about 35 KB and NETX.EXE uses 77 KB of conventional memory in the workstation. If the workstation has 1 MB of memory, you can load the NETX.COM functions into the expanded memory between 640 KB and 1 MB. Use the EMSNETX.EXE program instead of NETX.COM for this purpose.

If the workstation has more than 1 MB of memory, you may wish to load the NETX.COM functions into extended memory. This is the memory above 1 MB. The XMSNETX.EXE program is used instead of

NETX.COM to load the network shell into extended memory. You will need to load a memory manager, such as Microsoft's HIMEM.SYS, before you load XMSNETX.EXE.

EMSNETX.EXE and XMSNETX.EXE are provided by Novell on the WSGEN diskette.

Configuring IPX.COM

The IPX.COM file must be configured to match the jumper or switch settings on the NIC. The configuration steps are as follows:

1. Prepare a DOS boot disk (usually either drive A: or C:). If the disk is not formatted, use the DOS FORMAT /S command to format it.
2. Make a working copy of the NetWare disk that is labeled WSGEN. Use the DOS DISKCOPY command to make the copy.
3. If there are driver files supplied with the NIC, copy these onto the WSGEN diskette you made in step 2. The driver files are identified by the extensions *.LAN* and *.OBJ*. For example, the Interlan NI5210 NIC driver files are E5210SH.OBJ and E5210SH.LAN.
4. Run the WSGEN program. For example, place the WSGEN diskette into drive A: on the workstation and type *A:WSGEN*.

Following several introductory screens, there is a screen that lists the available NIC drivers (see Figure 5.6). The NIC drivers you copied onto the WSGEN diskette will be listed as well as the drivers provided by Novell. Use the arrow key to move down the list to highlight the NIC driver you want to use. Each listing has the name of the driver, the version, and the version date. Once your selection is highlighted, press the ENTER key to make the selection. If the driver you need is not in the list, press the INSERT key to access additional driver files. These files are on a separate diskette labeled LAN_DRV_.001, which you must place in the appropriate floppy drive.

Figure 5.6 shows the NetWare NE2000 driver as the selection. Once you press ENTER from this selection, the screen in Figure 5.7 is displayed. This screen shows the options for the NIC. The options you select must correspond to the NIC settings you used when the card was installed. (Refer to "Installing the Network Interface Card," in this chapter.)

In many cases, option *0:*, shown on the screen in Figure 5.7, is the best selection. Option 0: is the least likely to conflict with other devices in the workstation. (Like some network administrators, you may prefer to install the NIC after running WSGEN. This allows you to decide on

```
         <Escape> = Cancel   <F1> = Help   <Alt><F10> = Exit

 Select the driver that matches the network board in your workstation.

     3Com 3c503 EtherLink II  v3.01EC (901101)
     3Com 3c505 EtherLink Plus (Assy 2012)  v4.12EC (910117)
     3Com EtherLink/MC 3C523  v2.36EC (901207)
     IBM LAN Support Program Driver  v2.60 (901031)
     IBM PCN II & Baseband  v1.15 (900905)
     IBM Token-Ring  v2.60 (901022)
     NetWare NE/2  v2.02EC (900718)
     NetWare NE1000  v3.02EC (900831)
     NetWare NE2000  v1.05EC (900718)
   ▼ NetWare Turbo RX-Net  v2.11 (901217)

       Highlight the correct driver; then press <Enter>.
       If the driver you want is not listed, press <Insert>.
```

Figure 5.6 *WSGEN Screen Showing the NIC Drivers to Be Selected*

the best jumper and switch settings with the card in front of you, in case the settings you first select are not available on the WSGEN screen in Figure 5.7.)

Figure 5.8 is the last WSGEN screen. It displays the driver configuration settings you have selected and it prompts you to generate the network software, IPX.COM.

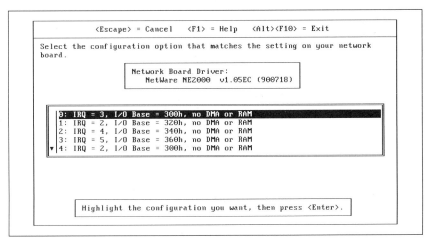

Figure 5.7 *WSGEN Screen Showing the Driver Options to Select*

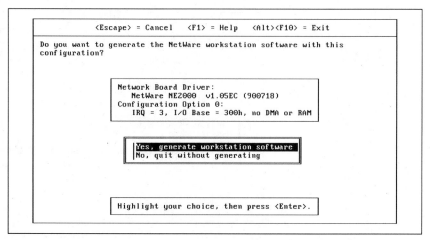

```
         <Escape> = Cancel    <F1> = Help    <Alt><F10> = Exit

 Do you want to generate the NetWare workstation software with this
 configuration?


              ┌──────────────────────────────────────────┐
              │ Network Board Driver:                     │
              │    NetWare NE2000  v1.05EC (900718)        │
              │ Configuration Option 0:                   │
              │    IRQ = 3, I/O Base = 300h, no DMA or RAM │
              └──────────────────────────────────────────┘


              ┌──────────────────────────────────────────┐
              │ Yes, generate workstation software        │
              │ No, quit without generating               │
              └──────────────────────────────────────────┘


              ┌──────────────────────────────────────────┐
              │ Highlight your choice, then press <Enter>.│
              └──────────────────────────────────────────┘
```

Figure 5.8 *WSGEN Screen Showing the Configuration Values Selected*

CONFIG.SYS

Each workstation will need a CONFIG.SYS file on its boot disk. This file is loaded automatically at the time the workstation is booted. CONFIG.SYS is a text file that loads device drivers and DOS environment characteristics. For example, WordPerfect requires that DOS enable 20 files to be open at the same time. This is accomplished by placing the statement *FILES=20* in the CONFIG.SYS file. The CONFIG.SYS file will usually contain four statements:

1. DEVICE=ANSI.SYS A screen driver used by many software applications. (*Note*: When this statement is used, copy the ANSI.SYS file from the original DOS disk to the workstation boot disk.)

2. SHELL=COMMAND.COM /P /E:1024 A command that increases the DOS environment size and prevents problems caused by the need to set **environment variables** for a program. (Environment variables are used to enable DOS to find files needed by it or by programs. The SHELL command is available only in DOS versions 3.2 and above.)

3. BUFFERS=20 Most software applications require a minimum number of 512 byte buffers for storing data on the workstation. Twenty buffers are enough for the normal range of software applications.

4. FILES=20 This command determines the number of files that can be open (on the workstation) at the same time. Most software applications require 20 or fewer open files.

A fifth statement is needed if you use a memory manager. For example, the memory manager HIMEM.SYS would be implemented by the statement *DEVICE=HIMEM.SYS*.

NET.CFG

If you use the IPXODI.COM driver, create a NET.CFG file on the workstation. NET.CFG will also work with the IPX.COM driver, as will a file called SHELL.CFG. But SHELL.CFG does not work with IPXODI.COM, so NET.CFG is more versatile. NET.CFG and SHELL.CFG are configuration files that help establish the NetWare environment. Some commonly used environment parameters are:

1. File handles: The number of network files the user can have open at the same time.
2. Local printers: A command that tells the network how many printers are connected to the workstation. (Workstation printers are called local printers.) A LOCAL PRINTERS = 0 statement is used when there is no workstation printer. (Otherwise, the workstation will "hang" when jobs are sent to the local printer.)
3. Preferred server: A statement that is needed on networks with more than one file server. It is used to indicate which server the workstation normally accesses. For example, a network might have a server named ACCT and another server named SALES. The statement *PREFERRED SERVER = SALES* will cause the workstation to log into the SALES server.

The NET.CFG file on your workstation might have the following command stream:

```
PREFERRED SERVER = SALES
LOCAL PRINTERS = 0
```

NETBIOS

Some applications are written to use the IBM communications protocol, **NETBIOS**. NETBIOS is a protocol developed by IBM for its PC LAN system. Novell provides a NETBIOS emulator in the file NETBIOS.COM, which simulates the NETBIOS protocol for applications that require it. If it is needed by an application, copy NETBIOS.COM to the workstation boot disk. NETBIOS.COM requires a companion file called INT2F.COM that must be on the boot disk, too.

AUTOEXEC.BAT File

You can automate the log-in process on the workstation by creating an AUTOEXEC.BAT file, which is a text file with a stream of commands. The commands are executed after the workstation loads DOS. A typical AUTOEXEC.BAT file will have the following command stream:

```
IPX

NETX        (For the version of DOS on the workstation; or
            EMSNETX.EXE or XMSNETX.EXE.)

NETBIOS    (If needed.)

INT2F      (If needed.)

F:

LOGIN
```

In this command stream, IPX and NET5 are used to load the network driver and shell. NETBIOS and INT2F are optional. They can be removed from the command stream if there are no applications that require them. The F: statement changes to the first network drive. The LOGIN command is used to access the user's NetWare account.

The Boot Disk

The files we have been discussing go on the workstation's boot disk. The boot disk is the disk (usually drive A: or drive C:) that the workstation uses to load the OS software, such as the DOS COMMAND.COM file, when it is powered on. The boot disk will have the following files:

```
IPX.COM

NETx.COM

CONFIG.SYS

AUTOEXEC.BAT

NETBIOS.EXE     (If needed.)

INT2F.COM       (If NETBIOS is used.)

NET.CFG
```

This set of files will work for Ethernet and ARCNET, but token-ring networks require an additional file, ROUTE.COM, on the boot disk. See Appendix A for sample CONFIG.SYS and AUTOEXEC.BAT files.

Diskless Booting

There are hardware configurations where boot disks are not used. In these configurations, the NIC has a remote reset boot PROM chip. In diskless configurations, the boot files are on the file server. Novell provides a utility called DOSGEN to copy the remote boot files onto the file server.

Creating an ODI Boot Diskette

As mentioned in the section on IPXODI, you may need to configure the workstation for a network that uses two protocols, such as TCP/IP and IPX. Use the following steps to create a boot diskette for use with IPXODI:

1. Prepare a DOS boot disk (usually either drive A: or C:). If the disk is not formatted, use the DOS FORMAT /S command to format it.

2. Copy the following ODI files located in the DOSODI subdirectory of the WSGEN diskette to the boot disk.

   LSL.COM This is the Link Support Layer software.

   NIC Driver Copy the NIC driver if it is provided by Novell or copy the driver supplied by the NIC vendor. For example, if you are using the NE2000 NIC, the driver file would be NE2000.COM

   IPXODI.COM This file manages communication between workstations.

   NETBIOS.EXE and INT2F.COM Copy these files if you will need them for software applications on the file server. (Consult the application software vendors' information on requirements.)

   ROUTE.COM and LANSUP.COM Copy these files if you are using a token-ring network.

3. Copy the appropriate NETX.COM file from the WSGEN directory. If the workstation has expanded or extended memory, then use XMSNETx.EXE or EMSNETx.EXE from the boot disk instead of NETX.COM.

4. Create a CONFIG.SYS file to specify the files and buffers parameters. Files should equal 20 or more.

5. Create an AUTOEXEC.BAT file and copy it to the boot disk. On an Ethernet network, the file would contain the following commands:

```
LSL

NE2000       (Or specify the name of the NIC driver if you
             are using a NIC other than the NE2000.)

IPXODI

NETX         (For the version of DOS on the workstation; or
             EMSNETX.EXE or XMSNETX.EXE.)

F:

LOGIN
```

The LSL command loads the LSL.COM file. The next command (in our example it is NE2000) loads the driver for the NIC. IPXODI loads the ODI network driver for the IPX and other protocols on the network. NETX is the NETX.COM shell for the workstation's version of DOS. Or you may substitute XMSNET or EMSNET if you plan to load the shell in extended or expanded memory. The F: switches to the NetWare login drive and LOGIN is used to log into the file server.

6. Create a NET.CFG file and copy it to the boot disk. This is an optional file, but you should plan to create it. The NET.CFG file enables you to document the configuration of the NIC and the protocol used. An example NET.CFG file could have the following commands for the NE2000 NIC.

```
LINK DRIVER NE2000

INT=2

PORT=320

FRAME=ETHERNET_II
```

The example shows that the NIC is using an Interrupt of 2, a PORT address of 320, and a frame (packet) type of Ethernet II.

Logging Into the File Server

The AUTOEXEC.BAT file on the boot disk contains the LOGIN command, which is used to log into the file server. The workstation will log in from the F: drive, or from the first available network drive. When the login command is used, the file server will prompt for the user's account name and password. A successful login is indicated when no error messages are displayed.

If the login process is not successful, the problem can be traced by examining the software and hardware settings on the workstation. Some examples of where to start are included in the following sections.

Problems with IPX

One source of problems is the NIC configuration. Check to be certain that the IPX or IPXODI configuration settings match those of the jumpers on the NIC. If there is a configuration mismatch, the workstation will display an error message about the mismatch, or it will hang. To check the driver settings, enter *IPX I* or *IPXODI I* at the workstation. The "I" switch displays the driver configuration.

If the NIC and software driver configurations match, try moving the NIC to another slot on the computer's bus. The original slot may be faulty. If you are still having problems, test the NIC to determine if it is damaged. Most NIC vendors supply diagnostic software. Replace any damaged or questionable NICs.

Connectivity Problems

Another type of problem is related to connectivity. This type of problem is indicated when you see the message, "File Server Not Found." The message means you have a bad cable connection or the file server is not on the network. Ensure the NIC is connected to the cable and that the cable is properly terminated and grounded. Cabling and connector problems require going to every connection on the network to examine the connections. A loose connection, a bad connector, or a break in the cable will cause workstations to be unable to find the file server.

Novell provides a utility called COMCHECK for testing the connectivity of the NIC and cable. COMCHECK uses IPX.COM, which means that IPX.COM must be loaded on each workstation to be tested. Also, make sure the cable is properly installed and connected to each workstation. COMCHECK does not require that the file server be running. Use COMCHECK any time a cable problem is suspected. Figure 5.9 illustrates the COMCHECK screen.

Memory Problems

A memory-related problem can also prevent the workstation from logging into the file server. If you are using EMSNETx.COM or XMSNETx.COM, be certain you have a memory manager loaded for expanded or extended memory access.

The DOS environment memory can also cause problems for the workstation. DOS environment memory is used to store DOS variable names and their values. For example, some software applications require a TEMP variable for temporary files. This variable is set by the DOS command *SET TEMP=C:*. The presence of several SET environment commands plus network commands can use up environment space. When

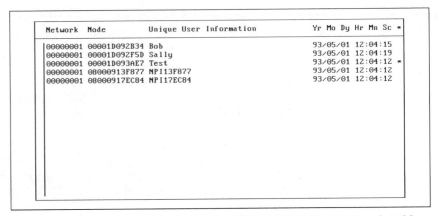

Network	Node	Unique User Information	Yr Mo Dy Hr Mn Sc *
00000001	00001D092B34	Bob	93/05/01 12:04:15
00000001	00001D092F5D	Sally	93/05/01 12:04:19
00000001	00001D093AE7	Test	93/05/01 12:04:12 *
00000001	08000913F877	NPI13F877	93/05/01 12:04:12
00000001	08000917EC84	NPI17EC84	93/05/01 12:04:12

Figure 5.9 *COMCHECK Utility Indicating That IPX.COM and Network Cable Are Functioning*

the environment space is used up, the workstation will begin displaying error messages about the environment memory. The environment space is set by default to 160 bytes (depending on the version of DOS).

To increase the DOS environment space, add the following command to the CONFIG.SYS file: *SHELL=C:\COMMAND.COM /P /E:1024*. In this example "C:" is the disk location of the DOS COMMAND.COM file. The "/P" switch tells DOS to run the AUTOEXEC.BAT file when the workstation boots. The "/E:1024" switch increases the environment memory to 1024 bytes. If 1024 is not enough, it can be increased to a larger number.

Summary

This chapter begins with an introduction to workstations, focusing on desktop computers that connect to a file server. Application software requirements are considered as they influence the selection and setup of the workstation. Memory is an especially important workstation requirement, since there must be enough memory for the network software and software applications.

Each workstation requires hardware and software configuration. The NIC is configured by setting the appropriate jumpers or switches on the circuit board. The network IPX software is configured to match the settings on the NIC. Using the WSGEN program to generate IPX.COM is illustrated through example steps and WSGEN screens. The implementation of IPXODI is also described, since many networks have several protocols in addition to the Novell IPX protocol.

The network shells NETX.COM, EMSNETX.EXE, and XMSNETX.EXE are described along with the use of memory managers. Many workstations make use of memory management so there is more memory available to run application programs.

As you configure the workstation, you will likely create boot files so that access to the file server is automatic for the user. Example boot files have been provided in the chapter for use with different workstation setups.

Once the workstation is prepared, problems may result in accessing the network. Several steps are presented for solving problems, including the use of Novell's COMCHECK program for testing network connections.

Key Terms

Conventional Memory   The memory that DOS can address on a workstation; ranges from 0 KB to 640 KB.

Environment Variable   DOS enables you to reserve environment space in a workstation's memory to store system variables used by a program. The variables enable the program to function more effectively—for example, by permitting the user to direct temporary files to a specific location.

Expanded Memory   The workstation memory that is between 640 KB and 1024 KB (1 MB). Portions of this memory can be used to store network software and other programs, if memory management software is used.

Extended Memory   The workstation memory that goes beyond 1024 KB (1 MB). It is used with the aid of memory management software.

Internal Routing   The process of sending packets between networks—for example, between an Ethernet and an ARCNET network.

Internetwork Packet Exchange (IPX)   A data transmission protocol used by NetWare. It permits the transmission of message packets or requests between a Novell file server and workstations.

NETBIOS   A communication protocol used by IBM. Some applications are written for a NETBIOS environment. Novell provides a program, NETBIOS.COM, that simulates this protocol.

NetWare Core Protocol (NCP)   A protocol that provides file server access services such as logging on, security checking, and print services.

Network Driver   The IPX or IPXODI file used by NetWare that enables the workstation to communicate with the network and to send and receive network packets of data.

Network Shell   A network program that interprets commands sent to or from a workstation. The shell determines if a command should be forwarded to DOS (or the workstation operating system) for action, or if it should be forwarded to NetWare.

Sequenced Packet Exchange (SPX)   A NetWare protocol that permits support functions for applications programs. It enables program-to-program communication, as might be used to handle data errors or recovery from network interruptions.

Workstation   A desktop computer connected to a host mainframe, a minicomputer, a file server, or another desktop. A workstation has its own CPU, can process data, and can manipulate file information. It may be a Unix-based computer, a DOS, computer, a Macintosh, or another type of computer.

Questions and Exercises

1. Find out the hardware interrupts for a workstation's hard drive, video, and two serial ports. What interrupts would be free for use with a NIC you plan to install in that workstation? What would happen if you configure the NIC so it conflicts with the hard drive interrupt?

2. Explain the concepts of conventional, expanded, and extended memory.

3. What types of software are typically run in conventional, expanded, and extended memory? Which types of memory require a memory manager? Find two commercially available memory managers and describe how they work.

4. What hardware configuration would you recommend for a DOS workstation to be connected to a Novell file server? Explain your recommendations.

5. Explain how a FAX board might conflict with a NIC in a DOS workstation.

6. Explain the function of IPX.COM. If your organization has multiple versions of IPX.COM reflecting different NIC settings, how would you determine the settings of a particular IPX.COM? What could you do as a network administrator to keep track of the different IPX.COM versions?

7. What versions of NETX.COM are available, and when would each be used? What are the alternatives to NETX.COM?

8. Why would it be helpful to have IPX.COM and NETX.COM built into future versions of DOS? What would be the disadvantages?

9. You are about to configure workstations for an Ethernet network and an ARCNET network. Explain the differences between the configurations of IPX.COM and NETX.COM.

10. You have purchased a NIC that does not have a driver supported by Novell. Explain what you would do to use the NIC-supplied driver with WSGEN.

11. When a workstation is powered-on, it goes through a bootup process. There is also a boot process for logging into a network. Explain the boot process during power-up and when the workstation logs into the network.

12. You are interested in determining if a memory manager would be useful for your workstation. Explain the benefits of using a memory manager. Are there any disadvantages to using a memory manager? What utilities are available in DOS or from third parties that will enable you to determine how workstation memory is being used at a given time?

Setting Up the File Server

Chapter Objectives

The objectives of this chapter are the following:

- To explain how to set up a file server.
- To show how to design an effective file server directory structure.
- To explain how server directories are managed.
- To show how to establish users and groups.
- To explain login scripts.

Introduction

Setting up a file server requires a combination of planning and technical skills. The planning involves gaining an understanding of the purpose of the file server. A server intended for accounting users will need to be set up differently than a server for a student lab in a college. The accounting server will have critical business data with an emphasis on access security. The student lab server will have programs to aid students with their homework, and access security will be more open so all kinds of students can use the server.

The technical skills required to set up a server include creation of directories, creation of users, establishing security, and installing software. This chapter explains the planning and technical skills needed to build a file server.

Process Overview

There are five basic steps involved in the file server set-up process:

1. Determine the use for the server.
2. Design and implement the directory structure.
3. Establish security for directories and files.
4. Create user accounts on the file server.
5. Create user and system login scripts.

Each of these steps is explained in the sections that follow.

File Server Use

Every file server is purchased for a particular use or combination of uses. Before you set up the file server, consult with the intended users. Find out what software applications will be placed on the server and how they will be used. This information will help guide you in establishing the **directory structure**, user accounts, and security options.

For example, a file server intended for office use might have WordPerfect word processing, Lotus spreadsheet processing, and an electronic calendar. As you work with the users, you will need to know how they intend to use the applications. How many copies of WordPerfect and Lotus will be needed? How many people intend to use the calendar? Are there defined workgroups within the office, such as accounting or customer service? Do certain workgroups wish to share their WordPerfect or Lotus files? Are specific files such as accounting spreadsheets confidential? Will an office assistant need access to his or her supervisor's account to check the calendar?

These are just a few of the questions that will arise. Make a list of questions and issues to discuss with the users. Also, plan to hold additional conversations as you are setting up the file server. It is easier to set up the file server with the users' needs in mind from the beginning than to make extensive changes later.

Creating a Manageable Directory Structure

Before installing software, it is essential to develop a plan for organizing the directories on the file server. Without such a plan, directories will quickly get out of hand. No one will know what software is where, which directory contains the most recent version of a program, or what software is mingled with other software in a given directory.

A directory structure is a system used to store and find files on a file server's hard disk. There are three components of a NetWare directory: volume, directory, and subdirectory. As we mentioned in Chapter 4, a volume is a logical unit of disk space. A single volume can span more than one disk. Your directory structure will be easier to manage if you match single volume to single disk, where possible.

If you have only one file server disk, then there will likely be only the *SYS*: volume for the system files, user files, and all other files. If you have three hard disks on the server, you might select to isolate activities by volume. The first disk would be SYS: and it would contain the NetWare system, utility, and print spooler files. Another volume might the called *USRS:* and would hold directories for each user's account. The third volume might be the *APPL:* volume to hold all software application programs.

Dividing volumes into this structure gives you many options for security, so it is possible to secure specific files and directories, but not others. Or you may want to secure an entire volume from all but a given group. For example, you might have a sensitive accounting volume, *ACCAPPL:*, that has programs meant only for the accounting department of a business.

Each volume is divided into directories and the directories may contain subdirectories or files or both. Volumes, directories, and subdirectories form a hierarchical structure for storing files in an organized manner. Think of each volume as a master filing cabinet with a limited number of drawers. Each drawer represents a major area of work, the drawers themselves containing subareas of work. Major areas on the APPL: volume might include software applications like WordPerfect, Lotus 1-2-3, FoxPro database, and Calendar. Each of these would form the directories on that volume. The WordPerfect directory would contain files, such as the WordPerfect program file. The same directory might contain subdirectories for graphics files, printer drives, and other WordPerfect utilities.

Figure 6.1 is a sample directory structure for a file server. The hierarchical structure enables you to designate a path to each file. A path to the WordPerfect program file might be: *BUS\APPL:WORD\WP.EXE*. In this path, the name of the file server is BUS and the volume name is APPL:. WORD is the WordPerfect directory and WP.EXE is the program file.

NetWare allows the path to be designated by the forward slash (/) or the backward slash (\). Contrast this convention to DOS, which only permits the backward slash in a path statement.

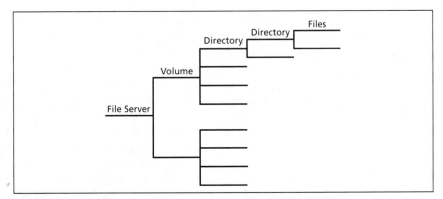

Figure 6.1 *File Server Hierarchical Directory Structure*

NetWare System Directories

NetWare creates four directories at the time the file server is generated: SYSTEM, PUBLIC, LOGIN, and MAIL. All four directories are on the SYS: volume. Figure 6.2 shows the basic directory structure.

The files in the NetWare created directories have a specific purpose. Some are operating system files and some are utility files for users. The SYSTEM directory has the network operating system, utilities to administer the file server, and bindery files with information about each user account. This directory is kept off limits to users other than the network administrator.

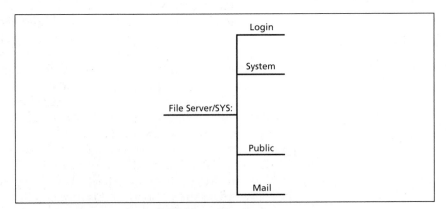

Figure 6.2 *NetWare Created Directory Structure*

The PUBLIC directory has utilities that can be used by all users. It contains programs that permit users to display and manage their directories, to see who is currently logged on, to set their password, and so on.

Each time a user account is created, a separate ID is established for that account. The ID is placed in the MAIL directory as a subdirectory. The username MARTIN might have the ID 2145780, which is also a subdirectory. This subdirectory will contain information used by the MARTIN account, such as an account login script, print job configurations, and mail data used by some types of mail programs. The login script is a text file that enables the user to create a customized login sequence.

The LOGIN directory has utilities to log into the file server. It may also contain programs to monitor software licensing and login security.

Directories Added by the Supervisor

Your goal is to create a directory structure that makes software installation easy and that supports the backup of critical files. To help you, Novell designed the NetWare operating system to support DOS workstations and the DOS file structure. NetWare has enhanced the DOS file structure to allow for multiuser access and for security.

Many of the rules that apply to DOS directories apply to NetWare directories. For example, in DOS the directory and file names use the 8.3 format so that a directory or file has up to 8 characters in the name and up to 3 characters in the optional extension. The file name should use alphanumeric—letter and number—characters.

Directory names should be logical and as short as possible. Logical names enable you to group files in a meaningful way. For example, a directory with the name WORD would contain Microsoft Word program files. A directory containing utility programs would be called UTILS. Creating directories with short names is useful because it reduces the characters to be typed. The result is a savings in time and a reduction in typing errors.

Directories should also be grouped by the type of files they contain. Program execution files are protected so they can be executed but not copied or deleted from the file server. Program files and associated support files will be kept in a protected directory that is backed up on an occasional basis (since program files do not change as frequently as data files). Data files will be kept in directories where the files can be copied, deleted, or updated. The data file directories will be backed up frequently, in case a file is deleted by accident or a file update is incorrect.

DOS Directories

NetWare supports all DOS versions beginning with DOS version 3. When a workstation boots with a particular version of DOS, there must be a corresponding DOS directory on the file server for some versions of NetWare, such as NetWare 2.15. There are not only multiple versions of DOS but versions from vendors that require separate directories. For example, separate directories are created for IBM DOS and for Compaq DOS.

Figure 6.3 is one example of a logical DOS directory structure that will support three versions of MS or PC DOS and one version of Compaq DOS.

DOS files are placed in subdirectories under the PUBLIC directory. The DOS utilities have functions similar to those in the NetWare utilities and are subject to the same level of network security.

Application Directories

The application directory structure is designed to support those applications that workstations will access from the file server. The directory structure supports DOS, Windows, OS/2, and Macintosh applications. As you design the directory structure, consider installation and update needs. For example, if you use WordPerfect, take into account the need to add future upgrades. Also, new graphics files are offered by WordPerfect and by third parties. Give WordPerfect its own directory and

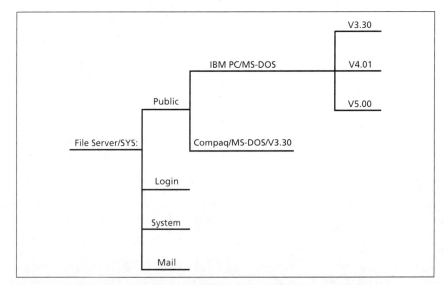

Figure 6.3 *DOS Directory Structure to Support Multiple DOS Versions*

create a subdirectory for the WordPerfect graphics. At upgrade time, the WordPerfect files will be easy to find. New graphics will also be easy to install.

DOS and Windows software applications should be in separate high-level directories. Within each directory, there should be subdirectories for specific applications. For example, WordPerfect would be in a subdirectory under the DOS application directory. Macintosh and OS/2 applications should be on separate volumes. Figure 6.4 shows an example directory structure for a network that has DOS, Windows, OS/2, and Macintosh applications.

Data Directories

The data files for applications should be placed in directories that are separate from the applications executable files. This is done so that the executable files can be protected against accidental alteration or deletion.

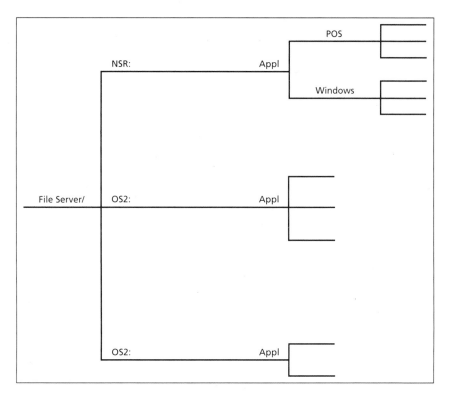

Figure 6.4 *Application Directory Structure to Support DOS, OS/2, Windows, and Macintosh Volumes*

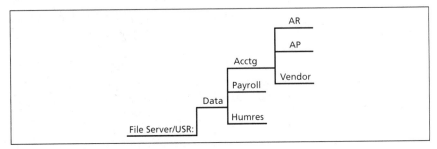

Figure 6.5 *Data Directories Structure for Three Departments*

For example, if you have Lotus users, they will create and update files containing Lotus spreadsheet data. Several users may wish to access a group of Lotus files to view or to update data. These files will be placed in data or production directories that allow access to one or more groups of authorized users. Some users may have authorization to update and create files, while others will have view access only. The issues of access and security determine the data directory structure.

Figure 6.5 is an example of directories for three departments with data stored on the file server. One department is accounting with sub-directories for accounts receivable (AR), accounts payable (AP), and vendor information (VENDOR). Another department is payroll and the third department is human resources.

User Directories

User directories, also called **home directories**, store a user's personal files. Personal files such as memos, letters, and other individual data are stored in the user's home directory. The user may also store customized *set* files for applications such as WordPerfect and Lotus 1-2-3. The user's home directory will often have the same name as the user's login name. For example, Joe Smith with user name JSMITH would have a home directory called JSMITH.

The home directory is seen by the users as a logical hard drive on the file server. The home directory is usually given a limited amount of disk space that the user must manage. Most users will have the option to create their own subdirectories under the home directory. Figure 6.6 is one example of a user directory structure.

Creating Directories

The DOS command that is used to create a directory is *MD* or make directory. The same command will work in NetWare. For example, let's create the directory *USR:\APPS\WP*.

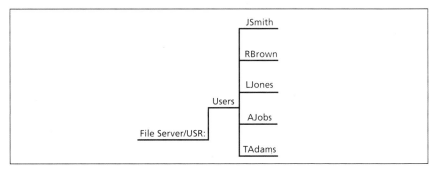

Figure 6.6 *User Directory Structure*

The first step is to be on the USR: volume. You determine what volume you are on by using the **MAP** command. MAP is a NetWare utility much like the DOS PATH command but MAP functions with file server and volume names. To change to volume USR: enter *MAP USR:*. To create a directory on the USR: volume called APPS, you would enter, *MD APPS*.

To create the WP subdirectory, you need to move into the APPS directory by using the *CD* or change directory command: *CD APPS*. Once you are in the APPS directory, enter *MD WP* to create the WP subdirectory. You can use the CD command to return to the root level of the USR: volume. The command *CD..* moves up one level, and *CD...* moves up two levels.

If you choose to remove a directory, first make certain it contains no files. Move one directory above the directory you want to remove and use the *RD* command for remove directory. To remove the WP directory in our example you would type *CD..* to move from the WP directory to the APPS directory. Type *RD WP* from the APPS directory.

Using FILER to Create Directories

The FILER utility enables you to view and modify information about volumes, directories, subdirectories, and files. FILER permits files to be copied, renamed, or deleted. It is used to manage the file server directory structure and to display or modify access rights to files and directories. Because FILER is in the PUBLIC directory, it is available to all users. FILER is started from any directory by entering *FILER*. An illustration of the FILER menu and submenus is presented in Figure 6.7.

When the *Current Directory Information* option is selected, FILER makes available data on the directory from which it was initially invoked,

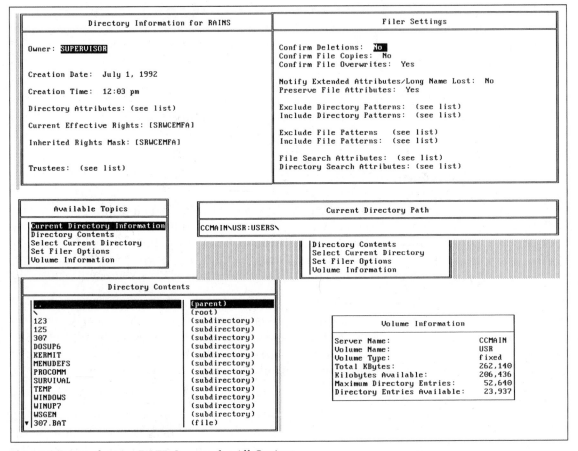

Figure 6.7 *Introductory FILER Screens for All Options*

or the directory to which it is currently pointing. Once the *Current Directory Information* selection is made, FILER displays a screen offering the following information about the directory:

- Creation date
- Creation time
- Directory attributes
- Current effective rights
- Inherited rights mask
- Trustees

The creation date and creation time are the date and time when the directory was established. The directory **attributes** refer to qualities of the directory—for example, whether it is to be hidden or set up to prevent deletion. Current effective rights to the directory are rights such as the ability to read the directory, write to it, and so on. The inherited rights mask shows the maximum rights that anyone can have in accessing the directory. The trustees option lists all users and groups who have trustee rights in the directory. (Attributes, inherited rights masks, and trustee rights are discussed later in this chapter.)

The second option on the menu in Figure 6.7 is *Directory Contents*. This option displays the files and subdirectories within the directory. It also gives you the ability to manage any of the subdirectories or files shown. This includes the ability to create or delete files and subdirectories.

The third option on the FILER menu is *Select Current Directory*. This option is used to switch to another directory or subdirectory from which the FILER options can be executed. An entry box is displayed at the top of the screen with the current directory. To change to another directory, modify the directory in the box with the backspace key and enter the correct current directory. The box can also be used to create a directory. For example, if you enter USR:\APPS\QPRO4 in the box, FILER will create this directory if it does not already exist.

The fourth selection on the FILER menu, *Set Filer Options*, is used to establish default options for managing files and directories. For example, you can set a default option to request confirmation before a file can be deleted or overwritten.

The last FILER option, *Volume Information*, shows the file server name, the name of the volume, the type of volume, the total volume size, the amount of volume space left, the maximum number of directory entries, and the number of directory entries available for use. FILER is a powerful utility because it can be used to delete a file or an entire directory; it can also be used to copy a directory and all of its subdirectories.

Using SYSCON to Create User Home Directories

SYSCON, or *SYS*tem *CON*figuration, utility is available for public access as is FILER. SYSCON is a multipurpose system management utility that is referenced throughout this book. One important management function of SYSCON is to create users. Another function is to create a home directory for each user. Every user should have a home directory where they can store personal files. SYSCON can be set with a default option to create a home directory for each new user. To set

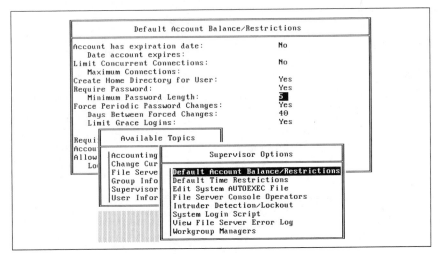

Figure 6.8 *SYSCON Default/Restriction Screen Showing Current Restrictions Applied to Newly Created Users*

the default option logon as the SUPERVISOR. Start SYSCON by entering *SYSCON*. On the beginning SYSCON menu, select *Supervisor Options*. Next, select *Default Account Balance/Restrictions*. A screen is displayed showing the current default balances and restrictions (see Figure 6.8). Select the *Create Home Directory for User* option and enter *YES*. Use the ESC key to save the default option and to exit SYSCON. Note that NetWare utilities use the ESC key to back out of menus.

Now that the default is set, SYSCON will prompt you to verify creation of the user's home directory each time a new user is created.

Managing Directories

NetWare has several directory management utilities in addition to FILER and SYSCON. They are DSPACE, NDIR, CHKDIR, RENDIR, LISTDIR, and MAP.

Limiting User Space with DSPACE

It is important to ensure that the file server cannot be immobilized because a user has suddenly consumed all of the available disk space. DSPACE is a utility to limit user file space. This utility is started by entering *DSPACE*.

On the first DSPACE screen, select *User Restrictions*. This option limits the amount of space on a volume. For example, when users are created, they should be limited to writing to their home directory and

```
Novell Disk Usage Utility  V3.56           Saturday  May 1, 1993  2:04 pm
                  User RAINS On File Server CCMAIN

    Av  Users on Server CCMAIN
   Cha ▲        User Disk Space Limitation Information
   Use
   Dir
            User:    GUEST

            Volume:  USR

            Limit Space:      Yes

      ▼     Available:      1024 Kilobytes

            In Use:            4 Kilobytes
```

Figure 6.9 *DSPACE Screen Showing the Space Limitation for GUEST on Volume USR:*

perhaps a data directory. If these directories are on volume USR:, then you should specify this volume along with the user. Figure 6.9 shows the current space used by user GUEST.

NDIR

NDIR, or *N*etwork *DIR*ectory, works like the DOS DIR command. NDIR lists the files and subdirectories in a directory. The list of files can be sorted by name, file size, date created, date last accessed, date last archived, file attributes, or owner. The command structure for NDIR is:

    NDIR [path] [options]

Use the forward slash (/) to separate options. NDIR/HELP displays information about the NDIR options. When used without any options, NDIR displays all of the files in a directory in alphanumeric sequence followed by the subdirectories.

RENDIR

RENDIR, or *REN*ame *DIR*ectory, allows you to change the name of a directory. You must be in the parent directory to use this command. The format of RENDIR is:

    RENDIR currentdirectory TO newdirectory

CHKDIR

CHKDIR, or CHecK DIRectory, shows the space available and how much space is in use for the directory and also for the volume. If the CHKDIR user does not have a space restriction, the space available for the volume is the same as for the directory. Figure 6.10 shows what would be displayed by entering CHKDIR from the directory \USERS\RAINS.

```
H:\>chkdir

Directory Space Limitation Information For:
CCMAIN\USR:USERS\RAINS

      Maximum        In Use      Available
      586,956 K      449,080 K   137,876 K    Volume Size
                     21,888 K    137,876 K    \USERS\RAINS
```

Figure 6.10 *Screen Showing CHKDIR Information for RAINS*

LISTDIR

LISTDIR, or *LIST DIRectory*, provides information about directories contained in the current directory. LISTDIR without options lists the subdirectories. One useful option is /A, which displays all subdirectories, inherited rights mask, and creation dates.

MAP

MAP is used to display, modify, and create drive mappings. When MAP is typed alone, the current drive mappings are displayed. There are three general types of drive mappings: local drives, network drives, and search drives. The local drives are those that belong to the workstation. They are typically drives A: through E:. The last workstation drive is determined by the DOS *LASTDRIVE* command that is used in the CONFIG.SYS file on the workstation. If the LASTDRIVE command is not used, then the first network drive will be F:. If, for example, the CONFIG.SYS statement LASTDRIVE=C: is used, then the default network drive will be drive D:.

Network drives are NetWare drives that can be defined from the default drive letter, such as drive F: to drive Z:. When a network drive is mapped, this means that the user can switch to the designated drive to access any programs or data files on that drive. For example, a subdirectory containing Lotus 1-2-3 might be mapped as drive R:. Once the user switches to drive R:, he or she can run Lotus 1-2-3 programs and the printer and setup files in Lotus 1-2-3. If the Lotus 1-2-3 subdirectory has the path SYS:APP/LOTUS, then the mapping is established by the following command:

```
MAP R:=SYS:APP/LOTUS
```

Search drives work like network drives. In both, subdirectories are mapped to specific drive letters. The difference, though, is that programs with .EXE and .COM extensions can be accessed without switching to the

MAP   **125**

network drive with the path containing the programs. For example, if a search drive is established for WordPerfect, then the WP command to start WordPerfect can be used from any drive. Search drives are mapped in the following way:

```
MAP S3:=SYS:APP/WP50
```

In this instance, search drive 3 (S3) becomes drive X:. This is because search drive mappings begin with the last letter of the alphabet. Search drive 1 is mapped to drive Z:, search drive 2 is mapped to drive Y:, and so on. Up to 16 search drives can be mapped. The DOS prompt command can be used to determine the directory level you are in at a given time. Type *SET PROMPT PG* at the DOS prompt.

The NetWare map command will show how each drive is mapped. To display the drive mappings, type *MAP* at the DOS prompt. Figure 6.11 provides an example of the output from the MAP command. Here, the first search drive is drive Z:. Often there will be several search drives that you will not want to replace. To add a new search drive for Z: without deleting an existing mapping, you would enter:

```
MAP INS S1:=USR:TEMP or MAP S16:=USR:TEMP
```

The MAP INS command inserts the new mapping USR:TEMP before the previously mapped search drives, shifting the other drives down the search path. In this example, USR:TEMP becomes drive Z:. The previous Z: drive mapping becomes drive Y:.

```
H:\>map
        Drive  A:    maps to a local disk.
        Drive  B:    maps to a local disk.
        Drive  C:    maps to a local disk.
        Drive  D:    maps to a local disk.
        Drive  E:    maps to a local disk.
        Drive  F: = CCMAIN\SYS:  \LOGIN
        Drive  G: = CCMAIN\USR:USERS  \
        Drive  H: = CCMAIN\USR:USERS\RAINS  \
        ------
        SEARCH1:   = Z:. [CCMAIN\SYS:PUBLIC  \]
        SEARCH2:   = Y:. [CCMAIN\USR:APPL\MSDOS\V5.00  \]
        SEARCH3:   = X:. [CCMAIN\USR:APPL\MARXMENU  \]
        SEARCH4:   = W:. [CCMAIN\USR:  \APPL]
        SEARCH5:   = V:. [CCMAIN\USR:  \APPL]
        SEARCH6:   = U:. [CCMAIN\USR:  \APPL]
        SEARCH7:   = T:. [CCMAIN\USR:  \APPL]
        SEARCH8:   = S:. [CCMAIN\USR:WINAPPS  \]
        SEARCH9:   = R:. [CCMAIN\USR:NETMGMT\NETUTILS  \]
        SEARCH10:  = C:\BATCH
        SEARCH11:  = C:\DOS
        SEARCH12:  = C:\LWP
```

Figure 6.11 *Current Drive Mappings Displayed with MAP*

The MAP utility provides great flexibility for accessing files. Its basic command structure is:

```
MAP [option] [drive:=path]
```

One useful command variation is the following:

```
MAP *1:=USR:USERS/%LOGIN_NAME
```

This statement will map the first available network drive to the user's login directory. %LOGIN_NAME is a NetWare variable that represents the user's name. For example, when JSMITH logs in, this user's first network drive would be mapped to USR:USERS/JSMITH.

Another useful command statement is:

```
MAP S:=T:
```

This statement will map drive S: to be the same as drive T:.

The MAP ROOT command is another variation of the MAP command:

```
MAP ROOT H:=USR:USERS/%LOGIN_NAME
```

This mapping creates a path that is treated like a root directory. In this example, drive H: would be treated as the user's root directory. From drive H: the *CD* command would not change to the \USERS directory, because the directory, \USERS\usersname, would be considered to be the highest level. This feature is useful when security concerns require that the user be limited in directory access.

Implementing a Security System

A network provides for distributed computing and data access. Therefore the network operating system must provide security to ensure that users do not have access to unauthorized data and applications. NetWare provides three levels of security: login and password, rights security, and attribute security.

Login and Password Security

Each user must have a NetWare user name to log into the file server. The user name may be the user's last name, first initial and last name, or some other combination of characters that identify the user.

On most file servers, users must also enter a password to access their account. The password function is optional and is enabled by the network manager.

The username and password security control who can log-on, when they can log-on, and from which workstation. SYSCON is the primary utility for implementing log-in security. The network manager uses SYSCON to create users and to optionally require the user to have a password. The supervisor can also set the days of the week and time of day when the user can log-on. The ability to set the workstation address (or addresses) from which users can access their accounts is another optional function of SYSCON. The address is taken from the network interface card of each workstation designated to access the account.

Passwords can be an effective means of security as long as users are taught not to share their passwords and to avoid leaving password information where there is public access. When passwords are required, the password should be at least five characters. NetWare accepts passwords from 2 to 45 characters.

The network manager can use SYSCON to require that users change their passwords at regular intervals, such as every 40 days. Figure 6.12 shows the SYSCON options for setting the user account restrictions for passwords. If the option *Require Password* is set to *No*, then the remaining fields are set to blank.

It is not always necessary for each user account to have a password. Some accounts may be designed for public access. A network of computers in a library or in a school may be designed for public use. For example, students in a classroom or school lab may not keep their data files on the network. Instead, they may access word processing or spreadsheet software and write their files to a floppy disk. The user accounts

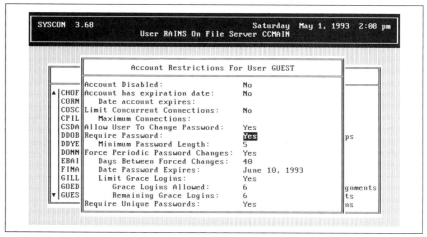

Figure 6.12 *SYSCON Screen Showing User Account Restrictions When Password Is Required*

they access may be generic, such as Station1, Station2, and so on. Their access to the network can be made available through menus, so that log-on procedures are automatic.

On any Novell file server, the supervisor account must always be passworded. This account is used by the network manager and it has privileges to all Novell functions, directories, and files.

At least one other account besides the supervisor account should be given supervisor privileges. If the supervisor forgets his or her password and there is no supervisor equivalent user, the only way to allow the supervisor to log-on is to reload the operating system. A supervisor equivalent account has all the rights of a supervisor and should be passworded. For NetWare applications where security is important, you should limit the number of workstations that can log into the supervisor and supervisor equivalent accounts.

Figure 6.13 shows the levels of security and how the levels interact. The supervisor can use default security or customize each level to protect the file server data.

Netware Trustee Rights Security

After users are logged into the file server, they have access to directories and files based on **trustee rights** and the **inherited rights mask** (IRM). The trustee rights determine the ability to read, delete, view, and update files and directories. These rights are presented in Table 6.1.

Any combination of trustee rights can be assigned to a user or a group of users. Trustee rights are assigned to the directory or to files in a directory.

The inherited rights mask supersedes trustee rights. A trustee will have only rights that are allowed by this mask. For example, if users have trustee rights to write to a directory, but not inherited rights to write to the directory, then they cannot write to that directory. Inherited rights also can be modified for specific files. For example, the inherited rights mask to the directory DATA might be R and F, where R permits users to read the files and F permits them to display the files (file scan) in the directory. The directory might contain the following files: BUDGET.DAT, PAY.DAT, PERSONS.DAT, and CHECKS.DAT. The supervisor has the option to grant W (write) rights to a specified user for only the BUDGET.DAT and PERSONS.DAT files. This user would then be able to modify these two files, but not the PAY.DAT or CHECKS.DAT files.

Inherited and trustee rights can be assigned to each user, but it is easier to create user groups and assign inherited and trustee rights to the group.

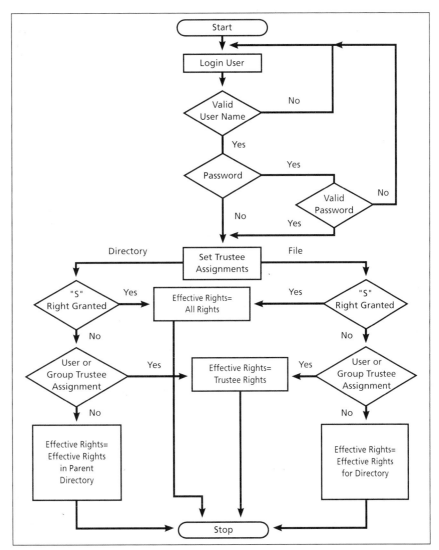

Figure 6.13 *Levels of Security and How They Interact*

Assigned rights flow down the directory structure. For example, if you assign R and F (Read and File Scan) rights to the directory APPL, each APPL subdirectory will have R and F rights. Trustee rights are assigned by using the SYSCON, FILER, or GRANT utilities. The inherited rights mask is managed by using the FILER and ALLOW utilities.

Table 6.1 File and Directory Trustee Rights

Trustee Right	Full Name	Description
A	Access control	The user can modify the trustee list of a directory or file, as well as the inherited rights mask.
C	Create	At the directory level, the user can create files and subdirectories. When assigned to a file trustee, the user can salvage a deleted file.
E	Erase	At the directory level, the user can delete the directory. At the file level, the user can delete the file.
F	File scan	At the directory level, the user can view the names of files when scanning with the DIR or NDIR commands. For files, the user can view the file on a scan of a file.
M	Modify	The user can rename a directory/file or change the directory/file attributes.
R	Read	The user can open and read existing files in a directory. At the file level, the user has the right to read and open a specific file.
S	Supervisor	The user has all rights to the directory, its files, and all subdirectories within the directory. At the file level, the user has all trustee rights to the file.
W	Write	The user can open and write to all the files in the specified directory. At the file level, the user can open and write to the specified file.

EFFECTIVE RIGHTS

Effective rights are those rights that the user has after trustee assignments are made and inherited rights masks are modified. The effective rights are summarized by the following rules:

• A user who has rights through trustee assignments made to the user, or group, or security equivalence to another user, has effective rights equal to the trustee rights no matter how the IRM is modified.

• When trustee rights are not assigned, the user's effective rights are determined by the IRM rights of the parent directory.

- When users are given supervisor equivalent rights, they have all rights to the directory, files, and subdirectories. These rights cannot be changed with the IRM.

ADDING TRUSTEE RIGHTS WITH GRANT

The GRANT command is used to modify trustee rights in a directory. This command is used from the DOS prompt and has the following structure:

```
GRANT RightsList [FOR Path] TO [USER or GROUP] Name
```

The parameters that can be used with this command include:

- **S** Supervisory
- **R** Read files or directories
- **W** Write to files or directories
- **C** Create new files or directories
- **E** Erase files or directories
- **M** Modify file or directory attributes
- **F** File scan
- **A** Access control
- **ALL** Grant all rights
- **N** Remove all rights
- **/SUB** Include granted rights to all subdirectories
- **/FILES** Put granted rights on all files

The /SUB and /FILE modifiers are placed at the end of the GRANT command as optional switches.

Let's look at two examples of how to set trustee rights in a directory. In the first example, the group EVERYONE is granted all trustee rights except the right to create subdirectories and change directory attributes. The directory is TEMP. The group EVERYONE is a group to which each new NetWare user is assigned.

```
GRANT R W C E F FOR USR:TEMP TO GROUP EVERYONE
```

The second example gives read and file scan trustee rights to the user RWILSON for files in the SYS:APP/LOTUS/DATA subdirectory.

```
GRANT R F FOR SYS:APP/LOTUS/DATA TO RWILSON
```

REMOVING TRUSTEE RIGHTS

REVOKE can be used to remove specific trustee rights for users or groups in a directory. The REVOKE options are:

- **S** Supervisory
- **R** Read files or directories
- **W** Write to files or directories
- **C** Create new files or directories
- **E** Erase files or directories
- **M** Modify file or directory attributes
- **F** File scan
- **A** Access control
- **ALL** Revoke all rights
- **N** Remove all rights
- **/SUB** Revoke rights from all subdirectories
- **/FILES** Revoke granted rights on all files

In addition to these parameters, REVOKE uses the modifiers FOR and FROM. The modifier FOR is used to specify the directory path. The modifier FROM specifies the group or user. The command structure is:

```
REVOKE RightsList [FOR Path] FROM [USER or GROUP] Name
```

The following example revokes write, modify, create, and file scan rights for the user group SALES in the directory SYS:APP.

```
REVOKE W M C F FOR SYS:APP FROM SALES
```

Revoking file scan rights can be a useful way to improve security on a file server. Users without file scan privilege cannot view the files in a directory. This limits a user's ability to inadvertently modify or delete files in that directory.

The REMOVE command completely removes all trustee rights to a directory. The format for this command is the following:

```
REMOVE [USER or GROUP] NAME [from path]
```

To remove trustee rights for all users from the directory USR:SYSTEM, you would enter:

```
REMOVE GROUP EVERYONE FROM USR:SYSTEM
```

Attribute Security

Attribute security is the third level of file server security. Attributes assign properties to files and directories that override trustee rights. Attributes restrict deleting, copying, writing, viewing, and renaming. FILER, FLAG, and FLAGDIR are used to modify the attributes of files and directories. The user must have the modify (M) trustee right in the directory to change attributes. A list of the directory attributes is presented in Table 6.2, and file attributes are presented in Table 6.3.

Table 6.2 Directory Attributes

Attribute	Full Name	Description
D	Delete	Prevents deletion of the directory.
H	Hidden	Hides the directory from DOS DIR, but NDIR will show the hidden directory.
P	Purge	Causes files in the directory to be immediately purged when files are deleted.
R	Rename	Prevents users from renaming the directory.
S	System	Hides the directory from DOS DIR, but NDIR will show the system directory.

Table 6.3 File Attributes

Attribute	Full Name	Description
A	Archive	Identifies files modified after the last backup.
CI	Copy Inhibit	Prevents Macintosh users from copying a file.
DI	Delete Inhibit	Prevents users from deleting directories or files.
X	Execute Only	Prevents copying of files with extensions of .COM and .EXE. This attribute cannot be changed. The files must be deleted then reinstalled.
H	Hidden	Hides directories and files from DOS DIR.
I	Indexed	Allows large files to be indexed for fast access.
P	Purge	Ensures that files are purged when they are deleted.

Table 6.3 *(cont.)* File Attributes

Attribute	Full Name	Description
RO	Read Only	Prevents files from being deleted or renamed.
RW	Read Write	Allows files to be deleted or renamed. RW is the default for files created on the file server.
S	Shareable	Allows more than one user to access a file at the same time.
SY	SYSTEM	An attribute assigned to system files and their directories. These files and directories are hidden from DOS DIR.
T	Transactional	Activates the transaction tracking system (TTS). It is used for database files so that incomplete transactions roll out in the event of a system failure.

Figure 6.14 shows the attributes of files in the directory WINUP7.

CHANGING FILE ATTRIBUTES WITH FLAG

The FLAG command is used to display or modify attribute designations for one or more files in a directory. The command format for FLAG is the following:

```
FLAG [Path/Filename [Options]]
```

```
H:\WINUP7>ndir
CCMAIN/USR:USERS\RAINS\WINUP7

Files:                 Size    Last Updated        Flags            Owner
------------------    --------  ---------------   ------------------  --------
BINDFIX     EXE      63,297   2-12-91   2:10p  [Rw---------------]  RAINS
NETAPI      DLL       7,168   6-24-91  11:05a  [Rw---------------]  RAINS
NETWARE     DRV     126,144  10-27-92   7:38a  [Rw---------------]  RAINS
NETWARE     HLP      34,348   2-12-92   3:12p  [Rw---------------]  RAINS
NWIPXSPX    DLL      30,016  10-31-92  12:53p  [Rw---------------]  RAINS
NWNETAPI    DLL     106,047   1-23-92   4:36p  [Rw---------------]  RAINS
NWPOPUP     EXE       4,208  10-28-92  10:32a  [Rw---------------]  RAINS
NWPSERV     DLL      11,616   8-02-91   1:22a  [Rw---------------]  RAINS
TASKID      COM       2,623  12-19-90   3:48p  [Rw---------------]  RAINS
TBMI        COM      17,089   7-10-91  12:27p  [Rw---------------]  RAINS
TBMI2       COM      17,999  12-04-91   2:46p  [Rw---------------]  RAINS
VIPX        386      24,362   9-04-92   1:01p  [Rw---------------]  RAINS
VNETWARE    386      10,093  10-19-92   3:55p  [Rw---------------]  RAINS
VPICDA      386      11,063   1-30-91  10:58a  [Rw---------------]  RAINS
WINUP7      DOC       5,695  12-08-92   3:08p  [Rw---------------]  RAINS

        471,768 bytes in   15 files
        499,712 bytes in  122 blocks
```

Figure 6.14 *NDIR Utility Showing File Attributes*

The following options can be used with FLAG:

- **RO**   Read only
- **RW**   Read write
- **S**   Shareable
- **A**   Archive needed
- **H**   Hidden
- **I**   Indexed
- **T**   Transactional
- **X**   Execute only
- **P**   Purge
- **N**   Normal or nonshareable read write
- **CI**   Copy inhibit
- **DI**   Delete inhibit
- **RI**   Rename inhibit
- **SY**   System
- **SUB** Flag all subdirectories in the directory
- **ALL** Assigns all but execute and copy inhibit attributes to files

The FLAG command can be used along with a path designation, to set attributes in a specified directory. When the FLAG command is used with no parameters, the current attributes are displayed. Note that the FLAG command can be used with the wildcard character (*). For example, if all .TXT files in the SYS:DATA\WP directory are to be flagged *shareable read write*, then the following command line would be entered:

```
FLAG SYS:DATA\WP *.TXT SRW
```

To flag all files in a directory as *shareable read only*, you would enter:

```
FLAG *.* SRO
```

Figure 6.15 shows the results of using the FLAG command.

CHANGING INHERITED RIGHTS MASKS WITH ALLOW

ALLOW is a command line utility that is used to view and change the inherited rights masks for attributes. You need to have access control trustee rights to use the ALLOW command. The ALLOW command has the following format:

```
ALLOW [Path [Rights List]]
```

```
H:\WINUP7>flag
        NETWARE.DRV         [ Rw - - - - -- - - -- -- -- -- -- ]
        NWPOPUP.EXE         [ Rw - - - - -- - - -- -- -- -- -- ]
        VIPX.386            [ Rw - - - - -- - - -- -- -- -- -- ]
        VNETWARE.386        [ Rw - - - - -- - - -- -- -- -- -- ]
        TBMI2.COM           [ Rw - - - - -- - - -- -- -- -- -- ]
        NWIPXSPX.DLL        [ Rw - - - - -- - - -- -- -- -- -- ]
        TBMI.COM            [ Rw - - - - -- - - -- -- -- -- -- ]
        VPICDA.386          [ Rw - - - - -- - - -- -- -- -- -- ]
        TASKID.COM          [ Rw - - - - -- - - -- -- -- -- -- ]
        NETAPI.DLL          [ Rw - - - - -- - - -- -- -- -- -- ]
        WINUP7.DOC          [ Rw - - - - -- - - -- -- -- -- -- ]
        NWNETAPI.DLL        [ Rw - - - - -- - - -- -- -- -- -- ]
        NWPSERV.DLL         [ Rw - - - - -- - - -- -- -- -- -- ]
        BINDFIX.EXE         [ Rw - - - - -- - - -- -- -- -- -- ]
        NETWARE.HLP         [ Rw - - - - -- - - -- -- -- -- -- ]
```

Figure 6.15 *FLAG Utility Showing File Attributes*

The path can be a drive letter or the directory name. The options are as follows:

- **R**   Read
- **W**   Write
- **C**   Create
- **E**   Erase
- **M**   Modify
- **F**   File scan
- **A**   Access control
- **N**   Allows no rights to be inherited
- **ALL**   Allows all IRM to be inherited, which is the default

If you enter ALLOW with no path or rights list, you will get a listing of the IRM for the files in the current directory, as shown in Figure 6.16.

In the example that follows the inherited rights mask is changed for the directory TEMP. All files and subdirectories in TEMP will have only read and file scan rights.

```
ALLOW USR:TEMP R F
```

SETTING DIRECTORY ATTRIBUTES WITH FLAGDIR

FLAGDIR is used from the command line to view and change directory attributes. The command format is as follows:

```
FLAGDIR [Path [Option]]
```

```
H:\WINUP7>allow
      Files:
            NETWARE.DRV                    [SRWCEMFA]
            NWPOPUP.EXE                    [SRWCEMFA]
            VIPX.386                       [SRWCEMFA]
            VNETWARE.386                   [SRWCEMFA]
            TBMI2.COM                      [SRWCEMFA]
            NWIPXSPX.DLL                   [SRWCEMFA]
            TBMI.COM                       [SRWCEMFA]
            VPICDA.386                     [SRWCEMFA]
            TASKID.COM                     [SRWCEMFA]
            NETAPI.DLL                     [SRWCEMFA]
            WINUP7.DOC                     [SRWCEMFA]
            NWNETAPI.DLL                   [SRWCEMFA]
            NWPSERV.DLL                    [SRWCEMFA]
            BINDFIX.EXE                    [SRWCEMFA]
            NETWARE.HLP                    [SRWCEMFA]
```

Figure 6.16 *ALLOW Utility Showing IRM*

The path can be a drive letter or the directory name. The following options apply to FLAGDIR:

- **D**   Delete inhibit
- **R**   Rename inhibit
- **P**   Purge
- **H**   Hidden
- **SY** System
- **N**   Normal resets the directory attributes to the default

The – and + characters are used with the option to either add or remove the option. For example, to add the hidden attribute to the directory TEMP, you would enter the following:

```
FLAGDIR USR:TEMP +H
```

Utilities for Identifying Security Holes

Any network with many users is susceptible to security problems. NetWare provides utilities to identify the potential security holes. These utilities are: RIGHTS, TLIST, USERLIST, WHOAMI, and SECURITY.

RIGHTS

RIGHTS is a command line utility that displays the effective rights of a user. The command is:

```
RIGHTS [path]
```

```
U:\APPL>rights
CCMAIN\USR:APPL
Your Effective Rights for this directory are [ R    F ]
   * May Read from File.                      (R)
     May Scan for Files.                      (F)
 * Has no effect on directory.

       Entries in Directory May Inherit [ R    F ] rights.
```

Figure 6.17 *RIGHTS Utility Showing Rights of GUEST in TEMP Directory*

Figure 6.17 shows the rights that user GUEST has in the APPL directory. Recall that even if the directory right indicates read-write attributes, a file in that directory that is flagged read only cannot be changed until the file is flagged read write.

To display the rights in your current directory, simply enter *RIGHTS*. If you want to display the rights you have in the directory SYS:APPS\WP, you would enter the following:

```
RIGHTS SYS:APPS\WP
```

TLIST

The TLIST command line utility lists trustees of a directory. Its command format is as follows:

```
TLIST [Path] [USERS or GROUP]
```

TLIST shows the user and group trustees of the directory specified. If no directory is specified, it lists information for the current directory. Figure 6.18 illustrates the information provided by TLIST.

USERLIST

The USERLIST command is used to present a list of currently logged on users. The display of information includes the connection number, each user's name, and his or her login time. If the /A option is used with this command, it adds information about each network address and each user node address.

```
H:\>tlist

CCMAIN\USR:USERS\RAINS
User trustees:
   RAINS                                    [ RWCEMFA] Al Rains
   GUEST                                    [ RW     ]
   ADMIN                                    [        ]
   -----
Group trustees:
   ADMIN                                    [ RW     ] Administration
```

Figure 6.18 *TLIST Showing Trustee Information for USERS\RAINS Directory*

WHOAMI

The WHOAMI command line utility is used to show log-on information about the user. The information shown includes the file server name, user name, connection number, and login time. If more than one server is attached, information is produced for each server. WHOAMI also shows group membership, security equivalences, effective rights, and other system information. The command format is as follows:

```
WHOAMI [ServerName] [Options]
```

The server name can be used to view user information on another server. The ALL or /A option displays all the information provided by WHOAMI. Figure 6.19 shows the information from WHOAMI/A.

SECURITY

The SECURITY utility scans all information on users and groups. It displays common potential security problems. Some of these problems are users without passwords, passwords that are too short, user accounts with no user login script, users with supervisor equivalent rights, users with trustee rights to the server root directory, and users with inappropriate access to key directories such as SYS:SYSTEM.

Only the supervisor can run the SECURITY utility, which is located in SYS:SYSTEM. The output from SECURITY can be several pages. The

```
H:\>whoami/a
You are user GUEST attached to server CCMAIN, connection 1.
Server CCMAIN is running NetWare v3.11 (250 user).
Login time: Saturday  July  3, 1993  10:05 am
You are security equivalent to the following:
     EVERYONE (Group)
     MARXMENUINTERNETLOG (Group)
     MARXMENUSTATIONINFO (Group)
     GROUPMAIL (Group)
     MAILUSERS (Group)
     PMSEND (Group)
You are a member of the following groups:
     EVERYONE
     MARXMENUINTERNETLOG
     MARXMENUSTATIONINFO
     GROUPMAIL
     MAILUSERS
     PMSEND
[         ]  SYS:
[ R     F ]  SYS:LOGIN
[ RW    F ]  SYS:SYSTEM/05000001.QDR
[ RW    F ]  SYS:SYSTEM/0B000034.QDR
[ R     F ]  SYS:PUBLIC
[    C    ]  SYS:MAIL
Press any key to continue ... ('C' for continuous)
```

Figure 6.19 *WHOAMI/A Utility Showing User Information*

easiest way to handle the output is to redirect it from the screen to a file that can be printed. To redirect SECURITY output to a file called RESULTS.TXT, you would enter the following:

```
SECURITY > RESULTS.TXT
```

Plan to run SECURITY two or three times a month or more to check on potential security problems.

Establishing Users and Groups

Once you have established directory creation and security procedures, you will need to create accounts for each NetWare user. Also, you will need to set up user groups. User group designations help reduce the work of managing user login scripts, trustee rights, and other file server resources. For example, if ten users need trustee rights to the directory, SYS:APPS\DATA\SALES, then the group SALES might be created. Each of the ten users is put into the SALES group, and the entire group is given the trustee rights to the directory.

There are three utilities for setting up users and groups: SYSCON, USERDEF, and MAKEUSER. SYSCON is menu driven and gives you the most versatility in creating users and groups. USERDEF and MAKEUSER work like DOS batch files. They contain a series of command line instructions for creating users in batch mode. SYSCON works well for managing single users, while USERDEF and MAKEUSER work well for creating several users who have similar set-up requirements.

Each time a user is created by these utilities, he or she will have at least two directories on the file server. One is a mail subdirectory contained in the SYS:MAIL directory. The name of the subdirectory is the same as the user's NetWare ID. If user AMARTIN has ID 5D000001, she will also have the mail subdirectory SYS:MAIL\5D000001. The mail subdirectory contains the user's login script, and it is used to process messages by some mail systems.

The second directory created for the user is a home directory where the user's personal files are stored. On a file server with a USR: volume for users' files, the home directory for AMARTIN might be as follows:

```
USR:USERS\AMARTIN
```

CREATING USERS AND GROUPS WITH SYSCON

SYSCON is the primary tool used by a supervisor to create a new account for a user. Figure 6.20 shows the SYSCON main menu screen and an example of each option on the screen.

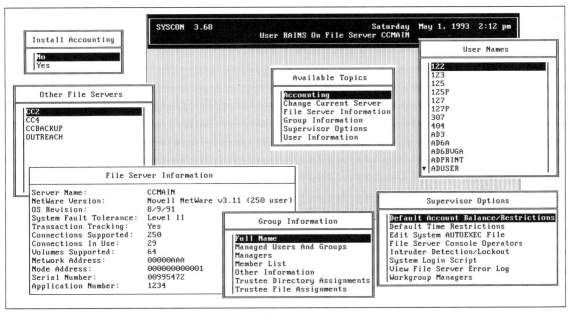

Figure 6.20 *Introductory SYSCON Screens for All Options*

The following paragraphs describe how to create a new user with SYSCON. The name of the user to be created is Jim Smith. In the process of adding Jim Smith as a user, the group STUDENTS will be created with Jim Smith as a member.

A popular naming convention is to use the first letter of the first name and append it to the last name. In this example, the user name for Jim Smith is JSMITH. Jim Smith also will be given a home directory with the name JSMITH.

Enter the command *SYSCON* to get started. The *Available Topics Screen* is displayed as shown in Figure 6.20. Select *User Information* from the menu, then select the *Default Account Balance/Restrictions* option. On a new system, SUPERVISOR and GUEST are automatically defined as users. To add a user, press the INS key. A box is displayed prompting for the user name. To create the user Jim Smith, you would enter JSMITH.

After you enter JSMITH, the *User Names* screen is displayed. Highlight the user you just created, JSMITH, and press the enter key. A box for the user's home directory is displayed, as shown in Figure 6.21. For the first user you create, it is necessary to specify the full path to the

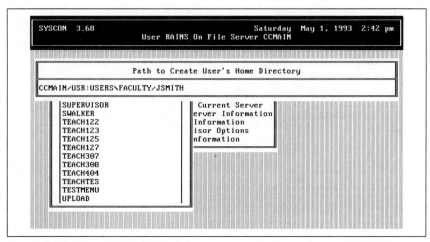

Figure 6.21 *Using SYSCON User Information Option to Create JSMITH Home Directory*

home directory. SYSCON uses this path as a default when additional users are created. As you create users after the first one, SYSCON will ask you to verify the path for each home directory.

JSMITH needs trustee rights to the directories he will be using. Granting trustee rights can be done on an individual basis or by groups. Since JSMITH is one of many students who will use the file server, it is easiest to grant trustee rights one time to the entire group of students. This saves time over granting trustee rights to each student individually.

Use the ESC key to access the *Available Topics* screen in SYSCON. From this screen, select *Group Information.* The group EVERYONE will be listed because it is created by NetWare at the time the file server is generated. Press the INS key to add a new group. A blank box is displayed where you can type in STUDENTS for the group name. When you press the ENTER key, two groups will appear on the list of groups, EVERYONE and STUDENTS. Use the cursor key to highlight STUDENTS and press ENTER. On the screen *Group Information,* select the *Member List* option. A box is displayed showing all users on the file server. Highlight JSMITH and press the ENTER key to add him to the group. Figure 6.22 illustrates the group screens in SYSCON.

Next, you will give the group STUDENTS trustee rights to the TEMP directory. On the *Group Information* screen, select *Trustee Directory Assignments.* A box displays the current directory. To designate the TEMP

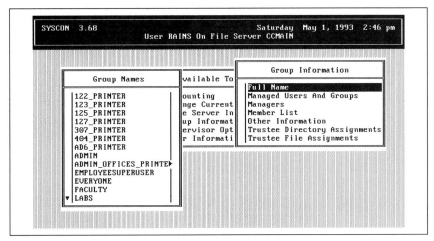

Figure 6.22 *Using SYSCON Group Information Option to Add STUDENT Group*

directory, delete the current directory and type the path to the TEMP directory, such as USR:TEMP. Press ENTER to designate the path you typed.

When trustee directory assignments are made to a group, each member added to the group has the trustee assignments of the group.

WORKGROUP MANAGERS

The network manager can assign the duties of user and group management to a **workgroup manager**. Workgroup managers have privileges to add users, change trustee rights, and perform other management functions for the groups and users assigned to them. The functions of workgroup managers are assigned through SYSCON with the *Group Information* and *User Information* options.

CREATING USERS WITH MAKEUSER

The network manager can create a large number of new users on the file server by initiating the MAKEUSER menu. This menu enables the network manager to create customized .USR files needed to establish users in a batch mode.

The MAKEUSER menu is started by entering MAKEUSER at the command level. This menu is reserved for use by the system supervisor and individuals who have supervisor privileges.

The *Create New USR File* option on the menu is used to start a new .USR file. The *Edit USR File* selection is available for the purpose of editing an existing .USR file. The *Process USR File* option executes the commands in a .USR file to generate new user information.

When the *Create New USR File* option is selected, MAKEUSER displays a blank editing screen. MAKEUSER commands are entered on the screen and saved in ASCII format. Normally, a .USR file is stored in an appropriate user subdirectory. For example, if there is a SYS:USER directory for all users and a SYS:USER\STAFF subdirectory, then the .USR file created to generate staff users will be stored in the SYS:USER\STAFF subdirectory. This subdirectory will also contain home directory entries for each user. For instance, if one of the user names is PJONES, then there will be a SYS:USER\STAFF\PJONES subdirectory that will serve as the home directory for user PJONES.

If the *Edit USR* File selection is taken, MAKEUSER displays a box for the path and file name of the .USR file to be edited. Editing is performed in a full-screen edit mode.

Once a .USR file is ready to be run, the *Process USR File* selection is made. A .USR file is then specified, and MAKEUSER proceeds to generate the specified users.

The MAKEUSER command selection includes options to specify account restriction information, to create groups, and to create individual users. Each command is prefaced by a pound sign (#) in the .USR file. The following is a summary of the MAKEUSER commands:

- **ACCOUNT_EXPIRATION** Specifies a date on which the account is to be disabled.
- **ACCOUNTING** Establishes the account balance and credit limit.
- **CLEAR** or **RESET** Clears keyword instructions that have been specified before the CLEAR or RESET instruction.
- **CONNECTIONS** Establishes the maximum number of simultaneous connections for an account.
- **CREATE** Creates specified accounts, including the user name, full name, password, group membership, and trustee rights.
- **DELETE** Deletes one or more existing accounts.
- **GROUPS** Assigns designated users to a group.
- **HOME_DIRECTORY** Creates the user's home directory.
- **LOGIN_SCRIPT** Specifies what script file (.LOG) is to be used as the user login script for one or more users.
- **MAX_DISK_SPACE** Establishes the maximum disk space to be available for one or more users.

- **PASSWORD_LENGTH** Sets the minimum length for a user password.
- **PASSWORD_PERIOD** Specifies how often (in days) the password must be changed.
- **PASSWORD_REQUIRED** Specifies that one or more users must have a password on their account.
- **PURGE_USER_DIRECTORY** Deletes the user's home directory.
- **REM** Prefaces a comment line to provide information about the contents of the .USR file.
- **RESTRICTED_TIME** Sets the times and days that specified users cannot access the file server.
- **STATIONS** Restricts the physical workstations from which a user account can be accessed.
- **UNIQUE_PASSWORD** Specifies that the user cannot reuse old passwords when changing the current password.

To create user JSMITH and add JSMITH to the group STUDENTS and set the expiration date to January 1, 1997, the MAKEUSER file would have the following statements:

```
#CREATE JSMITH
#GROUPS STUDENTS
#ACCOUNT_EXPIRATION 01-01-97
```

CREATING USERS WITH USERDEF

USERDEF is valuable for adding multiple users. This is a menu driven utility that creates users, creates login scripts, and establishes security and disk restrictions. When USERDEF is used, you can select a default template or create a custom template to use for creating users.

System Login Scripts

When a person logs onto the Novell network, the network first runs the **system login script**, then the user's individual login script. With prior thought and planning, the login sequence can be established to achieve two interrelated goals: low maintenance and clarity of performance.

Low maintenance calls for designing the login scripts so that it is easy to make modifications. This is done by accomplishing most of the login set-up work in the system login script, instead of in each user's login script. Minimize the commands in the user's login script. When you need to make changes to the log-in procedures, you will need to make changes only to the system login script. This is much easier than making repetitive changes to each user's login script, particularly when you might have to do this 20, 40, or more times.

Clarity of performance entails writing the login scripts so that they are internally documented and so that commands follow a logical sequence. This improves the ability to maintain the scripts after they have been written. Figure 6.23 contains an example of a system login script.

```
REM ** ESTABLISH DOS AND NOVELL CONTROLS **
BREAK OFF
MAP DISPLAY OFF
DOS SET PROMPT="$P$G"

REM ** ESTABLISH SEARCH DRIVES **
MAP S1:=SYS:PUBLIC
MAP S2:=SYS:APP\UTILS

REM ** DISPLAY GENERAL MESSAGE TO USERS **
FDISPLAY SYS:PUBLIC/MESSAGES/ALL.MSG

REM ** SET UP CUSTOMIZATION FOR GROUP ACCTING **
IF MEMBER OF "ACCTING" BEGIN
  MAP H:=SYS:USERS/ACCTING/%LOGIN_NAME
  CAPTURE P=0 NB NT TI=1 F=1
END

REM ** SET UP CUSTOMIZATION FOR GROUP MNGMENT **
IF MEMBER OF "MNGMENT" BEGIN
  MAP H:=SYS:USERS/MNGMENT/%LOGIN_NAME
  ENDCAP
  FDISPLAY SYS:PUBLIC/MESSAGES/MNG.MSG
END

REM ** SET USERS TO DEFAULT DRIVE H: **
DRIVE H:
```

Figure 6.23 *An Example of a System Login Script File*

Notice that the login script in Figure 6.23 is divided into several different sections, each separated by a beginning REM statement. (REM statements are used for comments.) The first section contains DOS and Novell controls that are standardized for all users. The BREAK OFF prevents users from exiting before the system login script is finished. The MAP DISPLAY OFF command suppresses display of the search drive mappings. And the DOS SET PROMPT="PG" sets the prompt sequence so it shows the directory path and the (>) prompt.

The next commented section establishes search drives. Search drive 1, or drive Z:, is mapped to the PUBLIC directory. Search drive 2, which becomes drive Y:, is mapped to an applications directory (SYS:APP\UTILS). The PUBLIC directory is normally mapped as the first search drive, since it contains commands each user will need to access.

It is best to establish a minimum of search drives. Network security is enhanced with fewer search drives, as is more efficient handling of the system. If you need a mapping to run an application or to access data, create it via a MAP INSERT statement in your menu system or in a batch file to run the application. Delete the mapping with a MAP REM once the application session has been completed. Keeping the number of search drives low yields more control over who can access which applications on the file server.

After establishing search drives, the login script in Figure 6.23 provides an opportunity to include a system-wide message to all users. This is accomplished through the statement: FDISPLAY SYS:PUBLIC/ MESSAGES/ALL.MSG. The text of the message is contained in the file ALL.MSG. Here is an opportunity to share information about the system with all users. The information might pertain to new software available, new employees, or anticipated "down" time for network maintenance. If there is no system-wide information to share, this statement can be commented out with an REM statement. Once a new message is prepared, the REM portion of the statement can be deleted so the message is displayed.

Another portion of the example system login script is an area for establishing customized procedures that pertain to specific groups on the file server. One set of statements is for the accounting (ACCTING) group, another is for the management (MNGMENT) group. The statements used for the accounting group include:

```
IF MEMBER OF "ACCTING" BEGIN
   MAP H:=SYS:USERS/ACCTING/%LOGIN_NAME
   CAPTURE P=0 NB NT TI=1 F=1
END
```

The block within the IF statement sets the user's home drive to H: and creates a map to the user's subdirectory. The identifier, %LOGIN_NAME, holds the specific user ID. The CAPTURE statement customizes printouts so they'll be spooled to Printer 0. In this instance, Printer 0 might be a shared laser printer connected to the file server. The set of statements for the management group is similar to those for the accounting group:

```
IF MEMBER OF "MNGMENT" BEGIN
    MAP H:=SYS:USERS/MNGMENT/%LOGIN_NAME
    ENDCAP
    FDISPLAY SYS:PUBLIC/MESSAGES/MNG.MSG
END
```

Here, the user's home drive is again set as drive H:. The ENDCAP statement is used to customize printing for this group. It assumes all management users have printers at their workstations. Finally, the statement FDISPLAY ACCT/SYS:PUBLIC/MESSAGES/MNG.MSG says to display a special message for management users only. This message might remind managers to have employee timecards in by a certain time.

The final statement in the example system login script sets the default drive to H:. Once the logged-on user is mapped to his or her home directory, this statement sets the default drive to that home directory.

User Login Scripts

User login scripts provide an opportunity to further customize network activities to individual users. This may entail calling special menus, specifying individualized printing parameters, or running a particular program.

As mentioned earlier, you can reduce system maintenance by performing as much customization as possible in the system login script. Place only those customizations that cannot be generalized in the system login script into the user login script. Figure 6.24 provides an example of a user login script.

Notice that the example user login script still contains internal documentation regarding what is being done. The script begins by calling user Scott's specialized menu. No map to the menu is necessary, because the menu's subdirectory was mapped into a search drive in the system login script. The #LOGOUT statement ensures that users are not thrown into the command level mode if they press the ESC key to exit the menu system. The last statement changes the session to the network home drive, which is drive F:.

```
REM ** RUN THOMAS SCOTT'S MENU **
#MENU TSCOTT

REM ** LOG OUT IF USER PRESSES ESC TO EXIT **
#LOGOUT

REM ** SET DEFAULT DRIVE BACK TO F: **
DRIVE F:
```

Figure 6.24 *An Example of a User Login Script File*

Summary

This chapter is an introduction to setting up a file server. Each file server is unique because it is set up to match how users work in a particular organization. Knowledge of an organization includes understanding the workstations, printers, applications, security needs, and work patterns of the organization.

A first step in establishing a file server is to determine the directory structure, including how many volumes will be needed, which directories should be placed on each volume, and how to designate subdirectories and home directories. NetWare tools such as FILER and SYSCON are introduced to help with directory management.

Another important step is to determine the security needs on the file server. Login and password security provide basic security on a file server. Files and directories are protected by the inherited rights mask, by trustee rights, and by file and directory attributes. FILER, GRANT, SYSCON, SECURITY, and REVOKE are some of the security management tools explained in this chapter.

Once security is in place, it is time to create users. SYSCON, MAKEUSER, and USERDEF are three user creation utilities. SYSCON is best for creating individual users. MAKEUSER and USERDEF are intended for batch creation of users.

The last topic of discussion is login scripts. Login scripts are written to help make the file server "user friendly." The system and user login scripts map drives, establish printer setups, display messages, and run utility programs for the user.

Key Terms

Attributes   Characteristics of directories or individual files. On a directory the attributes determine if the directory is hidden; if the directory can be deleted; if files are automatically purged from the directory when deleted; and if the directory can be renamed. File attributes determine if a file is read only; if the file can be updated; if the file can be copied or deleted; if the file can be used by more than one person at a time; and so on.

Directory Structure   The relationship of volumes, directories, subdirectories, and home directories on a file server.

Effective Rights   The rights a user has to a directory based on the combination of assigned trustee rights and the inherited rights mask.

Home Directory   A directory or subdirectory intended for a user's personal files on a file server. When a user account is created, a home directory is established for the user.

Inherited Rights Mask (IRM)   The maximum rights to a directory are determined by IRM. A user without supervisor privileges can have no more rights to a directory than those permitted by the IRM. The IRM supersedes trustee rights.

Login Script   A list of commands that are automatically executed upon login. The system login script has commands that affect all users on the server when logging in. The user login script affects only the individual user.

Map   A command that associates a logical NetWare drive letter with a directory. For example, the logical drive L: could be mapped to SYS:APP/WP. When you switch to drive L:, NetWare will place you in this directory. The MAP command enables you to create a mapping and to view current drive mappings.

Trustee Rights   A feature of NetWare that enables access rights to be assigned to any file server directory or subdirectory. The access rights are given to users and to groups. The rights govern whether or not a user can read, open, view, and create files, or perform other activities in a directory.

Workgroup Manager One or more users designated by a network manager to help manage certain users or workgroups. The workgroup manager has privileges to add users, change trustee rights, and modify login scripts for the group(s) he or she manages.

Questions and Exercises

1. Draw and label a hierarchical directory structure using the following information. Select logical names that also are DOS compatible. Include the default directories created during installation.

   • The file server name is PLAINS.
   • There are three server volumes—SYS:, VOL1:, and DATA:.
   • The DOS applications are WordPerfect, MS Word, Lotus 1-2-3, dBase, and FoxPro.
   • The user groups are SALES, ACCTING, MANGMNT, and OPER.
   • There are five initial users whose directories are 1A12345, 1B00000, 3C12345, 4D44444, 5E45678.

2. Explain the differences between data directories and application directories as they relate to management and security.

3. Briefly explain two functions of the utility FILER.

4. Explain how the commands DIR and NDIR differ. How are they the same?

5. What are the logical drive types supported by NetWare? How does each drive type assist the user?

6. What is the MAP command? Explain how it is used in NetWare.

7. You are considering the use of passwords to control access to the file server. Why would you use passwords? When would not having passwords be OK?

8. What commands are used to assign trustee rights? How do the trustee rights of a parent directory affect the child directory?

9. How do inherited rights masks affect access to directories and files?

10. What is the GRANT command that will allow JJONES read, write, and erase trustee rights to file server ACAD, volume DOSAPPS, and the APPL/WP51 directory? What is the GRANT command that will grant the same trustee rights to the group STUDENTS?

11. What utilities are used to change file and directory attributes? Provide one example statement for each utility and a brief explanation of what it does.

12. What utility is used to display a list of users who are logged on to the file server? What information does it provide?

13. Create an example system login script that does the following:

    • Maps search drives for the NetWare public utilities and for local customized utilities.

    • Maps each user to his or her home directory.

    • Sends a login message to users in the group EVERYONE.

    • Sends a login message to the group ACCT.

14. Create a user login script that will do the following while not canceling any of the system login script statements:

    • Creates a search drive for the directory SYS:APPS\LOTUS\ DATA.

    • Routes printouts to queue LASER.

    • Automatically runs the NPROT virus checking software on local drive C:.

Application Software: Selection and Installation

Chapter Objectives

The objectives of this chapter are the following:

- To discuss software compatibility and licensing.

- To explain the design of application software directories.

- To explain how application software is installed on the file server.

- To illustrate application software installation by using WordPerfect and Quattro Pro as examples.

Introduction

The guiding purpose of a LAN is to make a variety of applications available to users. Common applications are word processors, spreadsheets, databases, the DOS operating system, desktop publishing software, and communication and other specialized software.

Some applications will be available only to a single user, while others will be available to all users (depending upon licensing rights). The latter group of applications —those to be made available to many users—pose special challenges. In fact, the single most difficult aspect of establishing a LAN can be adapting application software to a multiuser environment.

This chapter focuses on how to install a variety of application software beginning with the selection of the application, enforcing licensing, use of the application directories, developing a methodology for installing applications, and installation of software.

Selecting Application Software

There are three general categories of applications: **standalone**, **network-aware**, and **network**. The standalone applications are written for a single computer. These applications often will run in a network environment much like they would run on a single microcomputer. The desktop publishing software Pagemaker is an example of this kind of software. Its use of program and temporary files has always been intended for a single computer. Single versions of PageMaker will run on a network, but Pagemaker has not been designed for network use. Another example of a standalone application is Lotus 1-2-3 Version 2.01. This early version of Lotus 1-2-3 required system access files that were not designed for network use.

Network-aware applications do not make full use of network functionality, but they also do not require special system files or special set-up arrangements to operate. A user can use an application on several network computers without having to load a special system file. Network-aware applications, however, do not recognize network utilities like network printing.

The desired application for a LAN is the network application. Network applications are written to take advantage of network printing, network file handling, and network application license monitoring. Some network applications require that a network operating system be present before the application can be installed. Two examples of network applications are Quattro Pro and WordPerfect. Both are written to use network printing and file-handling capabilities.

Licensing of Application Software

When you purchase an applications package for a network, you are given a license to use the software only according to the vendor's stipulations. Normally, the license does not include the option to alter the software, to make copies for use by others, or to run the software on more computers than the license authorizes.

When you purchase software, read the vendor's licensing restrictions and plan to follow these restrictions. Many vendors now offer site licensing for their software. You may be able to purchase a site license for all users in your organization. Or a site license may be available for individual file servers, so that all users of a server can use the software. Even when server- or site-licensed versions are purchased, know and follow the vendor's licensing restrictions. The same applies to shareware and public domain software.

Several Novell-compatible software products are available to help the network manager adhere to software licensing restrictions. When installed, these products will monitor the number of users of a particular software application. If there are only five licenses for a particular application, these packages will enable the network to prevent more than five people from accessing that specific application.

SiteLock from Brightwork and Meter from Saber are commercial **metering** applications. Both control how many people can access designated applications at the same time. They also keep statistics on the utilization of applications that can be put into report format. The statistics can help you determine if more software licenses should be purchased for a given application.

Another good practice is to take steps to prevent software from being copied from the network. This is done by setting flags and trustee rights. For example, flag files as shareable read-only (SRO) and set directory trustee rights to read (R) and file scan (F). These actions will prevent files from being altered.

One way to protect software from unauthorized copying is to flag .EXE files (the program files) with the execute only (X) attribute. When flagged as execute only, these files can only be run; they cannot be copied.

The use of menus also limits unauthorized copying of files. You can set up the file server so that users access software through a menu system, such as the commercial Saber menu system. Design the menu system so that the user cannot operate from the system prompt (>). Each user's access to software is from the menu only.

The most foolproof way to prevent copying of files is to have diskless workstations. This makes it physically impossible to copy files from the file server.

You should also post notices informing users of the copyright laws that apply to the software on the file server.

Application Directory Structure and Management

Before installing software, it is essential to develop a plan for organizing the directories on the file server. Without such a plan, directories will quickly get out of hand. No one will know what software is where, which directory contains the most recent version of a program, or what software is mingled with other software in a given directory.

A plan for organizing directories also makes security setup and software installation easier. Here are some simple rules for establishing directories and subdirectories:

- Limit your root directory to the minimum number of entries.
- Avoid putting application software in the Novell-created directories: PUBLIC, SYSTEM, MAIL, LOGIN.

- Identify versions of the application software in the directory name.
- Establish major directories, such as APP, for applications; put specific applications in their own subdirectories under the major directory.
- Do not install two different applications in the same subdirectory.
- Keep a record of what software is installed on the LAN, including license authorizations.

A plan for organizing directories should include minimizing entries in the root directory. Entries in the root directory should not exceed what can be displayed on one screen. Think of the root directory as a master filing cabinet with a limited number of drawers. Each drawer represents a major area of work, with the drawers themselves containing subareas of work. Major areas on a given file server might include software applications, network utilities, user directories, and user data.

The applications directory, as an example, can be divided into a host of subdirectories, one for each software application. There might be a LOTUS3 subdirectory for Lotus 1-2-3 version 3, a DBASE4 subdirectory for dBase version 4, and a WP51 subdirectory for WordPerfect version 5.1.

Figure 7.1 shows how subdirectories in WordPerfect might be allocated within an applications directory. As shown in the figure, specific files for an application can be placed in another subdirectory under the individual application subdirectory. Macros and set files (default settings) for WordPerfect can be placed in an APP\WP51\MACROS subdirectory, and graphics files can be placed in an APP\WP51\GRAPHICS subdirectory.

In Chapter 6 we discussed how access to a directory is gained by granting trustee rights. The trustee rights granted to a parent APP directory will flow down through application directories below APP. For

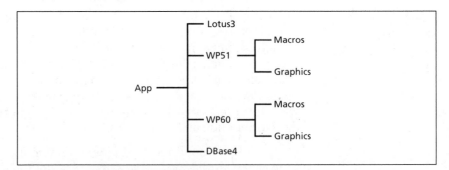

Figure 7.1 *An Applications Directory*

example, if the trustee rights for a user or group are shareable read-only for APP then these would be the trustee rights for APP/WP51. The directory structure as shown in Figure 7.1 reduces installation time because it makes assignment of trustee rights easy.

Having the proper directory structure also makes upgrading applications easy. For example, you may want to upgrade WordPerfect from version 5.1 to version 6.0. The WordPerfect 6.0 files would be placed in a WP60 subdirectory and the 5.1 version would remain in its WP51 subdirectory. This practice allows you to continue with the older version of WordPerfect until you are trained on the new version. Once the training is complete, you simply delete the WP51 directory (back it up first, in case you need to retrieve files later).

Software Installation Concerns

Not all software is intended for a LAN or multiuser environment. Before installing a software application on a Novell LAN, find out if it is intended for LAN use. Some applications are written specifically to be used in a network environment. Some are not but can be adapted to run on a LAN. And some software is not intended for LAN use, or even for adaptation to a LAN.

The considerations above are important because a single software package can make a LAN act unpredictably. As a rule, software that is not intended for LAN use, or adaptation to a LAN, should not be put on the LAN. LAN use is likely to be in violation of the vendor's intention for that software, and the risk is simply not worth the effort.

Another rule to follow is always to test software applications before making them available in a production mode. Here are several guidelines to follow when testing software:

- Test the software when the LAN is not in a production mode, or at least when no critical user activities are taking place.
- Test the software by logging in several users simultaneously and have them all try the software at the same time.
- Test the software on all of the workstation/printer configurations where it will be used.
- Test all menus involving the software.
- Test the software by operating it as it was not intended to be operated; try to simulate common user mistakes.

One very important consideration while testing software is to determine how much memory is required for an individual workstation to use the software. Some applications, such as computer-aided design

(CAD) packages, require a large amount of memory in the workstation. Use of these packages may have to be limited to specific workstation sites.

Another memory issue is whether the memory requirements of an application will interfere with the operation of the workstation. For example, the memory requirements of an application may cause the IPX.COM file on the workstation to fail, act erratically, or even hang the workstation. Often this means there is not enough memory for the IPX.COM file, any **terminate-and-stay-resident** (TSR) files, and the application itself. Or it may mean the application is addressing the same range of memory addressed by the IPX.COM file.

In the first case, where there is too much loaded into memory, the solution may be to clear any TSRs out of memory. Another approach is to experiment with the FILES and BUFFERS allocations in the CONFIG.SYS file. An additional step might be to increase the memory in the workstations where it will be used (if those workstations have less than 640 KB of memory).

Where there is an addressing conflict between the IPX.COM file on the workstation and the application, it may be necessary to generate a new IPX.COM file or to load IPX.COM in high memory.

DOS Workstation Concerns

When a DOS workstation boots, it loads the COMMAND.COM file and then configures the system using the CONFIG.SYS file. Next, the DOS commands in the AUTOEXEC.BAT file are run. All three files are important to any application used from a NetWare server. The version of DOS, along with the COMMAND.COM version, must be compatible with the application loaded from the file server. Many applications will not work with versions of DOS that are less than DOS 3.

Configuration settings in the CONFIG.SYS file must be set to run many types of software. For example, WordPerfect requires the ability to have 20 files open at the same time and it needs five buffers. The CONFIG.SYS configuration specifications for WordPerfect are FILES=20 and BUFFERS=5. Read the documentation for each application you intend to install for information about CONFIG.SYS requirements. Figure 7.2 shows a sample CONFIG.SYS file. This CONFIG.SYS file sets files at 55 and buffers at 30. The SHELL command in the example causes the workstation to look in the C:\DOS directory for the

```
FILES=55
BUFFERS=30
SHELL=C:\DOS\COMMAND.COM /E:1024 /P
DEVICE=C:\DOS\HIMEN.SYS /M:11
```

Figure 7.2 *CONFIG.SYS File Booting with DOS 5.0*

COMMAND.COM file; and the /E:1024 /P instructions cause DOS to reserve 1024 bytes for environment variables used by applications. The DEVICE C:\DOS\HIMEN.SYS statement loads a memory manager.

The AUTOEXEC.BAT file loads network files and logs the workstation into the file server. Figure 7.3 shows an AUTOEXEC.BAT file that begins with a PATH command to set paths to the BATCH, DOS, and NET directories. Next, it loads mouse software, network drivers, and the network shell into high memory with the LOADHIGH command. The F: command causes the workstation to access the F: drive on the file server. The LOGIN ENG/JWILSON command initiates login to the JWILSON user account.

Menus

Installed software can be run from a NetWare menu or from a third-party menu system. The NetWare system combines Novell menu commands with DOS batch file commands. A list of frequently used menu commands is presented in Table 7.1.

```
PATH C:\BATCH;C:\DOS;C:\NET
LOADHIGH C:\MOUSE\MOUSE SER1
LOADHIGH LSL
LOADHIGH NI5210
LOADHIGH IPXODI
LOADHIGH NETX
F:
LOGIN ENG/JWILSON
```

Figure 7.3 *AUTOEXEC.BAT File Booting with DOS 5.0*

Table 7.1 NetWare Menu Commands

Command	Description
%	A command placed in the left-most margin. It indicates that the text that follows is the title of the menu.
n,n,n	Three numeric values separated by commas can be placed after the menu title. The first two values determine the horizontal and vertical placement of a menu. The third value specifies the color. If no values are given, the menu is placed in the center of the screen with no color palette.
Left justified text	Text interpreted as a menu option, which appears under the title of the menu.
Indented commands	The menu system will attempt to execute any Novell or DOS command indented from the left margin. These include DOS commands, such as the clear-screen command (CLS). Or a DOS program can be run by giving the name of the program. A common Novell command is MAP INSERT. It is used to create a search directory to a program file.
!logout	A command that will log the user off. It must be indented from the left margin.

Menu command files are created in ASCII format and have an ".mnu" extension. To run a menu, type the MENU command followed by the name of the menu.

Many NetWare installations choose to create menus by using DOS batch files, instead of the NetWare MENU utility. DOS batch files are used because they are efficient, they easily show the process of starting applications, and there is no additional cost. Figure 7.4 illustrates a menu which is a text file created with an editor. Each option calls a DOS batch file.

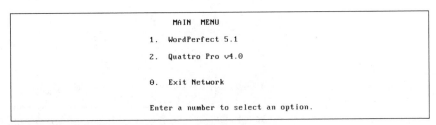

Figure 7.4 *Opening Menu for Accessing Applications*

Third-party menu systems are used also. Saber offers a complete menuing system that works along with the Saber metering software. The Hard Drive Menu (HDM) system is a shareware program that is used at NetWare installations.

Installation

The following sections describe important aspects of installing two popular applications packages, WordPerfect and Quattro Pro. These two examples illustrate how different software applications are installed on a NetWare file server.

Installing WordPerfect

WordPerfect is a network word-processing application that works equally well as a standalone application. WordPerfect takes full advantage of network printing capabilities and file-handling features.

Before you install WordPerfect, read the installation documentation that comes with it. To install the software, log onto an account with supervisor privileges or log onto the SUPERVISOR account from a workstation. Place the INSTALL disk in the floppy drive and enter INSTALL. The following is an overview of the installation steps:

1. Log onto the file server as SUPERVISOR.
2. Run INSTALL from the WordPerfect installation diskette.
3. Select the *Network Installation* option.
4. Select the WordPerfect files to install and the network drive where they will be installed.
5. Create a WP{WP}.ENV file to establish the WordPerfect operations environment.
6. Select and install the printer drivers needed for the printers on your network.
7. Exit the install program.
8. Create custom setup files for your users by running the SETUP function from within WordPerfect.
9. Flag the WordPerfect program and utility files as SRO.
10. Grant trustee rights to individuals and groups that will use WordPerfect.
11. Set up your metering software to limit access based on the number of WordPerfect licenses you own.

Figure 7.5 shows the installation options on the WordPerfect installation menu. From the list of options, select option 3, *Network*. Once the network installation is selected, there is another menu that prompts for information on the source drive and the destination drive. The source is the floppy drive on your workstation, and the destination is the network drive. In this example WordPerfect will be installed to V:\APPL\WP51. Figure 7.6 is the *Network Custom Installation* menu, which serves as a step-by-step check list. Option 4 is included to check the CONFIG.SYS and AUTOEXEC.BAT files. You do not need to run this option since it is for installation on standalone workstations. However, make certain each network workstation has files set to at least 20 and buffers set to 5 in the CONFIG.SYS file. If the files value is not set at 20 or higher, WordPerfect will display an error message when attempting to load at the workstation.

Option 5 in Figure 7.6 is used to customize the WP{WP}.ENV file. This file enables you to specify the type of network. When you select option 5, it displays the menu shown in Figure 7.7. Figure 7.7 is a list of network operating systems to select. Enter a *1* to select Novell NetWare. If you choose not to create a WP{WP}.ENV with the network selection, you can specify the network type when you start WordPerfect.

Option 6 on the *Network Custom Installation* menu in Figure 7.6 is used to select printers. Before you execute this option, consult with the network users on the types of printers they plan to use with WordPerfect. You can select as many printers as needed from the list presented by

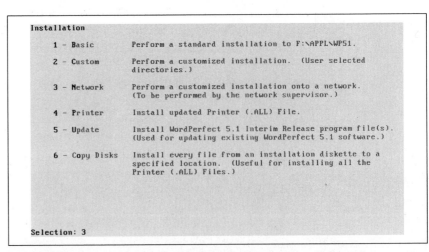

Installation

```
    1 - Basic        Perform a standard installation to F:\APPL\WP51.

    2 - Custom       Perform a customized installation.  (User selected
                     directories.)

    3 - Network      Perform a customized installation onto a network.
                     (To be performed by the network supervisor.)

    4 - Printer      Install updated Printer (.ALL) File.

    5 - Update       Install WordPerfect 5.1 Interim Release program file(s).
                     (Used for updating existing WordPerfect 5.1 software.)

    6 - Copy Disks   Install every file from an installation diskette to a
                     specified location.  (Useful for installing all the
                     Printer (.ALL) Files.)




Selection: 3
```

Figure 7.5 *WordPerfect Installation Screen Showing Install Options*

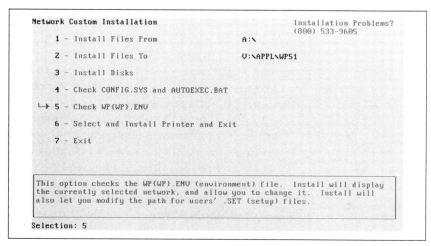

```
Network Custom Installation                          Installation Problems?
                                                      (800) 533-9605
        1 - Install Files From              A:\

        2 - Install Files To                U:\APPL\WP51

        3 - Install Disks

        4 - Check CONFIG.SYS and AUTOEXEC.BAT

    ↳  5 - Check WP{WP}.ENV

        6 - Select and Install Printer and Exit

        7 - Exit


   ┌─────────────────────────────────────────────────────────────────────┐
   │ This option checks the WP{WP}.ENV (environment) file.  Install will display │
   │ the currently selected network, and allow you to change it.  Install will │
   │ also let you modify the path for users' .SET (setup) files.           │
   └─────────────────────────────────────────────────────────────────────┘
     Selection: 5
```

Figure 7.6 *WordPerfect Network Custom Installation Screen Showing Install Options*

option 6. A printer driver is installed for each printer you select. If one of your printers is not listed, contact the WordPerfect Corporation to determine if they have additional printer drivers.

Once all of the printer drivers are installed from your selections, choose option 7 on the menu in Figure 7.6. This option completes the installation and exits the menu.

```
Check U:\APPL\WP51\WP{WP}.ENV file

        0 - Other
        1 - Novell NetWare
        2 - Banyan VINES
        3 - TOPS Network
        4 - IBM LAN Network
        5 - NOKIA PC-Net
        6 - 3Com 3+
        7 - 10Net
        8 - LANtastic
        9 - AT&T StarGROUP
        A - DEC PCSA
        B - 3Com 3+ OPEN

        * - No Network  (Single User)




     Selection: 1
```

Figure 7.7 *Screen Showing Network Option to Select for WordPerfect Environment File*

CUSTOMIZING WORDPERFECT

We have finished with the installation process and can now start WordPerfect to customize it. Change to the WordPerfect directory (in our example this would be \APPL\WP51) and enter *WP*.

Figure 7.8 shows the introductory WordPerfect screen. Notice at the bottom of the screen the line, *Username (Limit: 3 characters) : ___.* You are prompted for a three-character username. The username is used by WordPerfect to name its configuration or .SET file. The **.SET** file contains setup information for default parameters within WordPerfect. You can establish a .SET file for all users, or you can create special .SET files for individual users or groups. The .SET file will have in its name the three characters you specified on the introductory screen in Figure 7.8. For example, if you enter *ABC*, the file WPABC}.SET is created.

Once you are in WordPerfect, access the *Setup* menu by typing *SHIFT-F1.* The *Setup* menu shown in Figure 7.9 is displayed. Option 1, *Mouse*, is used to set parameters for use of a mouse with WordPerfect. Do not use this option unless all workstations on the network have identical mouse hardware. Option 2, for *Display* setup, is used to specify the monitor type at the workstation. Since most LANs are likely to have workstations with different types of monitors, do not change the display setup. WordPerfect defaults the setup to automatically determine the monitor type. Option 3, *Environment*, is used to customize backup

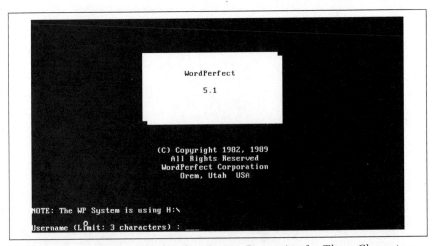

Figure 7.8 *Introductory WordPerfect Screen Prompting for Three-Character Username*

```
Setup

    1 - Mouse

    2 - Display

    3 - Environment

    4 - Initial Settings

    5 - Keyboard Layout

    6 - Location of Files




Selection: 0
```

Figure 7.9 *WordPerfect Setup Option Menu*

options, sound and cursor options, document management, save options, hyphenation, units of measure, and alternate keyboards. Figure 7.10 shows the *Setup: Environment* menu.

Two important options on this screen are *1 – Backup Options* and *3 – Cursor Speed*. Option 1 is used to set timed backups. This option automatically prompts WordPerfect to backup documents at specified intervals, such as every 15 minutes or every 30 minutes. Consult with your users regarding the need for timed backups.

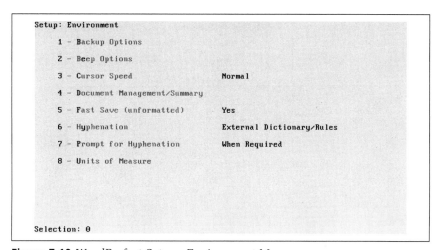

```
Setup: Environment

    1 - Backup Options

    2 - Beep Options

    3 - Cursor Speed                    Normal

    4 - Document Management/Summary

    5 - Fast Save (unformatted)         Yes

    6 - Hyphenation                     External Dictionary/Rules

    7 - Prompt for Hyphenation          When Required

    8 - Units of Measure




Selection: 0
```

Figure 7.10 *WordPerfect Setup: Environment Menu*

Option 3, *Cursor Speed*, is useful on some types of computers that have problems with WordPerfect's enhanced cursor speed. If some computers on your network have cursor problems while in WordPerfect, set this option to *Off.*

Once you have specified the environment, return to the beginning *Setup* menu in Figure 7.9. From here select option 6, *Location of Files.* This option determines the directories where WordPerfect will look for Speller, Thesaurus, and Graphics files. In our example file structure, the Speller and Thesaurus files are in \APPL\WP51. The Graphics files will be in directory \APPL\WP51\GRAPHICS (as discussed earlier in this chapter in the section Application Directory Structure and Management).

Once you have completed the *SETUP* menu, you need to select a printer driver. Press SHIFT-F7 to access the *Print* and *Options* menu. Figure 7.11 shows this menu. When you first access the menu Option S, *Select Printer*, will have no printer selection. Enter an *S* to select a printer.

The next screen is the *Print: Select Printer* screen. At the bottom of the screen there are several options. Select option 2, *Additional Printers.* This will present a list of printer drivers. Use option 1, *Select*, to add printer drivers to the setup. This is done by highlighting the desired printer and entering *1*. For example, one of the printer selections will be for the LaserJet Series II driver whose file name is HPLASEII.PRS.

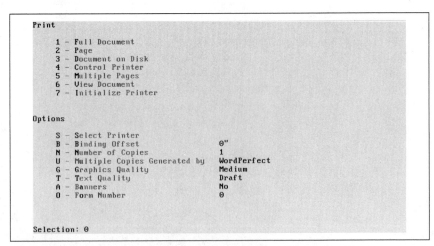

Figure 7.11 *WordPerfect Print Menu Showing That No Printer Has Been Selected*

Once the printer driver is selected you will need to edit the driver. Use option 3, *Edit*, from the *Print: Select Printer* screen to edit the driver. The edit option produces the screen shown in Figure 7.12. The first step is to change the port to which WordPerfect will print. The default is LPT1:. You need to modify the port so that WordPerfect prints to a network queue or file. Select option 2, *Port*, and enter *8* for *Other*. A prompt appears for a device or filename. You will need to enter the name of a print queue. Print queues are discussed later in this book. For now, keep in mind that print queues can be named for the room that contains the printer. In this example, the queue name is 122 for room 122 (see Figure 7.13).

Every time a user begins WordPerfect with the username 122, their printing will be sent to the file server, specifically a queue named 122. We will discuss queues and how to create them in later chapters.

You have the option to set up printer drivers for each printer on the LAN through WordPerfect. Use the *Print* and *Options* menu (press SHIFT-F7) to add as many print setups as needed. Consult your WordPerfect documentation for more information about WordPerfect installation and setup.

RUNNING WORDPERFECT

The next step is to create a DOS batch file or a menu from which to run WordPerfect. The sample batch file shown in Figure 7.14 can be run by itself, as part of a larger batch file, or as a modular batch file called by

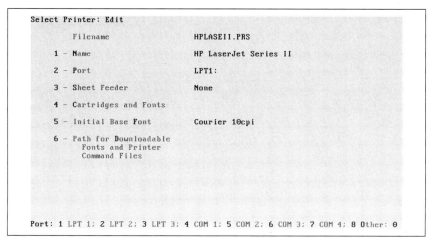

```
Select Printer: Edit

          Filename              HPLASEII.PRS

    1 - Name                    HP LaserJet Series II

    2 - Port                    LPT1:

    3 - Sheet Feeder            None

    4 - Cartridges and Fonts

    5 - Initial Base Font       Courier 10cpi

    6 - Path for Downloadable
        Fonts and Printer
        Command Files




Port: 1 LPT 1; 2 LPT 2; 3 LPT 3; 4 COM 1; 5 COM 2; 6 COM 3; 7 COM 4; 8 Other: 0
```

Figure 7.12 *WordPerfect Edit Printer Menu for Selecting Port*

```
Select Printer: Edit

        Filename                 HPLASEII.PRS

    1 - Name                     HP LaserJet Series II

    2 - Port                     LPT1:

    3 - Sheet Feeder             None

    4 - Cartridges and Fonts

    5 - Initial Base Font        Courier 10cpi

    6 - Path for Downloadable
        Fonts and Printer
        Command Files




Device or Filename: 122
```

Figure 7.13 *WordPerfect Edit Printer Menu for Selecting Print Device or Filename*

another batch file. The first statement clears the screen and places the cursor at the top left portion of the screen. The PAUSE statement gives users time to insert their disk in a floppy drive that is determined by the DOS variable %DRIVE%. %DRIVE% can be set in the system login script, the user login script, or in the AUTOEXEC.BAT file.

The CD V:\APPL\WP51 command is used to modify search drive five, which is V:. You could use the MAP command instead, which would be MAP S5:=SYS:APPL\WP51. However, it is more efficient to avoid MAP in this instance because MAP must be downloaded from the file server. The CD command is DOS resident so it executes quickly and

```
CLS
ECHO LOADING WP51....INSERT YOUR DATA DISK IN %DRIVE%
PAUSE
CD V:\APPL\WP51
%DRIVE%
WP/NC/NT=1/U-ABC/D-%DRIVE%
CD V:\APPL
H:
```

Figure 7.14 *A Sample Batch File to Launch WordPerfect*

does not require moving the MAP utility from the file server to the workstation. MAP is about 50 KB. Multiply 50 KB times the number of applications and the number of users; and you can see a significant reduction in network traffic by not using MAP. The logic behind creating one or two search drives and reusing them with DOS statements is a matter of speed and efficiency.

The %DRIVE% command in Figure 7.14 changes to the default drive, such as drive A: where the floppy resides. It also becomes WordPerfect's default drive.

WordPerfect can be started with many switches or parameters. In this example, the *NC* switch disables the cursor speed option. You may want to use the NC switch for workstations that load terminate-and-stay-resident programs. The *NT* switch establishes the type of network. NT=1 is for Novell file servers. If you earlier created a WP{WP}.ENV file, you do not need to use this switch. The *U-ABC* switch instructs WordPerfect to use the WPABC}.SET file that has default parameters.

The *D* switch in Figure 7.14 directs WordPerfect to write its temporary files on the specified drive. WordPerfect creates several temporary files when it starts. These files are used for print buffering and other temporary operations. In this example, the files will be written to the drive specified in the %DRIVE% DOS variable. During proper use, these files are deleted when WordPerfect is exited. (If WordPerfect is not exited correctly, it will display the message, "Are Other Copies of WordPerfect Running?". You answer with an *N* so that the old temporary files are deleted and new ones created.)

After WordPerfect is exited (see Figure 7.14) the batch command CD V:\APPL changes the search drive five to the \APPL directory. The H: command takes users back to their home directory.

There are at least as many ways to run an application on a network as there are on a local hard drive. This example, with the use of DOS variables, allows one rather simple set of batch commands to be used by a variety of users in different rooms using different printers.

FLAGGING WORDPERFECT FILES

Once the installation is complete, the last step is to flag the WordPerfect files so they cannot be changed. This should be done for all program-related files except the setup files. Flag the program files as SRO (shareable read-only); flag the setup files as SRW (shareable read-write). The following two FLAG commands will first flag all files as SRO and then change the set files to SRW:

```
FLAG *.* SRO
FLAG *.SET SRW
```

Use SYSCON or the GRANT command to give users access to the directories. For example, you can use the GRANT command in the following way:

```
GRANT R F FOR USR:\APPL\WP51 TO EVERYONE
```

Installing Quattro Pro

Installing Quattro Pro begins with setting up the directory structure. The second step is to install the software.

QUATTRO PRO DIRECTORY STRUCTURE

Figure 7.15 shows a directory structure that can be used for Quattro Pro. The QPRO directory has all the program files while the FONTS directory has the font files. QPRONET has the user access files that all users must use to run Quattro. Each Quattro user will also have configuration files in the user directory.

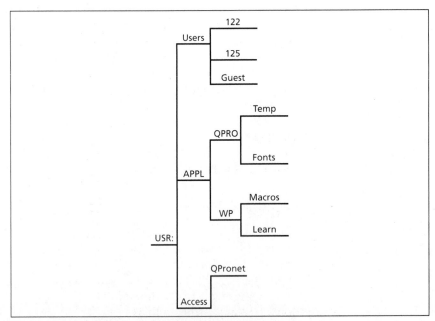

Figure 7.15 *A Recommended Directory Structure for Quattro Pro*

STEPS FOR INSTALLING QUATTRO PRO

The following is an outline of the steps used to install Quattro Pro 4.0.

1. Run the INSTALL program on the Quattro Pro v4.0 diskettes. The source drive is either A: or B: and the destination drive is a network drive, such as V:\APPL\QPRO.

2. Supply the following information after the files are copied to the server.

   - The type of display monitor that will be used.
   - The company name, the name of the network manager(s), and the serial number on the INSTALL diskette.
   - The directory path for the file QPRO.NET.
   - Whether you wish to modify the AUTOEXEC.BAT file. (Answer *NO* for the network installation.)
   - The network printer type. (This can be modified later.)
   - The WYSIWYG graphics mode to use. (Answer *No* to WYSIWYG if some network users do not have EGA or VGA monitors. The EGA and VGA users can change this parameter when they run the program.)
   - Whether to install the program for MS Windows (Answer *No* to installing for Windows.)
   - The character set to use. Choose *Standard U.S.* for the Bitstream Character Set.

3. From the application directory (V:) run QPUPDATE.EXE to add the program serial numbers so all licensed users can access Quattro Pro at the same time. Special LAN packs for Quattro Pro can be ordered with serial numbers for additional users as your network grows.

4. Copy all files with the .RF extension from the V:\APPL\QPRO directory to \APPL\QPRO\TEMP; delete the .RF files from V:\APPL\QPRO.

5. Create .MP files in the \APPL\QPRO\TEMP directory by entering the following command from V:\APPL\QPRO:

   ```
   MPMAKE QUATTRO.MU F:\APPL\QPRO\TEMP
   ```

6. Run QADMIN.EXE to create print queues and Quattro Pro drive mappings for the network. Consult the *Quattro Pro NetWare Utilities* section of the Quattro Pro documentation for an explanation of options with the QADMIN.EXE program.

7. Copy the QUATTRO.MP and RSC.RF files from the \APPL\ QPRO\TEMP directory to each Quattro Pro user's directory. Use the copy capabilities of FILER or the NetWare NCOPY command to copy these files.

8. Create a Quattro Pro user group, such as QPROUSERS, using SYSCON. Give read and file scan trustee rights to QPROUSERS as illustrated by the following GRANT command:

```
GRANT R F FOR USR:APPL\QPRO TO QPROUSERS
```

Also, give read, write, create, modify, and file scan trustee rights to the FONTS subdirectory so that users can manipulate fonts within Quattro Pro:

```
GRANT R W C M F FOR USR:APPL\QPRO\FONTS TO QPROUSERS
```

And give read, write, and file scan trustee rights to the \ACCESS\QPRONET directory:

```
GRANT R W F FOR USR:ACCESS\QPRONET TO QPROUSERS
```

9. Ensure that the DOS SHARE.EXE program is loaded from the AUTOEXEC.BAT file executed at each workstation. (This requires that the command SHARE be one of the lines in the AUTOEXEC.BAT file.)

10. Flag all program files in the \APPL\QPRO subdirectory as read-only, so these files cannot be modified by accident. The following FLAG command illustrates this step:

```
FLAG V:\APPL\QPRO SRO
```

11. Make certain that all users have access trustee rights to their home directory. Use the SYSCON or FILER utilities to verify trustee rights for home directories. (Access rights are normally given when a new user is created.)

A FURTHER LOOK AT THE INSTALLATION STEPS: DIRECTORY STRUCTURE

Because application vendors, such as Borland, require a validation file, a directory must be created that gives users write access to the validation files. Some vendors require that the directory have a specific name. Since the application directory file should be flagged as read-only, it is necessary to create a separate directory for the validation files. The example in step 8 of the previous section uses the \ACCESS\QPRONET subdirectory for the validation files. In step 8, the Quattro Pro users group, QPROUSERS, is given read, write, and file scan rights to the \ACCESS\QPRONET directory so the validation files can be written to as required by Quattro Pro licensing.

MODIFYING THE AUTOEXEC.BAT FILE

For installation step 9, the DOS SHARE command is added to the AUTOEXEC.BAT file. The SHARE utility is used to lock data files from updates by two users at the same time. SHARE prevents data errors that might occur from this situation. SHARE should be executed by the AUTOEXEC.BAT file before the network programs are run.

INSTALLING CONFIGURATION FILES

Quattro Pro uses **set** files as does WordPerfect. These are called **resource** files instead of set files. You also have the option to customize Quattro Pro's menu to emulate Lotus 1-2-3.

Each user must have a copy of or access to an .RF resource file. Users who want to use the Lotus look-alike menu must have access to the .MP menu preference file. These files can be placed in each user's directory, or in directories to be accessed by specified groups. For example, the SALES group might consist of users who want the Lotus look-alike menu. Another group, such as TECHS, might want the regular Quattro Pro menu.

The MPMAKE utility in the QPRO directory is used to make the configuration (.RF and .MP) files. Once the files are created, they should be copied to the users' personal directories (or to a directory shared by a group). Remove all configuration files from the application directory so they cannot be used by mistake.

Once you have created configuration files for users, keep a back up copy of each file in a system administrator's directory, or back up copies to tape or disk. If a user deletes his or her file, you will be able to restore it quickly.

QUATTRO PRO DRIVE MAPPINGS

Network drive mappings for Quattro Pro should be created before starting the application. Figure 7.16 shows the drive mapping menu that is created by the command */Options | Network | Drive Mappings.*

In the example provided by this figure, one drive is mapped: H:. Another drive is in the process of being created. Once the drive letter (for

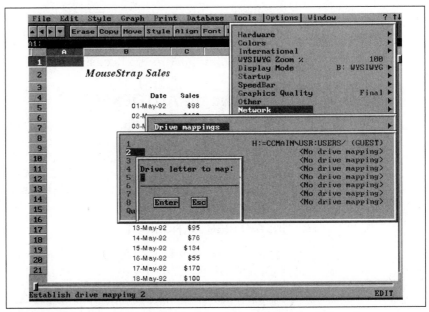

Figure 7.16 *Quattro Drive Mapping Screen Indicating the Network Drive Mapping*

example S) is entered there are a series of prompts for information about the user and the directory. Up to eight drives can be mapped. The */Options | Update* command makes these drive letters permanent.

To access files in a mapped drive, use the command */File | Retrieve*. The command displays the screen in Figure 7.17. To see the currently mapped drives, use the mouse to click on the *DRV* button. After you select a mapped drive, the files in that directory are displayed.

PRINTING IN QUATTRO PRO

The INSTALL utility configures the printer to print to the LPT1 parallel printer port at the workstation. If the user wants to print on a network printer, a change is needed. A network printer can be a printer attached to a workstation that is also used for network printing. Or it can be attached to a special network printing device, such as a Netport, that is directly connected to the network cable. (Networking of printing hookups is discussed later in the book.)

The default printer configuration is changed by using the command */Options | Hardware | Printers | 1st Printer | Device | Network Queue*. Figure 7.18 shows the options to select to change from the default LPT1

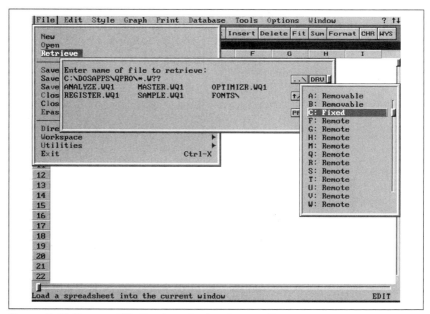

Figure 7.17 *Quattro File Retrieve Option Screen Showing "DRV" Button*

parallel printer to the *Network Queue*. Once the *Network Queue* option is selected, you enter the name of the file server that has the queue, such as CC MAIN. After the file server is selected, a list of the existing print queues is displayed. Select the desired print queue and the process is finished. The *Device* option in the *Type of printer* window will show, *Network Queue*. Use the command */Options | Update* to make this a permanent change.

With Quattro Pro, the users can select any printer connected to the network. They can make a rough draft on their workstation printers and send the final polished versions to a network laser printer or color plotter.

Quattro Pro uses a print manager to control the printing of files once they are sent to a print queue. Use the */Print | Print Manager* to access the Print Manager. Figure 7.19 is a screen showing the status of a print queue.

The queue and file server name are displayed on the status line at the bottom of the screen. The printer in Figure 7.19 is not ready or else the status at the top of the screen would be *Active*, indicating that the printing is in process.

Print Manager allows users to monitor, delete, or put print jobs on hold.

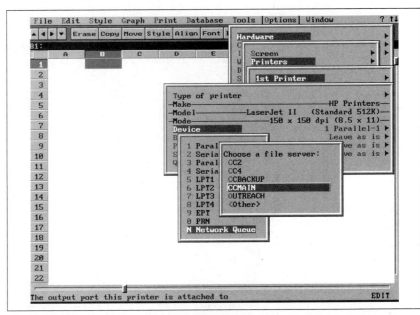

Figure 7.18 *Quattro Network Queue Screen Showing the Printer Setup*

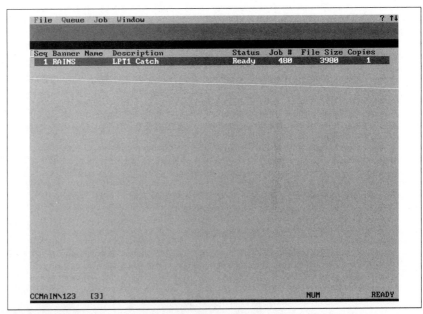

Figure 7.19 *Quattro Print Manager Screen Showing One File Waiting to Be Printed*

RESTORING LOST WORK

Work interruptions caused by power failures or equipment failures are taken in stride by Quattro Pro, even if you have not saved your work before the interruption. Quattro Pro can keep a running log of the user's keystrokes in a file called QUATTRO.LOG. The file can store from 1 to 25,000 keystrokes (the default is 200). To change the default value, use the command */Tools│Macro│Transcript*. A transcript box is displayed from which you enter / to display another menu. On the second menu, select the *Max History Length and/or Failure Protection* option and enter the desired value.

The restore process is started by retrieving the latest version of the spreadsheet (or you can begin with a blank spreadsheet if you did not save one). Enter */Tools│Macro│Transcript* for the second step for the restore. On the transcript listing, identify the most recent save or the beginning of the last work session. Use the */Begin block* and */End block* to select the keystrokes. Then select */Playback block*.

CREATING A QUATTRO PRO MENU

A batch file can be used as a menu for starting Quattro Pro. Figure 7.20 shows an example of a batch file, which simply maps the drives needed and starts Quattro Pro. Note that the batch file in Figure 7.20 creates one search drive to map to the ACCESS directory for user validation. When Quattro Pro is exited, the mapped drive is deleted.

```
CLS
ECHO  Place your data disk in %DRIVE%
ECHO.
PAUSE > NUL
ECHO  Space key to continue.
%DRIVE%
CD V:/APPL/QPRO
CD U:/APPL/QPRO/FONTS
MAP S8:=USR:APPL/ACCESS/QPRONET
V:Q
CD V:/APPL
CD U:/APPL
MAP DEL S8:
H:
```

Figure 7.20 *A Sample Batch File to Launch Quattro Pro v4.0*

Summary

As this chapter illustrates, the network manager must be familiar with many different software applications. He or she also needs a strong background in DOS as an aid for installing applications.

As a network manager, your first step is to examine potential software applications for network compatibility. Try to select applications that are designed for use on a network. Application licensing requirements are important also. Make certain you understand each application's licensing procedures. Plan to install metering software when needed to limit software use to the number of licenses you own.

Before installing any software, follow this chapter's recommendation to develop a plan for the file server directory structure. A well-designed directory structure makes software installation and upgrades easier. The directory structure can also be designed to reduce maintenance tasks, such as assigning and modifying trustee rights.

Software testing is important for the stability of the file server. Test all software before it is released to the users. The software testing should be done on every type of workstation that will be used with the software.

Installation information is provided for WordPerfect and Quattro Pro to illustrate how applications are installed. As these examples show, software installation is more complex on a network than on a standalone workstation. The network installation must be set up so that many users can access the software at the same time.

Key Terms

Metering Software   Software that is used to help the network manager adhere to software licensing requirements. It is implemented to prevent users from accessing more copies of specific software than permitted by the number of licenses owned. If 20 WordPerfect licenses are owned, the metering software prevents more than 20 users from accessing the software at the same time.

Network Applications   Software applications that are designed to work on one or more workstations.

Network-Aware Applications   Software applications that are able to run on a network and may even take limited advantage of some network features, but they are not designed specifically for use on a network.

Resource Files   Files used by programs such as Quattro Pro to establish default settings and other program features for the user.

Set Files   Files used by programs such as WordPerfect to establish printing options, default settings, and program options for the user.

Standalone Applications   Software applications that are not designed for network use and may not run on a network.

Terminate-and-Stay-Resident (TSR)   Programs that are written to remain in the workstation's memory, even when they are not in use. These programs are often started at any time by pressing a special key sequence.

Validation Files   Files that are used to allow access to individual software licenses. They ensure that use of a program is limited to the number of user licenses on the file server.

Questions and Exercises

1. Understanding copyright and licensing information is important. Find an application such as Quattro Pro or WordPerfect and read the licensing requirement. Summarize the licensing information. Can the application be installed on more than one computer? Can you make changes to the application? Can you sell the application? Can the application be installed on a network?

2. You are required to install the latest version of PCLOST, which is version 2.0. Version 1.0 is currently running on the network and users depend on it. Outline the steps you would take to install version 2.0 so that interruptions to users are minimized.

3. Create an AUTOEXEC.BAT file that calls a batch file to load the Novell network software. All the network files are in C:\NET.

4. Word processor XYZ requires that the NetWare CAPTURE command be run prior to starting XYZ so that network printing is used. XYZ does not allow the print queue to be changed once it is started. By contrast, WordPerfect allows the user to change the print queue from within WordPerfect. How does the user change the print queue from within WordPerfect?

5. Using an application at your location, create a batch file that will set the drive mappings and necessary variables to run the application and return users to their home directory when the application is finished.

6. In Quattro Pro version 4.0, it is possible for the user to create internal drive mappings. Explain how these are different from the drive mappings created with the MAP command. Is it possible to map a drive to another file server? If so, what steps would the user follow to map drives on two file servers at the same time?

7. You are installing Quattro Pro. Diagram the directory structure for this installation and include a group directory for data called GRPDATA. Only the group STAFF should have access to this directory. What command or commands would you use to assign the STAFF group read, write, and delete capabilities to the files in GRPDATA?

8

Network Printing

Chapter Objectives

The objectives of this chapter are the following:

- To explain DOS and network printing concepts.
- To explain how to use network printing tools.

- To illustrate network printing capabilities using three network printing solutions: NetWare's print server, Hewlett-Packard's Network Printer Interface, and Brightwork's PS-Print.

Introduction

Printing has always been a costly and labor-intense area of computing. In mainframe shops, printing has traditionally been centralized, with users obtaining printouts from the machine room personnel. Mainframe printers are large and expensive to maintain, and they require constant attention.

When personal computers became popular, many users purchased a printer to attach to the computer. This is expensive, too, due to the large number of printers purchased and the maintenance costs.

Local area networking offers a solution to printing woes because printers can be shared. Organizations can purchase high-quality printers for mutual use in workgroups. The cost of mainframe type printers is avoided as is the cost of purchasing a printer for each workstation.

On a LAN, shared printers can be attached to the file server or to a workstation, or connected directly to the network cable. Dot matrix, ink jet, color, and laser printers can be shared. Forms printers and plotters can also be shared on the LAN. Many combinations of network printers can be purchased for the same cost as yearly maintenance on one mainframe printer.

This chapter is a guide to network printing. It begins with an explanation of DOS and network printing concepts. The concepts are later put to work by exploring three solutions to network printing.

DOS Printing

The DOS PRINT command is used to print ASCII or **text files**. The print utility calls upon the computer's BIOS (Basic Input Output System) to send a print file one character at a time to the serial or parallel port of the computer. To print the file, MYFILE.TXT, you would enter *PRINT MYFILE.TXT* at the DOS prompt.

After you enter the print command, DOS asks if you want to print to port PRN (the parallel port, also called LPT1). This is the default port. Or you can direct printouts to a serial port by entering COM1 for serial port 1.

If the file is not an ASCII or text file, then it is necessary to print the file from the application used to create it, such as WordPerfect.

Many applications and later versions of DOS allow you to queue print requests (print requests are called **print jobs**). A **print queue** is a file that stores other files to be printed. Print queues are useful because they allow the user to send one or more print jobs to the queue and then continue working while the jobs print. While DOS prints the first copy, the other copies wait in the queue until it is their turn to print.

DOS print queues are limited by the amount of workstation memory (unless third-party software is used for printing). Many applications, such as WordPerfect, have special print queue handling software to overcome memory limitations. They create temporary print queue files on disk until print jobs are completed.

Network Printing

Network print requests from the workstation are routed through the network shell (NETx) to the file server. Each file server can have one or more print queues. A print queue can be linked to a specific printer or used for a specific type of form on a designated printer.

Print queue files are written to the file server disk. This means that print queue handling is limited only by the available amount of disk space.

Print jobs that are sent from the workstation to the file server are literally captured by the network shell. The shell grabs the file from any of the printer ports, LPT1, LPT2, LPT3, COM1, or COM2. The file is then sent to the file server's print management software.

Netware Printing Utilities

Network aware applications, such as WordPerfect, take advantage of network printing so there is little printer configuration necessary. For example, WordPerfect only requires information about which network print queue to use.

Applications that are not network aware require intervention for effective use of network print management tools.

NetWare provides several printing utilities to compensate for non–network aware applications. The following NetWare printer utilities are used to print, create queues, and monitor printing (see Table 8.1).

The first step in setting up print functions is to define the print queues. Every shared network printer will need a print queue. Print queues are defined in PCONSOLE. A print queue is really a subdirectory in the SYS:SYSTEM directory where print jobs are stored until they are sent to the printer.

Some print jobs may require special use of a printer, or special printer characters. For example, a CAD print job may need to have the

Table 8.1 NetWare Printer Utilities

Utility	Function
PCONSOLE	Creates, views, and manages print queues and sets up print servers.
PRINTDEF	Defines print devices and forms for use with PRINTCON.
PRINTCON	Defines print job configurations (queue, form, number of copies, and so on) used by PCONSOLE, CAPTURE, and NPRINT.
CAPTURE	Intercepts print jobs on the workstation and redirects them to the file server print queue.
ENDCAP	Ends the print job interception so that jobs are printed on the local workstation printer.
NPRINT	Prints designated ASCII files to a NetWare print queue.

printer work in graphics mode, or a word-processor file may need to print math characters. The PRINTDEF utility allows you to create a printer definition file that sets up the printer for graphics or special codes. PRINTDEF also is used to set up the printer for forms, such as an invoice or legal sized paper.

PRINTCON controls the printing environment by indicating factors such as which queue to use, the number of copies to print, and the type of data sent to the printer (ASCII or **binary**). When a form is defined in PRINTDEF, it is linked to a queue by parameters set in PRINTCON.

You will use CAPTURE frequently. It enables you to direct printing to network printers for applications that do not have network printing capabilities. NPRINT works like the DOS PRINT command, but it is more powerful. It enables you to print an ASCII file to a designated print queue.

PCONSOLE

Through PCONSOLE, users can add or delete print queues. Users can also monitor print jobs, delete print jobs, and specify which users have access to given queues.

The utility is entered by executing PCONSOLE from the command line in NetWare. Once PCONSOLE is executed, the menu in Figure 8.1 appears.

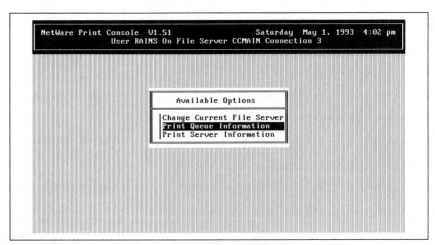

Figure 8.1 *PCONSOLE Screen Showing Available Options*

The first option on the menu, *Change Current File Server*, enables the user to attach other file servers. By using this option, it is possible to print files from more than one file server. Before a file server can be attached, a valid user name and password must be specified.

Besides attaching servers, this option provides the ability to log out of one or more file servers or to log into a different account on the same file server.

The second option on the PCONSOLE menu is listed as *Print Queue Information*. When selected, this option displays the print queues on the current server (see Figure 8.2). From here a new print queue can be created by pressing the INSert key. A print queue can be deleted as well. Print queue SALES_PRINTER is about to be created in Figure 8.2.

Additional information about a print queue is available by highlighting a specific queue name and pressing the enter key. When this is done, a *Print Queue Information* menu appears (see Figure 8.3) listing several options, which include the following:

- **Current print job entries** Lists all current print jobs waiting in the queue. When the option is selected, the PCONSOLE operator can place print jobs on hold, change the priority of printing, or delete print jobs.
- **Current queue status** Displays the number of entries in the specified queue, and the number of servers attached to the queue.
- **Currently attached servers** Displays the list of file servers attached to the print queue.

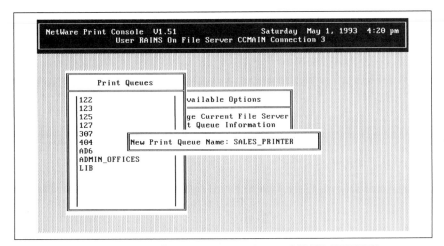

Figure 8.2 *PCONSOLE Used to Create Print Queue SALES_PRINTER*

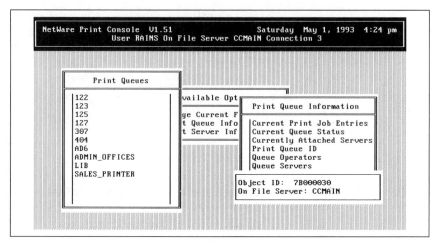

Figure 8.3 *PCONSOLE Showing the Object ID or Subdirectory Name for Print Queue SALES_PRINTER*

- **Print queue ID** Displays the object ID number, which every print queue is associated with. In Figure 8.3 the object ID for queue SALES_PRINTER is 16000020. The ID corresponds to a subdirectory, SYSTEM\16000020.QDR, where print jobs are sent for this queue.

- **Queue operators** Authorizes designated users as operators. All users except for the supervisor must be authorized as queue operators to access PCONSOLE and manipulate entries in the queue.

- **Queue servers** Specifies other servers that can access the print queue.

- **Queue users** Enables the PCONSOLE operator to authorize users to use the print queue. Except for the supervisor, only users who have been authorized can send a print job to a specific queue.

The last option on the menu in Figure 8.1 is *Print Server Information*. Several third-party software companies have written print server utilities for NetWare. Utilities like these enable remote workstations, print server boxes (such as Intel's NetPort), and print server cards (such as Castelle's JetPress) to act as **printer servers**. A print server processes print requests from multiple users and directs them to the designated printers. Printouts can be routed to printers attached to these devices, as well as to network printers attached to the file server. In this way, it is not necessary to obtain all printouts from the room containing the file server.

PRINTDEF

PRINTDEF is used to define and associate specific characteristics with a print device. For example, printer pitch, underlining, tabbing characteristics, landscape printing, and specific fonts can be set up for use with a certain printer. Once print characteristics are established for a printer, they can be associated with a print job configuration definition through the PRINTCON utility.

PRINTDEF is useful when an application does not provide **printer drivers** for specialized printer functions. Applications designed for a network such as WordPerfect do not require PRINTDEF. Many other non–network aware applications do require PRINTDEF. PRINTDEF is also used when ASCII files are printed with NPRINT or the DOS PRINT commands.

One important PRINTDEF function is to reinitialize a printer. For example, one user may send a print job requiring a small specialized font, such as 17 **cpi** (17 characters per inch) san serif (the font). If the next print job uses the printer's default mode, such as 10 cpi courier, it is necessary to reinitialize the printer to the default. PRINTDEF is used to send the character sequence needed to reinitialize the printer. (The reinitialize characters are different for each printer.)

To start PRINTDEF, enter the PRINTDEF command at the file server command level prompt. The *PrintDef Options* menu in Figure 8.4 is displayed. The first option in the menu, *Print Devices*, produces a second menu that supplies three options. The second menu, *Print Device Options*, is illustrated in the figure.

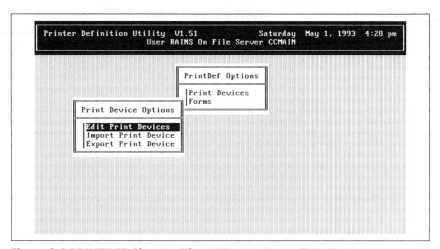

Figure 8.4 *PRINTDEF Showing Three Ways to Access Print Devices*

Before any print device options are available, they must be imported into PRINTDEF or created from scratch through the *Edit Print Devices* selection. The *Import Print Device* option is used to import existing print device files. The print device files are supplied with the NetWare operating system and are in the SYS:PUBLIC directory. These files have a ".PDF" extension for "printer device file."

Before importing a printer device file into PRINTDEF, list the .PDF files in the SYS:PUBLIC directory and determine which files to import. Next, enter PRINTDEF and take the *Import Print Devices* option from the Print Devices submenu. A box will appear into which the name of the directory, SYS:PUBLIC, is entered. Another box will appear with a listing of the printer device files. The *Import Print Device* option must be used for each printer device file to be incorporated into PRINTDEF.

Once a print device file has been imported, it can be edited using the *Edit Print Devices* option. When this option is selected, a list of the imported print devices is displayed. Any of these devices can be highlighted for editing. When one is highlighted to be edited, the menu in Figure 8.5 appears, offering two selections: *Device Modes* and *Device Functions.*

If *Device Functions* is selected from the menu, a list of the printer functions appears along with the printer control codes used to elicit

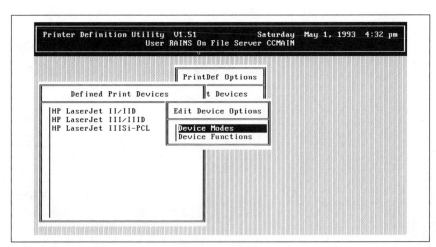

Figure 8.5 *PRINTDEF Showing Three Predefined Printer Devices*

each function. Information about printer control codes is contained in the individual printer manuals. Consult the manual for your printer or printers before editing any printer control codes. Also note that if there is no predefined printer device file for a particular printer, a new file can be created by specifying a device name on the Defined Print Devices list, which appears when the *Edit Print Devices* selection is made from the menu in Figure 8.4. Then select the *Device Functions* option on the menu in Figure 8.5 to add the desired printer functions and their corresponding control codes.

The *Device Modes* selection on the Edit Device Options menu in Figure 8.5 is used to establish specific print modes, such as condensed printing, landscape (sideways) printing, letter quality printing, and so on.

The predefined print device files imported into PRINTDEF come with a set of preestablished device modes. When *Device Modes* is viewed for one of these print files, a list of modes is displayed. Figure 8.6 shows the device modes that have been created for a Hewlett-Packard LaserJet II/IID. This list is also made available to the PRINTCON utility to specify a device and mode in a print job configuration. Each device mode is a set of one or more printer control codes that accomplish a given function. For example, a mode to perform landscape printing will have the given printer's landscape control code built into the mode.

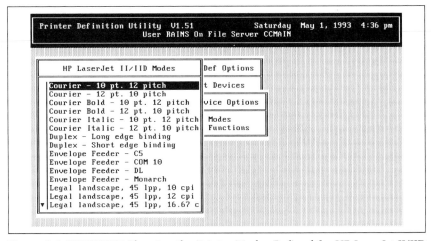

Figure 8.6 *PRINTDEF Showing the Printer Modes Defined for HP LaserJet II/IID*

The last option on the menu in Figure 8.4 is *Export Print Devices*. This option is used to export a device definition to another directory or to another file server. This is a useful option for those who wish to use a printer on another file server, and to make the appropriate device definitions available for that printer. Normally, the device definition is exported to the SYS:PUBLIC directory on the other file server. The export procedure requires having supervisor privileges on both file servers.

The last item on the *PrintDef Options* menu in Figure 8.4 is titled *Forms*. This option permits the user to create form specifications for use with the PRINTCON utility. When this option is selected, the system asks for the name of the form, such as "Checks" or "Grades." A number is then assigned by the user to the form to distinguish it from other forms. Forms can be numbered from zero to 255. Next, the length of the form in terms of lines per page is specified. Forms have a maximum of 255 lines. Finally, the width of the form is specified in characters. The maximum width is 999 characters wide.

Figure 8.7 shows that one form has been created, which has a form number of 0, length of 66 lines, and is 80 characters wide. The name of this form is "plain_8x11." To create more forms use the INSert key from the *Forms* menu and use the *Form Definition* menu to define the size of the form.

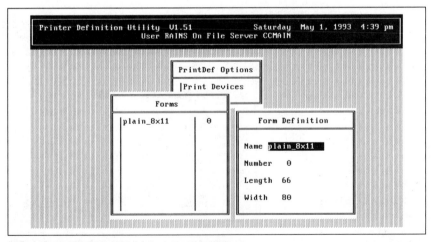

Figure 8.7 *PRINTDEF Used to Create a Form*

PRINTCON

PRINTCON is a utility menu that enables the user to establish print job configuration information. Print job information can be associated with specific print queues and printer numbers. The print job information that can be specified includes the number of copies to be printed, tabbing information, timeout count, and the decision to print a banner.

PRINTCON is begun by entering PRINTCON at the command level prompt in NetWare. At the start, PRINTCON displays the menu shown in Figure 8.8. The first option in the PRINTCON menu, *Edit Print Job Configurations*, is used to edit existing print job configurations and to create new ones. Since print job configurations are not automatically created by NetWare at the time the system is generated, the network manager must create the first configurations. It is not mandatory that a print job configuration be created for each printer and each queue. Creating print job configurations is simply a tool available to enable the network manager and the user to have more precise control over printouts.

Figure 8.9 contains a list of sample print job configurations. The figure shows that there are nine print job configurations and a new one, ADMIN_LASER, is about to be added.

Any print job configuration can be edited by highlighting the configuration, then pressing the ENTER key. Similarly, configurations can be deleted or renamed by using the DEL or F3 keys. New configurations are created by pressing the INSert key and specifying a name for the

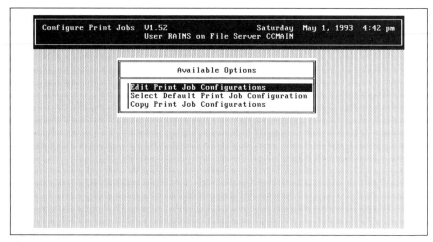

Figure 8.8 *PRINTCON Option Menu*

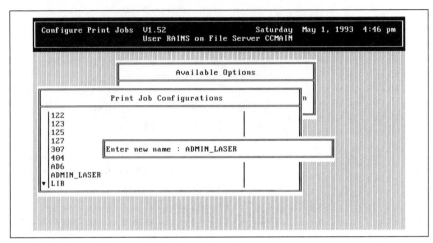

Figure 8.9 *PRINTCON Used to Create a Print Job Configuration, ADMIN_LASER*

new configuration (as in Figure 8.9). Once the configuration name is specified, an Edit Print Job Configuration menu appears, such as the example shown in Figure 8.10.

Starting with the left side of the screen, the first option shown in Figure 8.10 is *Number of Copies*. This option enables the user to enter the number of copies to be made for each print job. The maximum number of copies is 65,000.

Second on the menu is *File Contents*. This parameter presents two options: text and byte stream. The *Text* option is used when printing outside an application to send tabbing and any formatting characters within the document directly to the printer. The *Byte Stream* option is used when printing from within an application, such as WordPerfect or Microsoft Word. This option ensures that the formatting characters established by the application are used.

Tab Size sets the tabbing to a number from 1 to 18 at the user's discretion. This applies only to documents sent in the text mode.

The next option on the menu is *Suppress Form Feed*. Whether this parameter is set to "Yes" or "No" depends on whether the form feed is set by the individual application or the printer. Some applications automatically send a form feed, or blank form, after each print session. Some printers can be set to do the same thing. If the form-feed option is turned on in the software application or is set on the printer, then *Suppress Form Feed* should be set to "Yes." Otherwise, the form feed is set to "No."

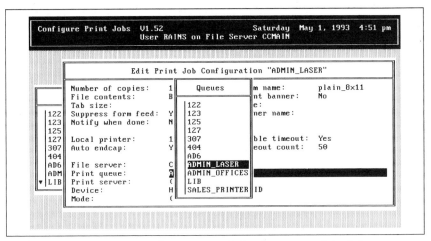

Figure 8.10 *PRINTCON Used to Assign a Print Queue to a Print Job Configuration*

The *Notify When Done:* option is set to "Yes" if you want users to receive a message that a print job has been sent to the printer. A "No" response means that no such message is sent.

The *Local Printer* option is used when the Capture command is in effect for the print session. This option specifies the workstation printer port from which the file will be captured (Ports 1-3).

The option, *Auto Endcap*, specifies when the file will print. If this parameter is "Yes," the printout is sent as soon as the program is exited, or as soon as the printer file is closed. If the parameter is marked "No," the job is printed as soon as an ENDCAP command is invoked, or when the printer timeout occurs (the "TI" option in the CAPTURE command). Note that this parameter is not in effect for local printouts. Set Auto Endcap to "Yes" if you plan to print data that requires frequent searches of the hard disk, such as a spreadsheet file.

File Server is an option used to specify which server will receive the printout. Viable servers are presented in a displayed list.

The *Print Queue* option is used to specify which print queue will receive the printout. Figure 8.10 shows an example list of print queues.

The option *Print Server:* enables you to direct the printout to a specific print server on the network.

The *Device* and *Mode* options are related to what has been defined through PRINTDEF. The *Device* option presents a list of predefined printer devices. The *Mode* parameter is used to specify which device mode will be used, such as compressed printing or landscape printing.

At the top of the right portion of the screen, the *Form Name* option is used to specify a form created via PRINTDEF. For example, in a school setting there might be special forms for printing grades and other forms for printing credit memos.

The option, *Print Banner*, provides the ability to specify that a **banner page** will be printed at the beginning of each printout. The banner page contains the name of the user and the name of the file that is printed. In this way, individual printouts can be identified.

The option *Name* is for the name of the user who sent the print job. The *Banner Name* option enables you to create a specific name on the banner. The banner can include 12 characters. If no name is provided, the name of the file being printed is used.

Next, the *Enable Timeout* option is used to specify when the file will be printed. If this parameter is marked "Yes," the file is printed at the end of the timeout parameter specified in the CAPTURE command. If it is marked "No," the time at which the file is printed is based on the *Auto Endcap* parameter. Like *Auto Endcap*, this option does not apply to local printouts.

The *Timeout Count* is used to specify the number of seconds to wait until the file is printed. The possible range is one through 1,000. For programs that pause to perform a data search, the range should be set relatively high—for example, for 60 seconds. This helps to ensure that all pages of the file are printed as a single group. Once the print job information has been completed, press the ESC key to save it and return to the menu in Figure 8.9.

The second option on the PRINTCON menu in Figure 8.8, *Select Default Print Job Configuration*, is there so an existing print job configuration is designated as the default. If a print job configuration is not specified (for instance, when you're using the CAPTURE or NPRINT commands), the default is used. When the *Select Default Print Job Configuration* option is selected, a list of print job configurations is displayed. The default is designated by highlighting the desired configuration and pressing the ENTER key.

The last option in Figure 8.8 is *Copy Print Job Configurations*. This is used to copy a user's defined configurations to another user. If one user creates a print job, it is not seen by other users. This is because print jobs created by users are stored in association with the specific user. However, the network manager can allow a user to use another's print job definition. This is done by copying one user's configurations to another user. Figure 8.11 shows that print job configurations will be copied from the Rains account to the Guest account.

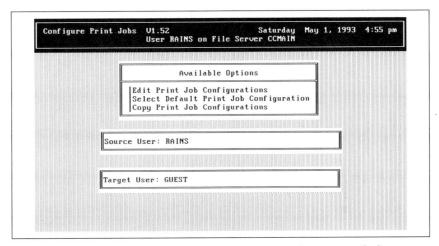

```
Configure Print Jobs   V1.52                    Saturday  May 1, 1993  4:55 pm
                       User RAINS on File Server CCMAIN

                        ┌──────────────────────────────────┐
                        │          Available Options         │
                        ├──────────────────────────────────┤
                        │ Edit Print Job Configurations      │
                        │ Select Default Print Job Configuration │
                        │ Copy Print Job Configurations      │
                        └──────────────────────────────────┘

                     ┌──────────────────────────────────────┐
                     │ Source User: RAINS                     │
                     └──────────────────────────────────────┘

                     ┌──────────────────────────────────────┐
                     │ Target User: GUEST                     │
                     └──────────────────────────────────────┘
```

Figure 8.11 *PRINTCON Used to Copy a Print Job Configuration File from Rains to Guest*

CAPTURE

CAPTURE is used to redirect print requests from the workstation printer ports to the network printers. CAPTURE is typically placed in the system or user login scripts so that printouts reach the proper destination. A series of parameters can be used with this command to control options, such as the following:

- Print queue
- Network printer number
- Print job configuration
- Number of copies to print

The most commonly used parameter options include:

- **P=n** Specifies the number of the network printer to receive the printout.
- **S=server** Indicates which server is to receive the printout.
- **Q=queue name** Determines which print queue is to receive the printout.
- **F=form** Indicates which form name or form number is to be used. (Forms are created through the PRINTDEF utility.)

- **C=n** Specifies the number of copies to print per print request.
- **J=job** Associates a print job configuration created through PRINTCON with the print request.
- **NB** Suppresses the generation of a banner page at the beginning of the printout.
- **FF** Indicates that a form feed should be issued after the printout.
- **NFF** Suppresses the form feed after the printout.
- **T=n** Sets tabbing for applications that do not have tabbing instructions included.
- **NT** Ensures that the tab characters in a document are not printed. NT should always be used for word processing and desktop publishing software. Also use NT whenever you print fonts.
- **TI=n** Specifies the length of time needed for the print job to get to the print queue before timing out. The timeout should be set higher for print requests that take longer than others to process, such as desktop publishing files and database files. For these types of printouts, the timeout may need to be as high as 30 to 60 seconds or more. The timeout parameter can be set up to 1,000 seconds.
- **SH** Indicates what CAPTURE parameters are currently in effect.

To send print jobs through a PRINTCON defined job set called ADMIN_LASER, you would enter the following:

```
CAPTURE J=ADMIN_LASER
```

In another example, the job is sent to print queue HP_LASER, with a timeout value of 30 and the specifications no banner and no tabs.

```
CAPTURE Q=HP_LASER TI=30 NB NT
```

The timeout value is important to ensure that there is enough time for a printout to complete. Documents that contain graphics such as diagrams or charts will need more time (30 to 45 seconds) than text-only documents (5 to 10 seconds). The NT value is specified so that the tabs or binary characters in the document are printed. NT prompts CAPTURE to print the document in byte or binary mode and to ignore the default NetWare tabbing parameter.

Once the CAPTURE command is invoked, it remains in effect until another CAPTURE command is issued or until an ENDCAP command is used. The ENDCAP command discontinues the capture of printer output at a workstation. It reverses the CAPTURE command, so a print request can be directed to a local printer connected to the workstation.

NPRINT

Individual files can be printed by using the NPRINT command. Like CAPTURE, this command comes with many print options that can be set by parameters. When you use the NPRINT command, first type NPRINT, then the name of the file to print, and last, the parameter you wish to use. The parameters include:

- **P=n** Used to specify the number of the network printer that will receive the printout.
- **S=server** Indicates which server receives the printout.
- **Q=queue name** Sets the print queue to receive the printout.
- **F=form** Indicates which form name or form number is to be used.
- **C=n** Specifies the number of copies to print per print request.
- **J=job** Associates a print job configuration created through PRINTCON with the print request.
- **NB** Suppresses the generation of a banner page at the beginning of the printout.
- **FF** Indicates that a form feed should be issued after the printout.
- **NFF** Suppresses the form feed after the printout.
- **T=n** Sets tabulation for applications that do not have tabulation instructions included.
- **D** Deletes the file after it is printed.

To print the file YEARLY.RPT, on Printer 1 with no banner and using print job configuration HP, enter this command statement:

```
NPRINT YEARLY.RPT P=1 NB J=HP
```

Three Printing Solutions

The sections that follow provide three solutions for **remote printing** on the network. Remote printing is printing at a location other than from the file server. The first solution is provided by Novell. It involves the use of print server software applications, PSERVER and RPRINTER.

Hewlett-Packard offers a hardware solution in the form of an interface card that is installed in the network printer. The remote printer connects directly to the network through the use of the card.

The third solution is PS-Print from Brightwork. This software gives the user the ability to send a print job to any of the print queues on the file server. PS-Print has a pop-up window showing a list of print queues for the user's selection.

All three are representative solutions and you should not discount other vendor products, such as Intel's NetPort and Castelle's LanPress and JetPress. There are several effective network printing solutions available.

Novell Print Servers

The printing solution offered by Novell enables you to connect printers directly to the file server and set up remote printers. Printers can be connected to the file server parallel and serial printer ports. This requires that printers be located near the file server.

Remote printing is accomplished by connecting printers to a workstation or to a print server box, such as the NetPort. The file server and remote printer solutions use the PSERVER software to move printouts to the right place.

The process for setting up printing is summarized as follows:

1. Set up the hardware.
2. Create the print queues or select existing ones.
3. Create the print servers.
4. Define the printers.
5. Assign the queues to printers.
6. Run the print server program.

Installing Printers

The first step is to connect printers to the file server, to one or more remote workstations, or to both. The number of printers that can be connected to a computer is limited by the number of parallel and serial ports.

For remote printing, identify the locations where printers need to be placed. The printers must be connected to a workstation that will log onto the file server, or they are attached to specialized boxes that connect directly to the network (note the manufacturer's instructions if you purchase this type of equipment).

Creating Print Queues

A print queue should be created for each remote printer. For example, if the printer is in room 201, the queue might be called RM201. Refer to the section on PCONSOLE for information on how print queues are created.

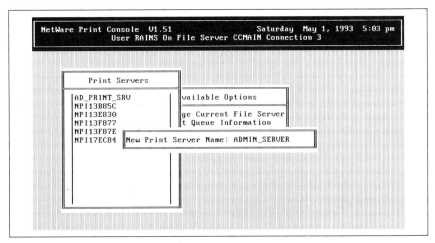

Figure 8.12 *PCONSOLE Used to Create Print Server ADMIN_SRV*

At the time the queue is created, designate the queue operators and queue users. The queue operator has the ability to delete print jobs from the queue and to change the priority of print jobs. The queue users are those who have the ability to use the queue. This can be individual users, groups, or all file server users (group EVERYONE). Figure 8.12 shows the menus used to assign a print server name.

Creating the Print Server	PCONSOLE is used to create a print server. Figure 8.12 shows a new print server being created. The name of the print server is ADMIN_SERVER.
Defining the Printers	Sixteen printers can be defined for a print queue. Figure 8.14 shows the options to define a printer. The first step is to select *Print Server Configuration* and *Printer Configuration*. Printers are numbered from 0 to 15, with Printer 0 used as the example in Figure 8.14.
Assigning Queues to the Printers	Once a printer is defined, assign a print queue to the print server. Figure 8.14 shows assignment of print queue SALES_PRINTER to print server ADMIN_SERVER.

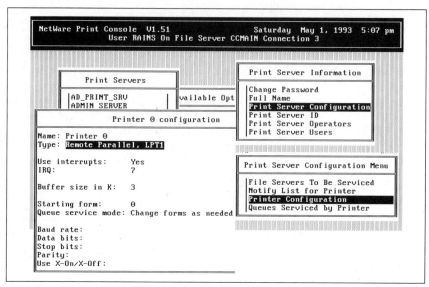

Figure 8.13 *PCONSOLE Used to Configure Print Server*

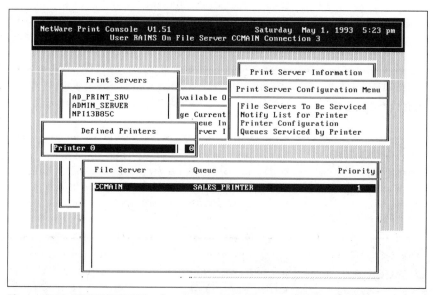

Figure 8.14 *PCONSOLE Used to Assign Print Queue SALES_PRINTER to Print Server ADMIN_SERVER*

Running the Print Server Program

The next step is to run the print server software provided by Novell. To print to a remote workstation that is dedicated as a print server, you would enter the following at the workstation:

```
PSERVER AD_PRINT_SRV 0
```

PSERVER is the application name and AD_PRINT_SRV is the name of the print server defined through PCONSOLE. The "0" is Printer 0 that is associated with the print server AD_PRINT_SRV.

Figure 8.15 shows the print server screen that is displayed at the remote workstation. This is one of two screens that show up to 16 printers and the printer status.

Hewlett-Packard's Network Printer Interface

The Network Printer Interface from Hewlett-Packard allows you to connect a Hewlett-Packard printer directly to the network. No dedicated workstation is required. Instead, the NPI card is installed in the printer, and the card is directly connected to the network. The network treats the printer similar to a workstation node. Since the printer is connected directly to the network, the data transfer rates are several times faster than printing data from a dedicated workstation printer port.

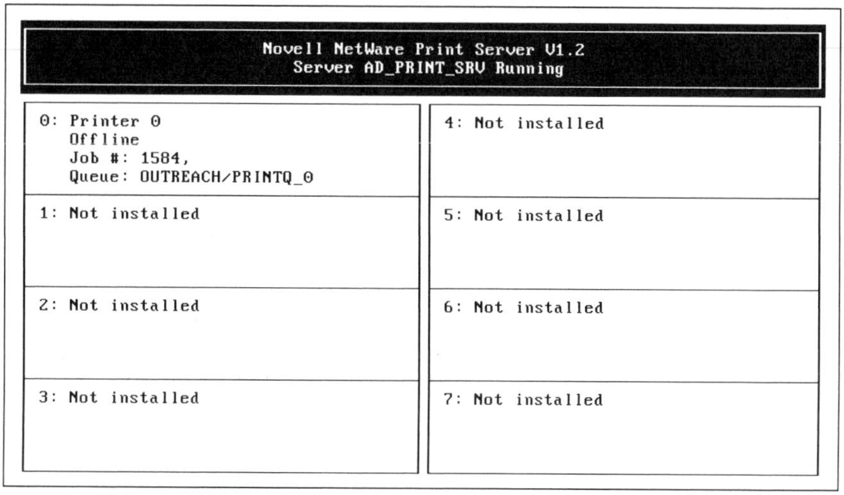

```
                  Novell NetWare Print Server V1.2
                    Server AD_PRINT_SRV Running

  0: Printer 0                        4: Not installed
     Offline
     Job #: 1584,
     Queue: OUTREACH/PRINTQ_0

  1: Not installed                    5: Not installed



  2: Not installed                    6: Not installed



  3: Not installed                    7: Not installed
```

Figure 8.15 *PSERVER Status Screen Showing Printer 0 Waiting for Print Job*

There are three steps to installing the Network Printer Interface:

1. Install the interface card in the printer.
2. Use PCONSOLE to create a print queue.
3. Configure the queue server.

Installing the Interface Card

The Network Printer Interface operates on Ethernet and token-ring protocols. Follow the installation instructions in the Hewlett-Packard documentation to install the interface card. Figure 8.16 shows the interface card and how it is installed.

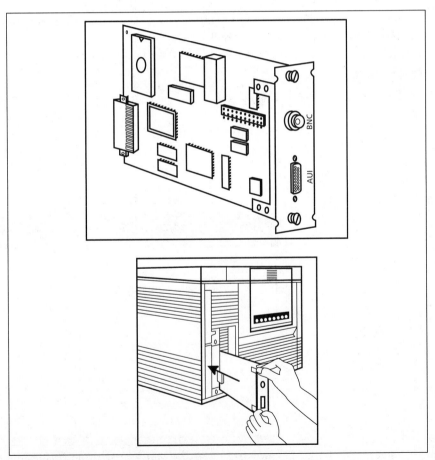

Figure 8.16 *Hewlett-Packard Printer Interface Card and How to Install It*

Creating a Print Queue

Use PCONSOLE to create a print queue for the printer. As mentioned in the PCONSOLE section, this is done by selecting the *Print Queue Information* option from the PCONSOLE menu. From the screen that displays print queues, press the INSert key and enter the name of the new queue in the dialogue box prompt (see again Figure 8.2).

Configuring the Queue Server

There are three steps to setting up a queue server:

1. Enable unencrypted passwords.
2. Invoke the print server name.
3. Start the Network Printer Interface.

Each of these steps is described in the sections that follow.

ENABLING UNENCRYPTED PASSWORDS

Many versions of NetWare expect passwords to be encrypted. To use the Network Printer Interface, the file server should be instructed to accept passwords that are not encrypted. This enables the print server to access the file server and users who are on file servers without password encryption. (The Hewlett-Packard manual recommends enabling unencrypted passwords.)

The command to unencrypt passwords is the following:

```
SET ALLOW UNENCRYPTED PASSWORDS=ON
```

This command is placed in the AUTOEXEC.NCF file that the file server reads when it boots-up. The AUTOEXEC.NCF file is changed by using the INSTALL NLM utility from the file server console or by using SYSCON from an account with supervisor privilege.

INVOKING THE PRINT SERVER NAME

The print server name is built into the interface card. When the interface card is installed and the printer is powered on, the interface card broadcasts its presence on the network. The printer interface card has a unique Ethernet network address, similar to a workstation on the network. The address is "hard-coded" on the interface card by Hewlett-Packard.

Figure 8.17 shows a list of Hewlett-Packard print servers and their names. The names all begin with NPI (Network Printer Interface). The print server name is broadcast by the interface card so that it is picked up by PCONSOLE.

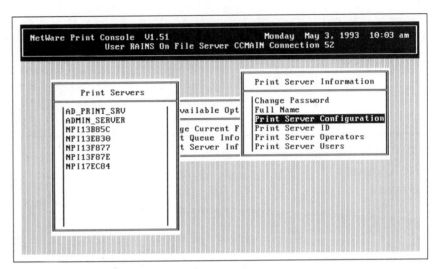

```
NetWare Print Console  V1.51                    Monday  May 3, 1993  10:03 am
                   User RAINS On File Server CCMAIN Connection 52

        ┌──────────────────────┐      ┌────────────────────────────────────┐
        │                      │      │   Print Server Information          │
        │    Print Servers     │      │ ┌──────────────────────────────────┐│
        │ ┌──────────────────┐ │      │ │Change Password                   ││
        │ │AD_PRINT_SRV      │ │vailable Opt│Full Name                     ││
        │ │ADMIN_SERVER      │ │      │ │Print Server Configuration        ││
        │ │NPI13B85C         │ │ge Current F│Print Server ID               ││
        │ │NPI13E830         │ │t Queue Info│Print Server Operators        ││
        │ │NPI13F877         │ │t Server Inf│Print Server Users            ││
        │ │NPI13F87E         │ │      │ └──────────────────────────────────┘│
        │ │NPI17EC84         │ │      └────────────────────────────────────┘
        │ │                  │ │
        │ │                  │ │
        │ │                  │ │
        │ │                  │ │
        │ └──────────────────┘ │
        └──────────────────────┘
```

Figure 8.17 *PCONSOLE Showing the Print Servers*

Each print server must be configured by the network manager using
PCONSOLE. To configure the print server, enter PCONSOLE and select
the *Print Server Information* option from the PCONSOLE *Available
Options Menu* (see again Figure 8.1). A list of print servers is displayed,
as shown in Figure 8.17. Highlight the print server you want to configure and press ENTER. From the next screen, *Print Server Information*,
select the *Print Server Configuration* option. The next screen will show
a list of 16 printers. The first time you select this option, none of the 16
printers will be configured. (The print server can have up to 16 configured printers, beginning with Printer 0.) To configure the first printer,
select Printer 0. This displays the configuration screen in Figure 8.18.

The first parameter on the screen in Figure 8.18 is *Name:*. The name
Printer 0 is entered here to define the first print server. The *Type:* option
indicates how the printer is connected to the network. For the Network
Printer Interface card, you specify *Defined elsewhere* for the *Type:* option
(since the printer is connected directly to the network there is no parallel or serial connection specified). Figure 8.19 shows the list of *Printer
Types*.

After the *Type:* option is entered, leave the remaining parameters
blank. These parameters, which include *IRQ:*, *Baud rate:*, and so on, are
used to define printers connected to the file server parallel or serial
ports.

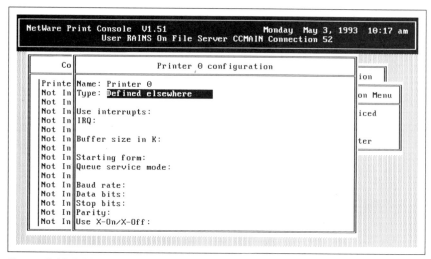

Figure 8.18 *PCONSOLE Used to Configure a Print Server*

STARTING THE NETWORK PRINTER INTERFACE

The next step is to run the Hewlett-Packard supplied program, PCONFIG, which configures and starts the Network Printer Interface. The *PCONFIG Main Menu* screen has two options: *1. Select Network Printer Interface*

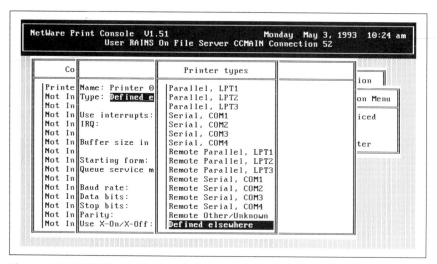

Figure 8.19 *PCONSOLE Used to Select the Type of Network Printer Connection*

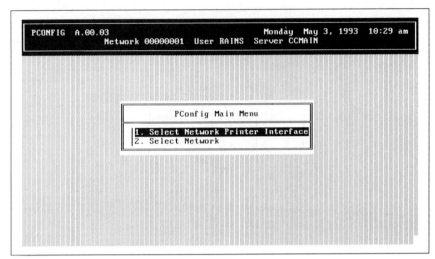

Figure 8.20 *PCONFIG Opening Menu*

and *2. Select Network.* These are shown in Figure 8.20. The first option is used to set up the printer interface. When this option is selected, the *Options Menu* in Figure 8.21 is displayed. Select option *1. Select/Configure Queue Server Mode* from the menu. When this option is selected the current status window is displayed as at the top of the figure. The status window shows the node name, which is print server NP117EC84 in our example. It also shows the operating mode (Queue Server), the name of the file server, and the printer status ("Waiting for Job"), which means there are no print jobs currently directed to the print server. The connection status message, "Logged in to File Server," means that the connection is successful. The printer and print server are ready to process print jobs.

The second option in Figure 8.21, *2. Select/Configure Remote Printer Mode,* is not used in our example. It is used in situations where the printer is attached to a workstation and the interface card is not in use.

The third option, *3. Reset Network Printer Interface*, is used when the printer will not print after a power problem or network disconnection problem. It resets the interface board so that it resumes accepting data from the network.

The Network Printer Interface can be used on more than one network. Refer again to Figure 8.20 and the option, *2. Select Network*. This option is used when you wish to share the network printer with users on another network—for example, when there are an Ethernet and an ARCNET network in the same area.

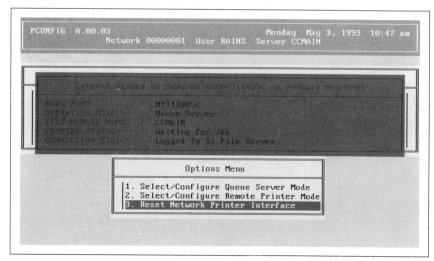

Figure 8.21 *PCONFIG Menu Used to Select/Configure Operating Mode*

If you decide to use the Hewlett-Packard Network Printer Interface, consult the installation manual for detailed information on configuration options.

Brightwork's PS-Print

Brightwork's PS-Print is a print solution that distributes print jobs to workstations with network printers. A unique feature of PS-Print is that it offers users a pop-up menu to control a printer or change printer options. The pop-up menu is memory resident and can be used from within applications, such as Lotus 1-2-3 or WordPerfect. Another feature is that PS-Print allows users to customize PRINTCON configurations without leaving a software application.

There are many PS-Print options for print queues and network printers. Portions of three software options are discussed in this chapter to provide you with an introduction: PSP-CFG, QueueIT, and PSP-CON. Refer to the PS-Print documentation for a more in-depth discussion of the software.

PSP-CFG

PSP-CFG (PS-Print configuation) is a configuration utility for print queues and printers. Our example begins with an illustration of how to configure print queues.

The first step is to create the desired print queues using PCONSOLE as discussed previously in this chapter. Next, use the PSP-CFG program

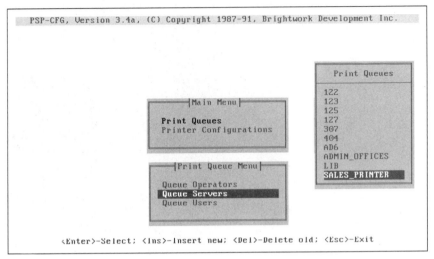

Figure 8.22 *PSP-CFG Used to Select Print Queues*

to assign a print queue to a remote printer (where the printer is attached to a network workstation). Figure 8.22 illustrates selection of the print queue, Sales_Printer. First, run PSP-CFG to access the *Main Menu*. Second, select the print queue, such as SALES_PRINTER. Once the print queue is selected, the *Print Queue Menu* is displayed. This menu is used to specify the queue operators, server, and users. The queue operators are those users or groups that can delete or change the priority of print jobs. The queue server is the NetWare queue server PSERVER.NLM that is loaded at the file server console. The queue users are all those entitled to use the queue, with the default set as the group Everyone.

Once the *Print Queue Menu* options are completed, the workstation printer is configured. Figure 8.23 shows the printer configuration screens, with the printer attached to the parallel printer port LPT1. The user receives a message when the print job is completed. The print queue will be scanned every ten seconds to determine if there is a new print job to process. The mode of service is from a print queue.

When several print queues are assigned to one printer, the queue operator can give each queue a priority to determine which jobs print first. For example, print queue Sales_Printer might be used by the sales office and would be assigned the highest priority. Print queue priorities are assigned from "Highest" to "Low." A print queue can be temporarily removed from service by assigning the "Disable" priority to the queue.

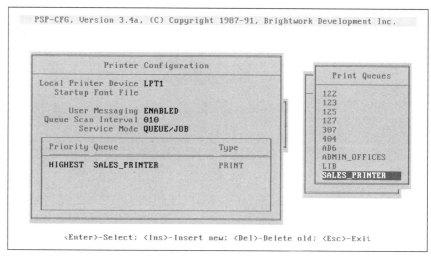

PSP-CFG, Version 3.4a, (C) Copyright 1987-91, Brightwork Development Inc.

```
          Printer Configuration                         Print Queues

Local Printer Device LPT1                                122
    Startup Font File                                    123
                                                         125
    User Messaging ENABLED                               127
Queue Scan Interval 010                                  307
    Service Mode QUEUE/JOB                               404
                                                         AD6
 Priority Queue                    Type                  ADMIN_OFFICES
                                                         LIB
 HIGHEST  SALES_PRINTER            PRINT                 SALES_PRINTER
```

<Enter>-Select; <Ins>-Insert new; <Del>-Delete old; <Esc>-Exit

Figure 8.23 *PSP-CFG Used to Configure the Printer*

QueueIT

QueueIT is a TSR program that runs at the user's workstation to control printing activity. For example, a user might be working on a Lotus 1-2-3 spreadsheet with the intention to print a rough draft on a dot matrix network printer. While the user is working, a department head asks for a polished preliminary copy to take to a meeting. A pop-up menu from QueueIT can be accessed while in Lotus 1-2-3 to redirect printouts to a network laser printer.

Figure 8.24 illustrates the QueueIT menu used to change print queues. In this example, the *Device Status* window shows that no print queue is selected. To change the print queue, the user moves the highlighted prompt to another queue on the *Print Job List* and presses the INSert key.

Figure 8.25 shows the current print configuration. This is the information that has been created through PRINTCON. QueueIT enables the user to temporarily change the printer configuration settings by using the *Customize Print Job Configuration* menu. The customized settings stay in effect for the current log-on session, but they go back to the original settings when the session is done.

PSP-CON

PSP-CON (PS-Print Console) is another pop-up menu TSR that is loaded at the user's workstation. It enables the user to stop a print job that is printing to cancel print jobs in the print queue, and to change the print queue, the printer form, and the sequence in which jobs will print. Figure 8.26 shows the options available in PSP-CON.

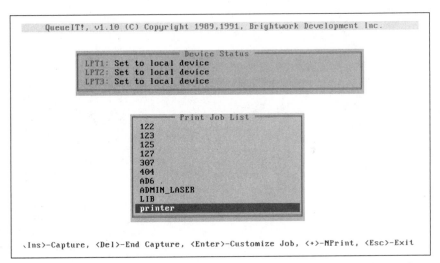

Figure 8.24 *QueueIT Used to Change the Current Print Queue to a Queue Set in Print Job "Printer"*

Another useful PSP-CON feature is the ability to send a font file to a printer. Many laser printers have software that is downloaded into the printer's memory for special fonts. PSP-CON can be used from within an application such as WordPerfect to download the fonts before printing.

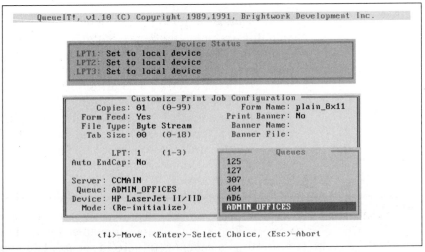

Figure 8.25 *QueueIT Used to Temporarily Change a Print Job Configuration*

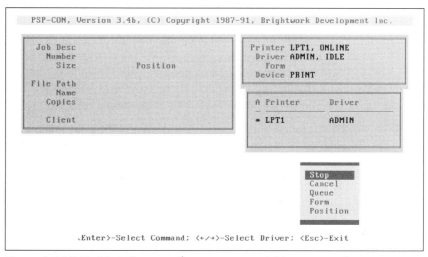

Figure 8.26 *PSP-CON Showing the Options Available to Control a Print Queue*

Summary

Network printing is critical to any installation. Versatile network printing capabilities give users productivity tools such as laser printers, fonts, and graphics for polished reports, letters, and charts.

This chapter explains network printing tools for network managers and users. It begins by comparing DOS printing with network printing. Network printing is more powerful and versatile than DOS printing capabilities.

Several NetWare printing utilities such as PCONSOLE, PRINTDEF, PRINTCON, CAPTURE, ENDCAP, and NPRINT are discussed. PCONSOLE is used to control print activities and to establish print queues. PRINTDEF and printer definition files are used to customize network printing for specific kinds of printers. PRINTCON customizes print job characteristics such as the number of copies to print, banner pages, and print queue selection. CAPTURE, NPRINT, and ENDCAP are used to control print parameters for software applications that do not use network printing capabilities.

Three example network printing solutions are presented, illustrating the versatility of network printing. The first solution is offered by NetWare. It involves the use of the NetWare PSERVER utilities for remote printing.

Hewlett-Packard offers a high-performance network printing solution called the Network Printer Interface. This interface card allows a printer to be connected directly to the network cable.

PS-Print from Brightwork gives the user extensive network printing control through the pop-up menu programs QueueIT and PSP-CON. The program, PSP-CFG, enables the network manager to customize use of print queues and printers with PS-Print.

Key Terms

Banner Page   An identification page that is available on some operating systems or printer software systems. Enables printouts to go to a designated person or place.

Binary File   A file format with special or machine-readable characters. It cannot be read by displaying it to the screen with the DOS TYPE command.

Cpi (characters per inch)   The size of a print font (the number of characters printed in an inch). For example, a small font is 16 cpi. Commonly used font sizes are 10 and 12 cpi.

Print Job   A print file waiting in the print queue until it is printed. Each time you send a printout from an application or print a file, a print job is created.

Print Queue   A waiting line or file where each job is sent to be printed in proper order. Print jobs are managed by placing them in a queue.

Printer Driver   Software that provides instruction codes to a printer. For example, WordPerfect comes with printer drivers for many printers to take advantage of font, style, size, and other special printer features.

Printer Server   Software and printing equipment, used to accept printing requests from multiple users and to process the requests so that they reach the designated printers.

Remote Printing   On a Novell network, printing from a printer not physically attached to the print server.

Text File   An ASCII file that does not have special characters used by a software application. Word processors, such as Microsoft Word, place special binary characters in files for tabbing, page setup, and other specialized characteristics.

1. Explain how DOS prints the ASCII file, AUTOEXEC.BAT, using the parallel port. Include the role of BIOS in your explanation. How is it possible to use the DOS TYPE command to print this file to a printer?

2. What is a network print queue and how is it used? Assume that Mary is working in her office and wants to send a WordPerfect document to a laser printer in another office. What role does the print queue have in this process?

3. Explain the PRINTDEF utility and give an example of why you would use it.

4. Explain the PRINTCON utility and how it is used with PCONSOLE and PRINTDEF.

5. Print queues are files on the file server. Assume that a print queue file name is 12345678. What is the complete directory path to this file?

6. NetWare printer utilities support printers connected to the file server and to remote workstations. What are the advantages and disadvantages of printing to the file server? What are they for printing remotely?

7. What is the relationship between a print queue and a print server, if any? Develop a system for naming print queues and print servers.

8. Research or determine the throughput speed of a parallel printer port on an 80386 computer. Compare it to the throughput of a specialized printer interface, such as the Hewlett-Packard Network Printer Interface.

9. The network manager assigns print queue operators and users. What can the queue operators do that the users cannot do? Who should be queue operators? Why?

NetWare and Windows Integration

Chapter Objectives

The objectives of this chapter are the following:

- To explain the hardware and software needed to run Windows.
- To explain four ways that Windows can be installed for use on a network.
- To illustrate how Windows is installed on a NetWare file server.
- To illustrate how network applications are installed in Windows.

Introduction   Microsoft Windows can transform the way you now use your workstation. It provides pictures, boxes, windows, icons, arrows, and other screen graphics so that using a workstation is more intuitive. These pictorial features are known as a **Graphical User Interface (GUI)**. Microsoft Windows combines these screen displays with a mouse interface so you no longer have to use the keyboard exclusively. You can use the mouse to click on pull-down menus or an icon—a small picture that represents a Windows application. You can also use the mouse to arrange the visual display of your screen so it matches the way you work.

Why invest in Windows? It can make your network users more productive. They will spend less time trying to access their applications and more time in the applications. For example, users can run WordPerfect and Lotus 1-2-3 at the same time, with each in its own window. They can jump between windows without exiting either application.

Windows provides a complete environment from which to run applications. It includes applications such as a calendar, a notepad, a calculator, a drawing program, a terminal emulator, a file manager, and a print manager.

Many popular applications are written to work from within Windows. Word-processing applications such as WordPerfect and Microsoft Word will run from Windows. The desktop publishing application PageMaker works from Windows. There are also CAD applications, applications for FAX documents, applications to access IBM mainframes, accounting applications, and many other applications designed for the Windows environment.

This chapter is an introduction to using Windows with NetWare. Once you complete the chapter, you will have an understanding of the hardware required to run Windows, how it is installed, and how software is installed to take advantage of its features.

Hardware Required for Windows

Even the experts do not agree on the best hardware platform for Windows. One reason is that Windows requires a large amount of memory for the workstation. Another reason is that some vendors' workstation products run Windows differently. The Windows workstation recommendations in this chapter are intended to emphasize the need for more workstation resources rather than fewer resources. Using this approach, the minimum workstation requirements for Windows are the following:

- An 80386 or an 80486 workstation with a minimum clock speed of 25 Mhz
- At least 4 MB of RAM
- An SVGA (Super VGA) video board with 1 MB of RAM
- An SVGA monitor
- A good mouse, such as those made by Microsoft, Logitech, or Mouse Systems
- A hard drive with at least 80 MB (depending on the number of applications you plan to install on the hard drive instead of from the network)

If you have users who plan to run applications that need a math coprocessor, purchase the 80486 workstation. This will provide the speed and computing capability needed for these types of applications.

Microsoft recommends 4 MB of RAM for your workstation. You may need more memory for some applications, such as for desktop publishing software.

SVGA is becoming a de facto standard for much software. Plan to purchase a monitor with good resolution, such as .31 dot (the size of the pixel) or smaller.

A high-quality mouse is as important as the keyboard. Select a mouse that enables you to navigate the screen pointer precisely and with the speed appropriate for the kind of work performed.

The size of the hard drive depends on where the applications are loaded. A large hard drive of around 200 MB is needed if the applications will reside mainly on the workstation. A small hard drive, of say 80 MB, will work if the applications are loaded from the file server. Many Windows applications require from 10 to 15 MB of disk.

The Workstation Operating System and Memory

A workstation that runs Windows will benefit from the use of MS DOS 5.0 or DR DOS 6. These versions of DOS offer memory managers that allow moving the network shells and the DOS operating system in and out of conventional memory.

As we discussed in Chapter 5, an 80386 or 80486 workstation can use three types of memory: conventional, expanded, and extended. Figure 9.1 illustrates memory for an 80386 workstation.

Workstation memory and memory management is vital for using Windows. Windows will not function if the workstation has too little memory available. Before installing Windows, you should thus verify the

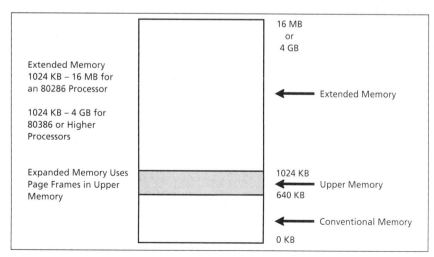

Figure 9.1 *Conventional, Expanded, and Extended Memory*

amount of memory at the workstation. DOS 5.0 has a memory utility that shows the memory statistics. Type *MEM* at the DOS prompt to display the amount of used and free memory on the workstation. The MEM command also comes with several switches for more detailed information. For example, the */program* switch shows the programs (such as the network shell) loaded in memory and the memory location of each program.

Some versions of Windows provide a similar utility to display workstation memory. To use this utility, enter *MSD*. Figure 9.2 illustrates the diagnostics available by using MSD. MSD has an *IRQ Status* option used to view IRQ interrupt information about the workstation. Figure 9.3 shows the information that is available by selecting *IRQ Status*. (Refer to Appendix A for a complete discussion of the information provided by MSD.)

Workstation Shells

If you have a NetWare network that was installed before Windows 3.1 became available, it is likely that your IPX.EXE network shell will need to be upgraded. Some older versions of IPX.EXE do not work with Windows.

During installation, Windows will detect the version of IPX.EXE installed at the workstation. Windows displays a message when it finds IPX.EXE versions that are out of date. The IPX version must be at least 3.21. The Windows install disks have IPX files that can be used on the

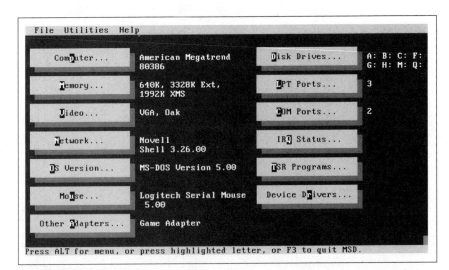

Figure 9.2 *Windows Diagnostic Utility MSD Opening Menu*

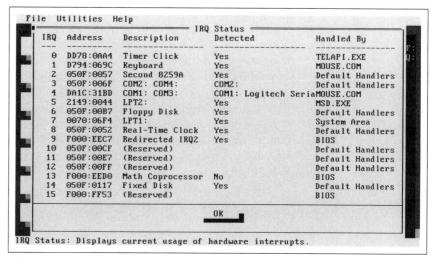

```
 File  Utilities  Help
                              IRQ Status
  IRQ  Address   Description        Detected             Handled By
  ---  --------- -----------        -------------------- ------------------
   0   DD78:0AA4 Timer Click        Yes                  TELAPI.EXE
   1   D794:069C Keyboard           Yes                  MOUSE.COM
   2   050F:0057 Second 8259A       Yes                  Default Handlers
   3   050F:006F COM2: COM4:        COM2:                Default Handlers
   4   DA1C:31BD COM1: COM3:        COM1: Logitech SeriaMOUSE.COM
   5   2149:0044 LPT2:              Yes                  MSD.EXE
   6   050F:00B7 Floppy Disk        Yes                  Default Handlers
   7   0070:06F4 LPT1:              Yes                  System Area
   8   050F:0052 Real-Time Clock    Yes                  Default Handlers
   9   F000:EEC7 Redirected IRQ2    Yes                  BIOS
  10   050F:00CF (Reserved)                              Default Handlers
  11   050F:00E7 (Reserved)                              Default Handlers
  12   050F:00FF (Reserved)                              Default Handlers
  13   F000:EED0 Math Coprocessor   No                   BIOS
  14   050F:0117 Fixed Disk         Yes                  Default Handlers
  15   F000:FF53 (Reserved)                              BIOS

                               OK

 IRQ Status: Displays current usage of hardware interrupts.
```

Figure 9.3 *MSD Utility Displaying the IRQ Setting for a Workstation*

workstation. These files are LSL.COM, IPXODI.COM, and NETX.COM, and they are used to support workstations with the ODI drivers. NetWare drivers and shells are discussed in Chapter 5.

AUTOEXEC.BAT and CONFIG.SYS Files

The AUTOEXEC.BAT and CONFIG.SYS files must be customized at the workstation to load the ODI shells into upper memory. The following is an example of the AUTOEXEC.BAT file:

```
SMARTDRV.EXE
PROMPT $P$G
PATH=C:\BATCH;C:\DOS;C:\;C:\ODI
SET TEMP=C:\WINDOWS\TEMP
CD\ODI LOADHIGH C:\MOUSE\MOUSE SER 1
LOADHIGH C:\ODI\LSL
LOADHIGH C:\ODI\E210DI
LOADHIGH C:\ODI\IPXODI
LOADHIGH C:\ODI\NETX
F:
LOGIN GUEST
```

In this example, the Windows SMARTDrive disk caching program is loaded to reduce the amount of time the computer spends reading from disk. The AUTOEXEC.BAT file then sets the DOS prompt so that the path is displayed followed by a greater-than symbol. A temporary directory, C:\WINDOWS\TEMP, is set for Windows temporary files created during use of Windows. Next, the mouse and network drivers are loaded into high memory, and the network shell is loaded into high memory. The drive is set to the network default F: drive, and the NetWare LOGIN command is executed to access the GUEST account.

The following CONFIG.SYS file sets the DOS environment for Windows:

```
FILES=55
BUFFERS=30
SHELL=C:\DOS\COMMAND.COM /E:1024 /P
DEVICE=C:\HIMEM.SYS /M:11
DOS=HIGH,UMB
DEVICE=C:\EMM386.EXE NOEMS
STACKS=9,256
```

In this CONFIG.SYS file, the number of open files is 55 and the number of buffers is 30. The workstation is directed to use the COMMAND.COM file in the C:\DOS directory and to allow 1024 bytes for environment variables. Next, the HIMEM.SYS memory manager is loaded. HIMEM.SYS provides access to extended memory and HMA (the high memory area is the first 64 KB of extended memory).

The DOS=HIGH,UMB command loads DOS into upper memory (using the HIGH parameter), and the UMB parameter enables DOS to support the use of upper memory blocks by the EMM386 memory manager. The DEVICE=C:\EMM386.EXE NOEMS command loads the EMM386 memory manager. EMM386.EXE is used to simulate expanded memory and to provide access to the upper memory blocks (UMB), which contain memory between 640 KB and 1024 KB. The parameter NOEMS allows the expanded memory manager to fill the empty portion of upper memory with extended memory so programs can be loaded high. NOEMS prevents the memory area from being allocated for DOS applications that use expanded memory.

The STACKS=9,256 command allows several program interrupts to stack up without hanging the workstation. Microsoft Windows recommends nine stacks, each with 256 bytes.

```
Conventional Memory :
Name                 Size in Decimal       Size in Hex
------------         --------------------  -------------
    MSDOS               19376    ( 18.9K)      4BB0
    HIMEM                1072    (  1.0K)       430
    EMM386               3232    (  3.2K)       CA0
    COMMAND              3392    (  3.3K)       D40
    E210DI               6784    (  6.6K)      1A80
    IPXODI              16272    ( 15.9K)      3F90
    NETX                43728    ( 42.7K)      AAD0
Total  FREE :          561152    (548.0K)
Upper Memory :
Name                 Size in Decimal       Size in Hex
------------         --------------------  -------------
    SYSTEM             183888    (179.6K)      2CE50
    SMARTDRV            28304    ( 27.6K)       6E90
    LSL                39056    ( 38.1K)       9890
Total  FREE :           62304    ( 60.8K)
Total bytes available to programs (Conventional+Upper) :     623456   (608.9K)
Largest executable program size :                            561152   (543.0K)
Largest available upper memory block :                        13744   ( 13.4K)
7602176 bytes total contiguous extended memory
    5185536 bytes available XMS memory
```

Figure 9.4 *DOS 5.0 MEM/C Command Used to Display Memory*

After you boot the workstation and execute the CONFIG.SYS and AUTOEXEC.BAT files, it is useful to run the MEM program to display free memory (see Figure 9.4). Note that the figure shows 13.4Kb bytes available in upper memory blocks. In this situation we have attempted to load too many programs into UMBs and are out of room. NETX would have been loaded into UMB but the workstation ran out of memory and so it was loaded into conventional memory. This happens automatically and no error messages are displayed.

Where to Install Windows

There are several ways to install Windows. The approach taken depends on the workstation hardware, the file server hardware, and the amount of control desired by the network administrator.

If the hard disk space on each workstation is limited, around 40 MB, then install Windows on the network. If file server disk space is limited (depending on the number of applications you have installed), then install Windows on each workstation.

The need to control each user's ability to change Windows configuration settings is an important factor, too. If very tight control is needed—for example, in a classroom—then Windows files are installed on the file server. If there must be flexibility in configuration settings, then consider installation at each workstation.

The location decision affects where you will install three groups of Windows files: shared files, user files, and the swap file. These files are described in the next sections.

SHARED FILES

The **shared files** include WRITE.EXE, the dynamic-link libraries (.DLL files), font files, help files, and device driver files. These files require about 16 MB of disk space on a file server. When installed on a workstation, they require 8 to 11 MB of disk space. The workstation installation requires less disk space because only those files used for one type of workstation are installed. On a file server, you will need to install several combinations of font files, device drivers, and so on.

USER FILES

The **user files** have information about each user's hardware configuration and desktop applications. This includes information about the monitor type, the type of mouse used, the printer port type, and so on. These files have the file extensions .INI, .GRP, and .PIF. Only one set of user files is needed when installed on the workstation. More than one set is needed when the installation is on the file server, so that each type of workstation is defined to Windows.

SWAP FILE

The Windows virtual memory manager uses the **swap file** to move information from memory to disk. The disk is usually the workstation's hard drive but can be a virtual disk in the workstation's RAM. The swap file can also be on the network's file server. Using the file server is discouraged. With the swap file on the server, traffic on the network increases and access time may be slow.

The Windows swap file requires at least 1.5 MB of disk space but works best with 5 to 10 MB of space.

FOUR INSTALLATION CHOICES

There are four choices for installing the server, user, and swap files. These choices, including their advantages and disadvantages, are described in the next sections.

1. **Installation with all files on the workstation:** The first method is to install all Windows files on the workstation. The network can be accessed from Windows, and network functions like file sharing and printer servers are available to Windows.

   Windows requires 8 to 11 MB of disk space for the workstation installation. Use this method if there are few Windows users on the network, if there will be portable computers attached to the network, if there is limited network disk space, or if users need control over their individual Windows setups. Just as each person's desk is organized differently, Windows users may want to configure their Windows functions differently for each workstation.

2. **Installation with all files on the file server:** The second way to install Windows is to place all files in a shared directory on the file server. Having the three types of files on the network results in poor performance because the swap file is on the file server. This type of installation may be needed when the network workstations do not have enough disk space for Windows, or when diskless workstations are used.

3. **Installation with the shared and user files on the file server:** The third way to install Windows is by placing the shared files in a common directory on the file server. The user files are installed in each user's home or personal directory, and the swap file is placed on the user's workstation hard drive or on a virtual RAM drive on the workstation.

   This method is very efficient from the standpoint of disk usage, performance, and file management. There is only one copy of the shared files on the network, users have access to their user files, and the swap file does not slow performance. Each user can manage his or her own user file (setup information), or the network manager can flag these files read-only so the user does not change the file.

4. **Installation with shared files only on the file server:** The fourth installation option is to place the shared files on the file server. The user and swap files are placed on the workstation's hard drive. This gives users control over their desktop setup for Windows. With the shared files on the server, a large portion of disk space is still saved on the workstation, since the user and swap files account for only a minor portion of the space required by Windows.

   Under most circumstances, you will likely follow option three, placing user and shared files on the file server. It provides the largest savings in disk space, gives the user control, and provides good performance. Option four is the next best choice but offers less savings on workstation disk space.

Installing Windows on the File Server

Windows has an installation utility, SETUP, that is easy to use. Before starting the installation, ensure that no one can send a message to the Supervisor account and interrupt the process. The best method is to select prearranged systems time and disable logins on the server. Logins are disabled by typing *Disable Login* at the file server console. If you must perform the installation while users are on, type *CASTOFF* from the Supervisor's account to turn off messages to that account.

RUNNING SETUP

The SETUP utility is run with various switches that determine how Windows is installed. Table 9.1 describes some of these switches. Consult the Windows documentation for more detailed information about all of the switches available with SETUP.

Table 9.1 Windows SETUP Switches

Switch	Function
/i	Ignores automatic hardware detection so the user is prompted to verify hardware settings on the file server or workstation.
/n	Sets up a shared copy of Windows from a file server to the workstation. This is run after Windows is installed on the file server.
/a	Runs the administrative installation of Windows to a file server by expanding and copying Windows disks to the file server.

Before you start installation, decide which SETUP switches you wish to use. You will also need to decide whether to use the *express* or *custom* setup. The express setup works well for most installations. When using the express installation, you will only need to provide information about printer and port connections.

The custom setup allows more control over the installation process. With this selection, SETUP asks you to verify hardware and software information detected on the workstation or to input your own setup information.

The installation example provided in the following sections shows how to set up Windows with the shared and user files on the file server and the swap file on the workstation.

SERVER SETUP

The first step in the example is to install files on the server by logging into the network as Supervisor and creating a Windows directory. For example, the directory might be T:\WINAPPS. Next, expand and copy the Windows disks to the file server by typing *SETUP /A*.

As soon as the Windows files are copied to the file server, flag them as shareable and read-only (FLAG *.* SRO). Users will be able to access but not change the files.

WORKSTATION SETUP

In this example, all of the shared and user files are copied to the file server and the swap file is copied to the workstation. Map the Windows directory to a search drive (for example, MAP S3: = \WINAPPS); run *SETUP /N* from the workstation.

Setup will attempt to detect the workstation's hardware and software configuration. Once the detection process is complete, Windows will display a screen showing what it detected (see Figure 9.5). The instructions at the bottom of the screen indicate that the present configuration can be accepted by using the ENTER key or the arrow keys can

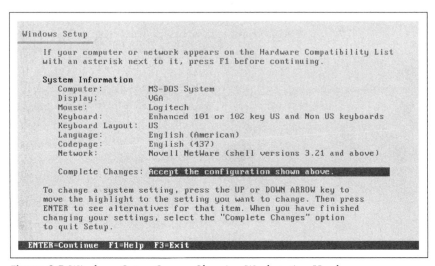

Figure 9.5 *Windows Setup Screen Showing Workstation Hardware Configuration*

be used to change a selection. During the detection process, Windows may determine that the workstation IPX file is not compatible. If this happens, upgrade the IPX file on the workstation.

Running the setup utility to install Windows on workstations is not difficult. Once you are through with the setup program, Windows is installed and ready to use.

The workstation installation starts with default settings for the Windows desktop environment. The environment includes layouts, icons, and the default applications accessible from Windows. These settings can be customized later from the user's home directory.

The desktop applications are put into a **shared program group** on the file server. These are applications grouped together for access by users. For example, there could be a group of network utilities put into a group to be accessed only by the network manager. Figure 9.6 illustrates groups of applications that are selected by clicking on the group icon. The groups are displayed across the bottom of the *Program Manager* desktop. The groups shown are *Accessories, Games, StartUp, Windows Resource Kit, Main,* and *Novell NetWare*. The *Applications* group has been selected and displays a window showing the applications in that group. If you

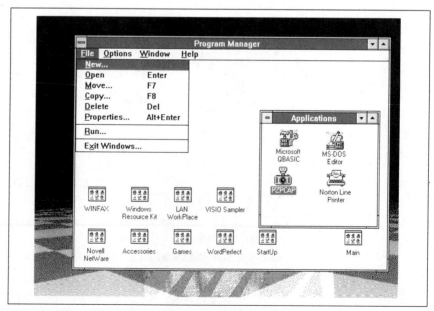

Figure 9.6 *Windows Program Manager Showng Program Groups*

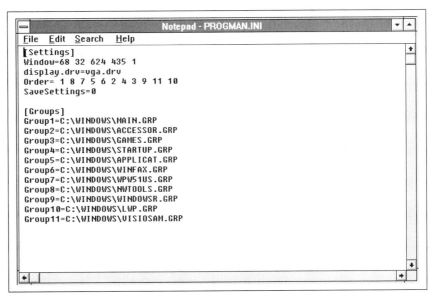

Figure 9.7 *PROGMAN.INI File, Which Windows Reads to Load and Place Group Icons on the Desktop*

select the *File* option at the top of the *Program Manager* screen, you will see that the *Copy* and *Delete* options are not available. This prevents users from making changes to the group. This is accomplished by flagging the Windows file PROGMAN.INI as shareable read-only so it cannot be changed. The file is found in the Windows network directory. Figure 9.7 shows the contents of PROGMAN.INI.

When Windows is started, the *Program Manager* reads the PROGMAN.INI file to determine which shared program groups to display. Notice that the desktop displayed in Figure 9.6 corresponds to the group information (Groups 1 through 11) in Figure 9.7.

Running Windows

Now that Windows is installed on the file server, how is this installation of Windows different from Windows on a standalone computer? A look at the File Manager and Print Manager is a good way to examine the differences. Two other Windows options, Windows Resource Kit and NetWare Workstation Services, deserve a look, too. These four Windows functions are presented in the sections that follow.

File Manager

The **File Manager** is a Windows function for displaying and managing files and directories. The File Manager is able to detect NetWare mapped drives and the local drives on the workstation. Figure 9.8 shows a screen displaying the mapped drives and the contents of subdirectory \LABS\404\WINDOWS on drive H:.

In this example, when the WINDOWS subdirectory is selected, the files are listed on the right side of the screen. Each file, such as the DOSPRMPT.PIF file, has several properties with which it is associated. Since this is a file on the network, there are file properties and network properties that can be displayed. Figure 9.9 shows the properties of the file. Notice there is a box for viewing the network properties of the file.

Selecting the network box displays another screen that shows the network file properties. Figure 9.10 illustrates the screen that displays network properties. The file in this example, DOSPRMPT.PIF, is shareable with the rename and delete options inhibited, which means it is flagged shareable read-only.

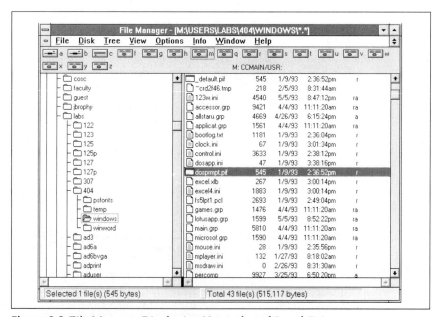

Figure 9.8 *File Manager Displaying Network and Local Drives*

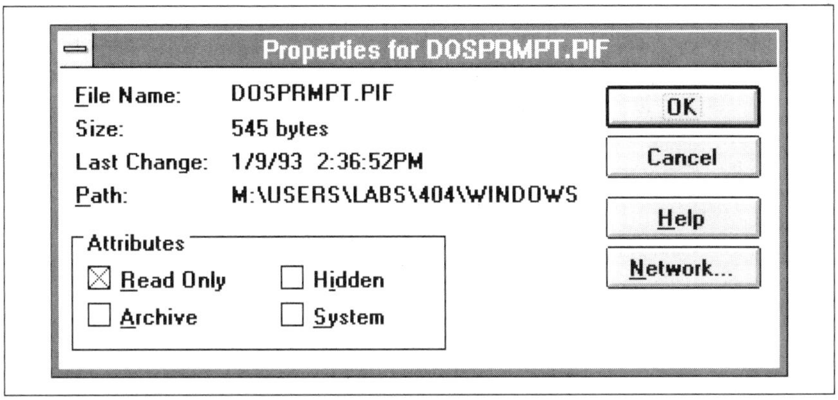

Figure 9.9 *File Manager Displaying Properties of a File*

Another useful network feature is that important date information about a file can be displayed. As shown in Figure 9.10, Windows provides information about the creation date of a file, when it was last accessed, when it was last updated, and when it was archived last.

Print Manager

Network printing is made easier by Windows **Print Manager**. Print Manager handles printing at the workstation printer and on the network printers. It does this by displaying two types of print queues: local print queues and network print queues. With Print Manager, you can pause a printout, set printing priorities, and delete printouts. Print Manager also enables you to go onto other applications while a job is waiting to be printed.

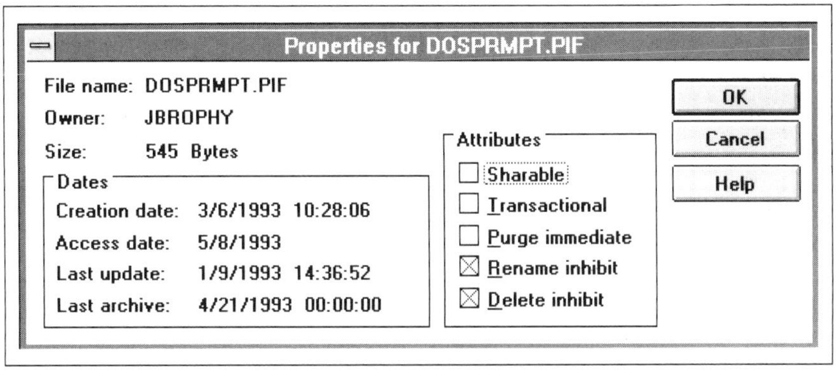

Figure 9.10 *File Manager Displaying Network Properties of a File*

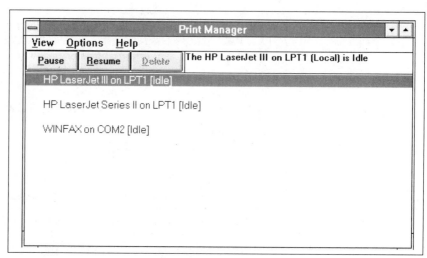

Figure 9.11 *Print Manager Showing Printer That Was Installed During Setup*

Figure 9.11 shows the printer selected during the Windows installation process. The screen in Figure 9.11 indicates that the printer is idle and printouts will be directed to a local (workstation) printer.

To obtain more information on how to configure Print Manager, click with the mouse on the *Help* option at the top of the screen. A help file is displayed with information on the printer configuration. Figure 9.12 displays part of the file with information on Print Manager.

Note the *Options* selection at the top of the Print Manager screen in Figure 9.11. Clicking on the *Options* selection displays the *Network Options* box as shown in Figure 9.13.

The *Network Options* box provides the choice of bypassing the Print Manager and directing all printouts to the network. This option is useful if network printing is handled through application programs, such as WordPerfect, and the Print Manager is not needed. When you click on the box next to *Print Net Jobs Direct*, all printing is directed to the network print queue and will bypass the Print Manager.

To set up printing directly to the network, it is necessary to select the print queue. This is accomplished by choosing the *Options* box from the *Print Manager* menu shown in Figure 9.11. Figure 9.14 shows the menu box used to select the print queue. When a print queue is selected, the next step is to connect the queue to Windows. Click on the *Connect* option to connect the queue selected. The queue chosen in Figure 9.14 is CCMAIN/SALES_PRINTER.

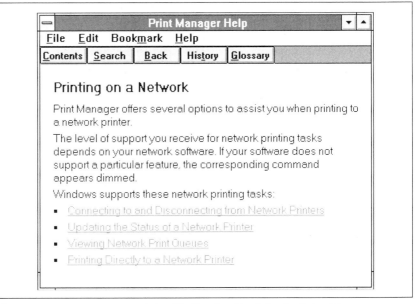

Figure 9.12 *Print Manager Help File Used to Explain the Print Manager*

Windows Resource Kit

The Windows Resource Kit is an add-on product from Microsoft that can be purchased to assist in managing the desktop. Some of the options provided with the kit are used to manage the workstation, while other options give the user easy access to network features. Figure 9.15 shows the options that are provided when the Windows Resource Kit is installed.

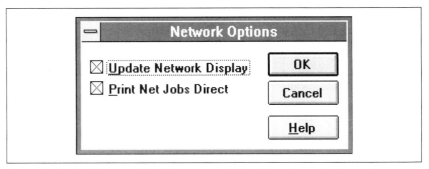

Figure 9.13 *Configuring Print Manager to Print Directly to the Network Print Queue*

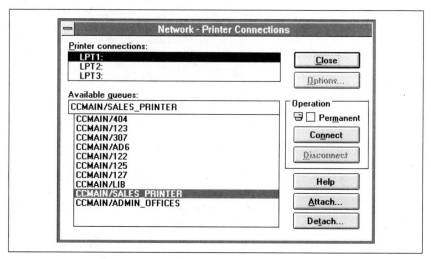

Figure 9.14 *Print Manager Printer Configuration Screen Used to Select the Network Print Queue*

Since Windows uses a large amount of memory, it is useful to be able to run a utility that graphically displays the status of the workstation memory. To do this, select the *System Resource Monitor* icon in Figure 9.15. Figure 9.16 illustrates the current status of the workstation memory.

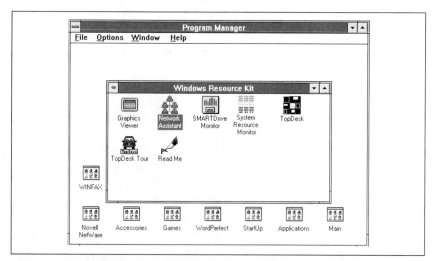

Figure 9.15 *Program Group Windows Resource Kit Screen Showing Utilities*

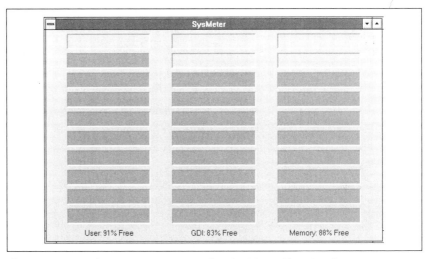

Figure 9.16 *Windows Resource Kit Utility SysMeter Showing Current Memory Usage*

The three columns show the amount of memory for user resources, graphics resources (GDI), and Windows program memory. On-line information about the System Resource Monitor, SysMeter, is obtained by pressing the F1 key on the screen shown in Figure 9.16. Figure 9.17 illustrates the on-line documentation.

Netware Workstation Services

Novell markets a Windows Workstation Kit that provides icon access to network services. The software and documentation is not included with Windows or NetWare and must be purchased separately. Figure 9.18 shows the utilities that come with the kit.

The options that come with the Windows Workstation Kit include:

- A map display
- A display of network printers
- A display of network attachments
- A userlist display
- A display of volume information
- A utility to set the account password
- Two utilities for sending and receiving messages

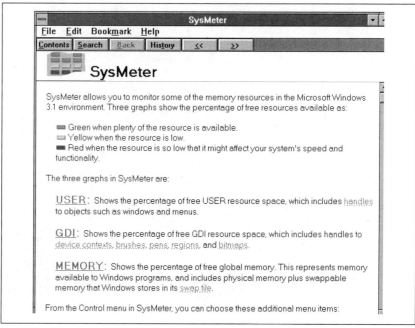

Figure 9.17 *Windows Resource Kit Help File Explaining SysMeter*

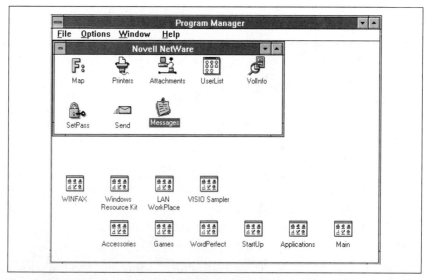

Figure 9.18 *NetWare Workstation Services Screen Displaying Network Utilities*

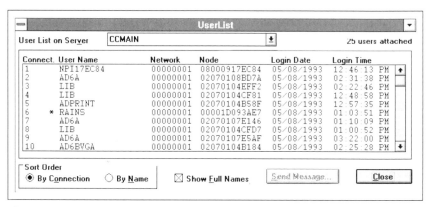

Figure 9.19 *NetWare Workstation Services Userlist Utility*

The *Userlist* option is particularly useful since it displays a list of users and provides the option to send a message to one or more users. *UserList* also has the ability to display users on more than one file server. Figure 9.19 shows the *UserList* screen.

Installing WordPerfect for Windows on a File Server

Installing software applications to run in Windows and on the network requires some advance planning. It requires an understanding of the different types of workstations on the network and of the work habits of the workstation users.

Installation of WordPerfect for Windows is used in this chapter to illustrate how an application is installed and configured. An outline of the installation steps is provided in Table 9.2.

Table 9.2 Installing WordPerfect for Windows

Step	Description
1	Prepare in advance for the installation by reading the documentation.
2	Run the WordPerfect Install program.
3	Install the printer drivers.
4	Modify the system login script to assign drive mappings.
5	Assign the trustee rights.
6	Customize the environment files.
7	Flag the program and set files.
8	Test the installation.
9	Document the installation for later reference.

WORDPERFECT DOCUMENTATION

Reading the manufacturer's documentation regarding the installation is the first step. Begin by reading Appendix M, Networking WordPerfect, of the *WordPerfect for Windows Reference*. Next, read the README.NET file on the WordPerfect diskettes. This file is an update to Appendix M. The README.NET file is displayed during the installation process.

RUNNING THE INSTALL PROGRAM

Start the installation by logging into the Supervisor account on the file server. With the WordPerfect install diskette loaded at the workstation, run the INSTALL program. Figure 9.20 shows the beginning installation screen. Start with option 8, *README,* to view the README file.

After completing the README file, select option 3, *Network,* to begin the network installation. Figure 9.21 shows the *Network Installation* screen. Use option 1 on that screen to indicate the source drive of the WordPerfect installation diskettes, such as drive B:. Option 2, *Install To,* is used to indicate where WordPerfect files will be installed. This option displays the screen in Figure 9.22. In this example, drives: is mapped to USR:WINAPPS/WPWIN, which is mapped before beginning the install by using the MAP ROOT command. MAP ROOT is used so that users cannot move to the parent directory. Files

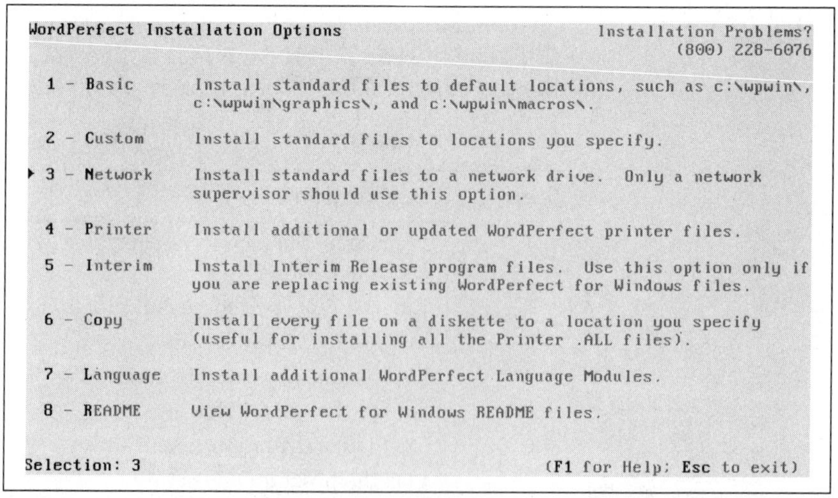

```
WordPerfect Installation Options                    Installation Problems?
                                                         (800) 228-6076

    1 - Basic        Install standard files to default locations, such as c:\wpwin\,
                     c:\wpwin\graphics\, and c:\wpwin\macros\.

    2 - Custom       Install standard files to locations you specify.

  ▶ 3 - Network      Install standard files to a network drive.  Only a network
                     supervisor should use this option.

    4 - Printer      Install additional or updated WordPerfect printer files.

    5 - Interim      Install Interim Release program files.  Use this option only if
                     you are replacing existing WordPerfect for Windows files.

    6 - Copy         Install every file on a diskette to a location you specify
                     (useful for installing all the Printer .ALL files).

    7 - Language     Install additional WordPerfect Language Modules.

    8 - README       View WordPerfect for Windows README files.

  Selection: 3                                    (F1 for Help; Esc to exit)
```

Figure 9.20 *Beginning Install Menu for WordPerfect for Windows*

```
WordPerfect Network Installation                    Installation Problems?
                                                        (800) 228-6076

   1 - Install From                  b:\

 ▶ 2 - Install To

   3 - Perform Installation

   4 - Check .ENV Files

   5 - Select Printer(s)

   6 - README

   7 - Exit Install


   ┌──────────────────────────────────────────────────────────────────┐
   │  The Install To option lets you specify the locations (such as c:\wpwin\ │
   │  and c:\wpwin\graphics\) where you want to install the WordPerfect files.│
   └──────────────────────────────────────────────────────────────────┘

 Selection: 2                                    (F1 for Help; Esc to return)
```

Figure 9.21 *Installation Program Performing the Installation*

for graphics, macros, and so on are to be installed in the directory format mentioned in earlier chapters. For example, the graphics files will be installed in directory USR:WINAPPS/WPWIN/GRAPHICS (the same as S:/WPWIN/GRAPHICS).

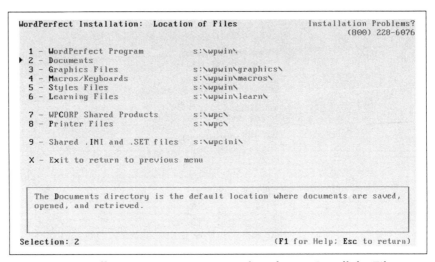

```
WordPerfect Installation:  Location of Files        Installation Problems?
                                                        (800) 228-6076

   1 - WordPerfect Program        s:\wpwin\
 ▶ 2 - Documents
   3 - Graphics Files             s:\wpwin\graphics\
   4 - Macros/Keyboards           s:\wpwin\macros\
   5 - Styles Files               s:\wpwin\
   6 - Learning Files             s:\wpwin\learn\

   7 - WPCORP Shared Products     s:\wpc\
   8 - Printer Files              s:\wpc\

   9 - Shared .INI and .SET files s:\wpcini\

   X - Exit to return to previous menu


   ┌──────────────────────────────────────────────────────────────────┐
   │  The Documents directory is the default location where documents are saved, │
   │  opened, and retrieved.                                            │
   └──────────────────────────────────────────────────────────────────┘

 Selection: 2                                    (F1 for Help; Esc to return)
```

Figure 9.22 *Installation Program Prompting for Where to Install the Files*

Option 3, *Perform Installation,* is selected next from the screen in Figure 9.21. This option copies the WordPerfect files to the file server.

As the files are installed, there are prompts for the type of keyboard to be used at the workstations. The choices are to install a keyboard layout that conforms to DOS command keystrokes or a keyboard layout to conform to Windows keystrokes. Since the installation is for Windows, choose the *1-CUA Keyboard* option. Figure 9.23 shows the WordPerfect screen explaining these options.

Once the files are copied to the server, a *Reminder* screen is displayed (see Figure 9.24). This screen is a reminder to flag the files as read-only; to grant appropriate trustee rights (such as read and file scan); to set up the AUTOEXEC.BAT and other startup scripts for WordPerfect use; and to designate a printer port for WordPerfect (such as a network printer queue).

The successful installation will create a Windows group called WordPerfect. This Windows group will display a screen with icons for WordPerfect, Speller, Thesaurus, and File Manager. Figure 9.25 shows the WordPerfect group.

Printer Drivers

The WordPerfect printer drivers are established by starting WordPerfect. Start WordPerfect by clicking on the WP icon in the WordPerfect group. There are several options displayed at the top of the

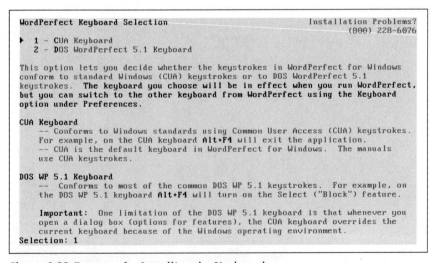

```
WordPerfect Keyboard Selection                    Installation Problems?
                                                       (800) 228-6076
 ▶  1 - CUA Keyboard
    2 - DOS WordPerfect 5.1 Keyboard

This option lets you decide whether the keystrokes in WordPerfect for Windows
conform to standard Windows (CUA) keystrokes or to DOS WordPerfect 5.1
keystrokes.  The keyboard you choose will be in effect when you run WordPerfect,
but you can switch to the other keyboard from WordPerfect using the Keyboard
option under Preferences.

CUA Keyboard
    -- Conforms to Windows standards using Common User Access (CUA) keystrokes.
    For example, on the CUA keyboard Alt+F4 will exit the application.
    -- CUA is the default keyboard in WordPerfect for Windows.  The manuals
    use CUA keystrokes.

DOS WP 5.1 Keyboard
    --  Conforms to most of the common DOS WP 5.1 keystrokes.  For example, on
    the DOS WP 5.1 keyboard Alt+F4 will turn on the Select ("Block") feature.

    Important:  One limitation of the DOS WP 5.1 keyboard is that whenever you
    open a dialog box (options for features), the CUA keyboard overrides the
    current keyboard because of the Windows operating environment.
Selection: 1
```

Figure 9.23 *Program for Installing the Keyboard*

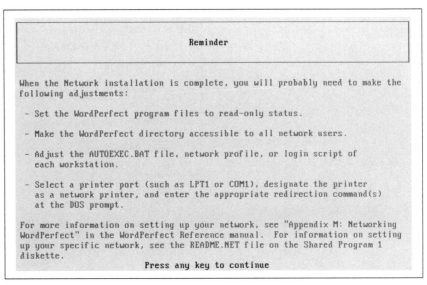

Figure 9.24 *Final Installation Screen Informing Network Supervisor How to Finish Installation*

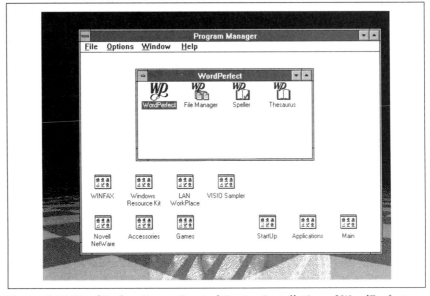

Figure 9.25 *WordPerfect Group Created During Installation of WordPerfect*

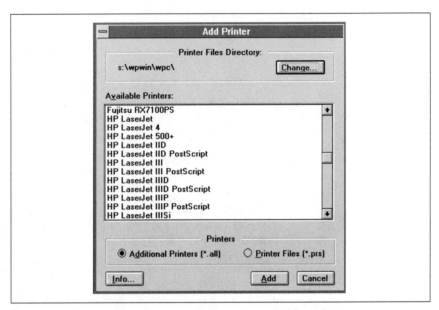

Figure 9.26 *WordPerfect Printer Selection Menu Used to Choose a Printer Driver*

beginning WordPerfect screen. Click on the *File* option. A pull-down menu of selections appears. Click on the *Printer configuration* selection. Figure 9.26 displays the *Printer Configuration* menu.

As the screen in Figure 9.26 illustrates, the printer files are in /WPC subdirectory. Use the arrow key to highlight and select the printer or printers that will be used with WordPerfect. Press the ENTER key to select each printer.

After a printer is selected, there is the option to use the WordPerfect or the Windows printer drivers. Figure 9.27 displays the next menu from which to select the printer driver. Choose the WordPerfect printer drivers. They are tailored for WordPerfect and perform better than the Windows printer drivers. Each printer must be set up before it is used. Click on the *Setup* option for each printer you install. The *Setup* screen is shown in Figure 9.28.

It is necessary to designate the printer port on the *Setup* screen. Click on this option. If the printer is to be used at one workstation only, designate LPT1, LPT2, COM1, or COM2 (LPT1 or LPT2 for parallel connections and COM1 or COM2 for serial connections). If the printer is a shared network printer, click on the *Network Printer* box.

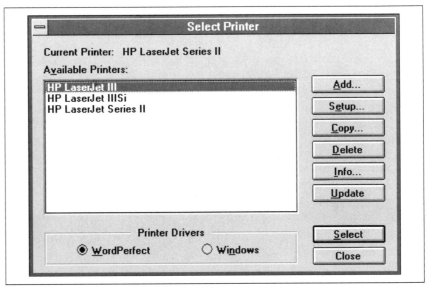

Figure 9.27 *Select Print Menu to Set Up the Printer*

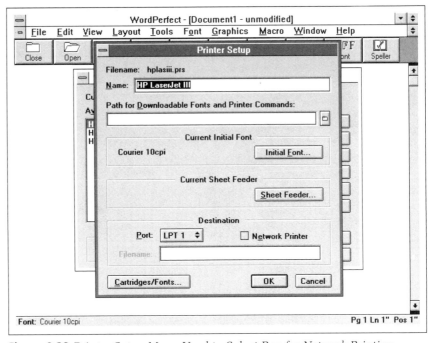

Figure 9.28 *Printer Setup Menu Used to Select Box for Network Printing*

SYSTEM LOGIN SCRIPT

The next step is to ensure WordPerfect will run as a shared application on the network. To do this, you will need to modify the system login script to include drive mappings for Windows and for WordPerfect. Figure 9.29 shows an example system login script. The script in that figure first turns the map display to off so that the network drive mappings are not displayed when a user logs in. The prompt command sets the DOS prompt to display the directory followed by the greater-than symbol. Next, the home directory is set for each user to USR:USERS/ %LOGIN_NAME, where %LOGIN_NAME is the NetWare value for the user's account name. After the home directory is mapped, the user's default directory is set to H: for the home directory.

There are three search drives mapped in the system login script. Each is mapped with the MAP ROOT command so that the users cannot move to the parent directory above each mapping. Search drive 1 is mapped to the public directory so users can access NetWare commands. Search drive 2 is mapped to the USR:APPL/MENUS subdirectory to permit users to execute a menu from which to start applications (for users who do not have Windows). Search drive 3 is mapped to the USR:WINAPPS/WIN subdirectory so users can start Windows.

TRUSTEE RIGHTS

Another step toward making WordPerfect a shared application is to set the trustee rights. Use the GRANT or SYSCON utilities to set trustee rights. To use SYSCON, start the utility and select the *GROUP* option.

```
REM ** SET ENVIRONMENT **
MAP DISPLAY OFF
DOS SET PROMPT="$P$G"

REM ** MAP TO USER'S HOME DIRECTORY **
MAP H:=USR:USERS/%LOGIN_NAME
DRIVE H:

REM ** MAP SEARCH DRIVES **
MAP ROOT S1:=SYS:PUBLIC
MAP ROOT S2:=USR:APPL/MENUS
MAP ROOT S3:=USR:WINAPPS/WPWIN
```

Figure 9.29 *An Example of a System Login Script for WordPerfect*

Modify the group EVERYONE to have read and file scan rights to the USR:WINAPPS directory. This gives rights to the Windows and WordPerfect directories for all users on the file server. If you want to limit rights to a specific group, such as SALES, then give read and file scan rights to SALES instead of to EVERYONE.

To use the GRANT command to assign read and file scan rights to EVERYONE, enter the following at the command line:

```
GRANT R F FOR USR:WINAPPS TO EVERYONE
```

ENVIRONMENT FILES

Several environment files must be created so that WordPerfect runs as a network application from Windows. The environment files are WP{WP}.ENV, WPC_NET.INI, WPC.INI, and WP{xxx.SET (the xxx represents the set file name, such as JAS for John A. Smith's set file). The set file serves the same function as the DOS WordPerfect set file described in Chapter 7. It contains information about printer setup, page layout, backup options, initial codes, and other options.

The WP{WP}.ENV file provides WordPerfect with start-up information, such as the type of network and where to find other environment files. This file is created during the installation of WordPerfect. An example WP{WP}.ENV file is the following:

```
/NT=1
/PS=s:/wpcini/
/NI=s:/wpc/
/WPC=s:/wpc
```

The /NT=1 line in the file informs WordPerfect that it is running on a Novell network. The /PS=s:/wpcini/ parameter instructs WordPerfect to look in the /wpcini/ subdirectory for the WordPerfect .SET files. The /NI parameter indicates to WordPerfect where to find the WPC_NET.INI file, such as in the /wpc subdirectory as shown in this example. The /WPC line informs WordPerfect where to find (subdirectory /wpc in this example) the WordPerfect Corporation Shared Products code. These are files shared by WordPerfect users.

When installed as a Windows application, WordPerfect uses several .INI files. These files are created by the WordPerfect installation process. The .INI files specify keyboard choices, button/bar configuration and options, File Manager, speller, thesaurus, short cut keys, and other customization options. For example, WPC.INI is a file created to customize WordPerfect for each user. This file also has product information that is used by

WordPerfect. The WPC_NET.INI file has network and product information needed by WordPerfect to run as a network application. The WPC.INI and the WPC_NET.INI files also are "product-global" files, which means they contain information common to all WordPerfect Corporation products.

FLAGGING FILES

Most of the WordPerfect files should be flagged as shareable read-only. This helps prevent their accidental deletion or modification. The .SET files, though, must be flagged as shareable read-write. Each user must be able to write to his or her set file to use the WordPerfect setup option.

Create a separate subdirectory for the .SET files and use the /PS command in the WP{WP}.ENV environment file to inform WordPerfect about where to find the files. Make certain all .SET files are copied from the WordPerfect program directory to the .SET file subdirectory. This subdirectory must have file scan and read-write trustee access rights for all WordPerfect users. (Refer back to Figure 9.22 to review the WordPerfect directories.)

TESTING

The testing phase is important for installation of any software on the network. At least five areas of testing should be completed: workstation access, printer configuration, security, program setup, and shared access.

Combined network and Windows applications require that all workstation types be tested for successful access. For example, if your network has IBM PS/2 80386, Gateway 80486, and Zenith 80486 computers, test Windows and WordPerfect on each machine. Test different monitor types, such as VGA and SVGA.

Printer configurations need to be tested, too. If the network has Hewlett-Packard and Okidata laser printers, test each with Windows and WordPerfect. Also test local workstation printers and remote network printers.

Test security by determining if any user can alter or delete Windows or WordPerfect program files. Can users access a directory where they should not have trustee rights? Can the users access and change files that are meant for access, such as a user's .SET file and data files?

Program setup is another area for testing. Run WordPerfect to verify the program can properly access the dictionary, the thesaurus, the drive used for data files, the macro files, and environment files. Ensure the printer setups are customized properly.

Test simultaneous use of WordPerfect to verify there is shared access. Log onto ten or more accounts from different workstations at the same time. Make certain each workstation has full access to WordPerfect and that workstation performance is satisfactory. Also determine that metering software is properly controlling access based on the number of licenses owned.

DOCUMENTATION

Document how WordPerfect has been installed. This will prove invaluable when disaster strikes—for example, when the file server loses a disk drive. The documentation will help you recreate the installation so that interruption to the users is at a minimum.

Create a chart showing the directory structure and drive mappings. Document the contents and location of environment files, such as the .ENV, .INI, and .SET files. Record information on how WordPerfect has been customized, what printer drivers are used, what macros have been created, and so on.

AFTER INSTALLATION

When you have completed all of the installation steps, WordPerfect is ready for release to the network users. Stay in contact with the users so you can provide modifications to meet their needs. There may be portions of the installation that will have to be changed as the users become more expert on the network, Windows, and WordPerfect.

Summary

Windows is a popular applications interface that is installed on millions of computers. The popularity has lead to extensive use of Windows on Novell networks. This chapter provides information about the network installation of Windows and about installing network applications to run from Windows.

The workstation requirements needed to run Windows are described, including the type of CPU, memory, and disk space. Installation of Windows involves determining what workstation resources are available. If the workstations have minimum disk storage resources, Windows files are installed on the file server. When the workstations have more disk storage resources, large Windows files, such as the swap file, are installed on the workstation.

Once Windows is installed, the user has access to features such as File Manager and Print Manager. File Manager makes it easy to view, copy, move, create, and delete user files on the network and on the workstation. Print Manager is used to direct print files to local and network printers.

Windows makes running applications easier by providing menu groupings, mouse capabilities, and icons. The installation of a Windows application is illustrated by using WordPerfect. The process is divided into ten steps that cover installing the software files, customizing the software, creating drive mappings and trustee rights, testing, and documenting the installation.

File Manager   A tool included with Windows that gives the user the ability to display, copy, move, and delete files.

Graphical User Interface (GUI)   An interface that uses graphics such as icons, boxes, windows, pictures, and arrows to make use of a workstation easier. Microsoft Windows is a GUI that lets users build their own menus and add PC functions through the use of icons.

Icon   A small picture or symbol that is a graphic representation of a Windows application or utility.

Print Manager   A Windows utility that enables the user to direct print files to workstation and network printers. Print Manager is also used to set printing priorities, to hold printouts, and to delete print jobs.

Shared Files   Files containing information used to configure Windows for device drivers, fonts, link libraries, and user help information.

Shared Program Group   A box on a screen that serves as a menu of functions (represented by icons) associated with one or more Windows applications. Shared Program Group screen displays can be customized by the Windows user.

Swap File   A file used by Windows to help free memory as needed. This critical file is disk storage that Windows uses to temporarily move data stored in memory onto a disk, until the information is again needed in memory by the CPU.

User Files   Windows files with information about each user's hardware configuration and desktop applications. The information includes monitor type, type of mouse, printer port type, and so on.

1. A company employee uses DOS and DOS applications. The employee is attempting to determine whether the current computer will be able to run Windows or whether they should buy another computer. What are the hardware issues that should be discussed with this user? What hardware configuration would you recommend?

2. To run Windows on a network requires having up-to-date versions of the network shells. What shells must be up-to-date and how would you determine the version?

3. Of the four ways to install Windows files, which way minimizes the total disk space needed on the network file server and workstations? Explain why. Which install method requires the most disk space on the network?

4. Explain the difference between the "/n" and the "/a" setup options for Windows. Include in your discussion an explanation of the workstation location and configuration.

5. When a workstation boots using the AUTOEXEC.BAT and CONFIG.SYS files, various drivers and memory managers are run. Some of these drivers, such as MOUSE.SYS and MOUSE.EXE, have different file extensions. Explain why there are two different mouse drivers and how each would be loaded.

6. The network administrator has the ability to install Windows so that all workstations see the same desktop display and so that the display cannot be changed by the user. Explain the benefits of having a single desktop display and how the administrator would go about preventing users from changing the desktop display.

7. Outline the steps needed to install a Windows application. The outline should be in three parts: (1) pre-installation activities, (2) installation activities, and (3) post-installation activities. Begin with how you would set up the directories. Confine the discussion to network specific issues.

Network Management

Chapter Objectives

The objectives of this chapter are the following:

- To show how to formulate a network administration plan.
- To explain NetWare Loadable Modules.
- To illustrate the use of network management utilities.

Introduction

While the LAN is in the installation and testing stage, take the opportunity to develop a plan for its administration. This plan will involve these steps:

- Establishing the duties of the **network manager**
- Selecting the network manager
- Training the network manager
- Establishing a back-up person for the network
- Defining network standards
- Developing a plan to prevent and solve network problems
- Establishing security procedures for the network
- Developing a network disaster recovery plan
- Creating a plan for user training
- Identifying ways in which users can report problems

- Purchasing equipment to help resolve network problems
- Finding ways to expedite growth and modifications in the network

When developing a management plan for the network, keep in mind that the network exists for users; it is their tool. In an industrial setting, this means it can become a cornerstone to facilitate the productivity of workers and management. Within educational settings, it is vital for classroom, laboratory, and general academic endeavors.

Users will quickly become dependent on the LAN to complete their work. When something goes wrong, they will expect a quick solution. And as their LAN expertise develops, they will have increasing expectations for LAN services, coupled with LAN growth. With an effective and responsive management plan, it will be possible to correct problems more quickly. Further, it will be easier to address the needs for increased services and growth.

Duties of the Network Manager

The network manager provides the link between the organization and the technical aspects of the LAN. If the network manager's duties are defined clearly, it will be easier for this person to keep the LAN operating reliably.

A primary duty of the network manager is to administer the *technical side* of the LAN. This entails setting up and maintaining hardware on the LAN. As mentioned earlier, the hardware consists of the file server (or servers), workstations, printers, modems, communication equipment, cable, cable connectors, uninterruptible power sources, and other equipment.

Once the hardware is installed, it is good practice to establish service contracts on network components such as the file server, workstations, printers, and other critical equipment. Preventive maintenance schedules, especially for printers and cabling, will ensure uninterrupted network performance.

On the technical side, the network manager plans the transition from the test phase of the LAN to full-scale production. This involves fully testing the NetWare operating system, establishing user directories, establishing access restrictions and file protection, invoking security measures such as passwords, and installing and testing application software. An added part of the transition to full production is converting data files from other computer systems to the LAN for use by specific LAN applications. The files requiring conversion may be from host computers or standalone desktop computers.

Another technical feature is the selection of LAN utilities to enhance access and performance of the LAN. For instance, utilities such as print server applications enable the network manager to establish remote printers at points other than the file server. Remote printing enables users to direct their printouts to any printer on the LAN, which reduces equipment requirements and permits the network manager to put a printer at any location on the LAN. Utilities such as a Novell Access Server or Remote2 software enable users to dial into the LAN through the telephone system. In this way, it is possible for the vice president of a company to access a LAN at a manufacturing site in Denver while working at his or her desk at corporate headquarters in New York.

There are also utilities that help with LAN maintenance activities, such as maintenance-menuing systems. These provide quick access to common maintenance functions, such as BINDFIX. There are also programs available that enable automatic deletion of residual log-on files, such as batch files associated with the Novell menu system.

The technical responsibilities of the network manager are as follows:

- Loading the NetWare software
- Installing NetWare updates and patches (for software problems)
- Creating new user accounts, user home directories, and user login scripts
- Creating and updating the system login script
- Designing and implementing the volume and directory structure
- Designing and implementing the security procedures
- Installing, updating, and testing software applications
- Providing user training, support, and documentation
- Monitoring the file server(s) and network for problems
- Providing for regular backup of all network files
- Planning and implementing hardware upgrades for file servers, server memory, workstations, and printers
- Performing regular maintenance activities such as running BINDFIX, deleting old files, archiving files, and updating server utilities

The network manager is responsible for both the technical and the business aspects of the LAN, maintaining familiarity with the use and the cost of the equipment, which can vary among vendors. Some less expensive components can be used instead of costlier ones. Some brands of cable may be as effective and reliable as other brands, but they may cost less.

Familiarity with upgrades to the NetWare operating system is another area that combines the technical and business sides. Novell is constantly upgrading and improving its products. The network manager is responsible for acquiring the latest versions of NetWare utilities. Many are available through subscription to the Novell forums on CompuServe, a nationwide dial-in service that offers forums, bulletin boards, electronic mail, shopping, and other services to subscribers. The LOGIN.EXE, MAP.EXE, SYSCON.EXE, IPX.EXE, and other NetWare utility upgrades can be downloaded to a workstation from CompuServe.

As the network grows, the network manager will have to make decisions about upgrading to new versions of NetWare. For example, is an upgrade cost effective?

The most important business responsibility of the manager is to work with other managers within his or her organization to develop a sound budget for the network. The LAN will become a backbone for accomplishing daily work tasks. Many departments and divisions in an organization will have an interest in LAN funding.

Another business function of the manager is to maintain relationships with vendors. The broader the range of vendors, the more likely it is the network manager will be able to take advantage of support and price differences among them.

Writing **requests for proposals** (RFPs) is another key business responsibility. An RFP outlines all of the organization's hardware and software requirements that must be met by a vendor. The completed RFP is sent to vendors. Vendors who believe they can meet the requirements in the RFP will submit a formal written response, showing how they intend to fulfill the requirements.

If the RFP is written well, it can be invaluable in a number of ways. First, it forces the organization to analyze its LAN needs as comprehensively and clearly as possible. Second, it enables vendors to determine if they can offer a solution to the organization's needs. Third, it provides a recourse if the vendor makes promises that are not kept, or if the vendor supplies equipment and services that do not meet the original specifications in the RFP.

When writing an RFP, it is particularly important to specify all equipment requirements in as much detail as is feasible. This includes requirements for mean time between equipment failure, software compatibility specifications, warranty needs, and statements showing who is responsible for hardware and software support (see Figure 10.1).

Even more important than developing RFPs and maintaining relationships with vendors is the necessity for the network manager to understand the environment in which the LAN will be used. In business, LANs may be used in a variety of areas: accounting, order entry, manufacturing, inventory, internal communications, or any combination of these. In the school environment, LANs may be used for teaching

- A description of the organization
- A description of the organizational goals to be fulfilled via the LAN
- Equipment specifications
- Equipment reliability requirements
- Equipment locations (including information about buildings that will house the equipment)
- All communication needs (including details about existing communication equipment)
- Software specifications
- Specifications regarding applications software
- Compatibility with specific Novell operating system environments
- Connectivity requirements with other LANs, mainframes, minicomputers, or workstations
- Software and hardware support requirements
- Warranty requirements

Figure 10.1 *Request for Proposal (RFP) Outline*

classes, for administrative functions, or for scientific research. If you understand the needs of the production environment, you will also understand how the LAN should be managed. For example, if a particular LAN is used to generate payroll, there will be critical times during each pay period when the LAN must function at its optimum level.

Part of understanding the production environment is developing direct communication lines with other managers whose areas are affected by the LAN. To a large extent, they will need to have an impact on how the LAN is managed and what applications are used on the LAN.

Training and documentation are particularly important responsibilities of the network manager, who has a vested interest in training LAN users and in providing documentation for software applications. The training role is as important as the technical role. Users need to know how to use specific software applications. They also need to know how to route printouts to the appropriate printers. And they need to know the basics of logging on, logging off, and using menus.

As users learn about basic operations, many will quickly gain an interest in developing more sophisticated applications skills. They will begin to see even more uses for the LAN and will ask that more applications be installed. New applications increase the demand for training.

Installing documentation on the LAN is a good way to address some of the need for training. There is a host of computer-aided training packages for commonly used applications such as Lotus 1-2-3, dBase, WordPerfect, MS Word, and PageMaker. Many of these packages offer training at beginning and advanced levels. The Novell user manuals can be installed on-line for convenient access.

Selection and Training of the Network Manager

Demands on the network manager necessitate finding someone with technical training in computer science or a related area, as well as experience in supporting microcomputer applications. It is also necessary to find an individual with experience in host communications, since many LANs are connected to host computers.

Knowledge of communication protocols and microcomputer internals is another important ingredient. The ability to test communication signals and the ability to upgrade microcomputers are two additionally useful skills. Strong writing and oral capabilities are also important.

Further, the network manager needs to be prepared to seek additional training and education to keep current in the field. New hardware architectures and enhancements to operating systems are a given in the networking business.

Establishing Back-up Personnel

In addition to the network manager, there must be back-up staff who can provide support when needed.

Back-up individuals need to know how to keep the LAN functioning smoothly. They need information about how to manage print queues, how to operate software, how to back up and restore LAN data, and how to diagnose problems. It is also important to have at least one back-up individual who understands the directory structure, how to create new users, how to write menus and login scripts, how to grant trustee rights, and how to use system functions such as SYSCON and PCONSOLE within the NetWare operating system.

Defining Network Standards

If there are no standard approaches to setting up a network, management of the network will quickly become chaotic. Standard approaches include ways of creating groups, writing login scripts, defining users, mapping search drives, and creating boot files.

Without standardization, the network will quickly get out of hand. For example, in the absence of planning and coordination of efforts, the directory structure can quickly become very complex. Standard applications programs may end up in any of several directories or subdirectories. Multiple versions of the same program may exist in different directories. As the complexity grows, it becomes more difficult to upgrade software, since one directory might hold several different sets of programs. The most recent version of programs may be difficult to separate from older versions, and mapping to the right directory will become problematic.

Standardizing Directories

A good place to start is in standardizing directories and subdirectories. Chapter 6 provides details about standardizing directories. Because of the importance for network management, this section reviews and expands on issues discussed in Chapter 6.

Novell NetWare creates four key directories: PUBLIC, SYSTEM, LOGIN, and MAIL. The PUBLIC directory stores utilities and programs used by the Novell network. This directory should be reserved strictly for software provided through Novell. For example, the directory provides a good location for installation of the on-line Novell manual documentation provided in the Folio program described later in this chapter.

The SYSTEM directory contains files and programs used by the NetWare operating system. Like the PUBLIC directory, this directory should also be reserved strictly for operating system files.

The LOGIN directory is used for log-in by users. It contains the LOGIN.EXE program, the SLIST.EXE program, and a few other utility programs. SLIST displays available file servers. Utilities from other vendors are placed in this directory if they are used for log-on activities.

The MAIL directory is used to store mail files for electronic communications. It also stores each user's login script and printer configuration files.

Other directories can be created by the network manager and authorized users as the need arises. First, develop a naming convention when establishing new directories or subdirectories. For example, applications such as word processors, spreadsheets, and database programs can be placed in an APP directory. Within the directory, there can be subdirectories for specific applications, such as WP for a word processor and DB for a database program. It is advantageous to keep the names of directories and subdirectories short by using descriptive abbreviations.

If you need to install more than one application package—for example, two different word-processing applications—create a subdirectory for each separate application. For instance, you may have purchased both Microsoft Word and WordPerfect for installation. You may also have copies of dBase or Paradox to install. Create separate subdirectories under an applications directory for each package.

Within each subdirectory, you may want to create yet another subdirectory. As an example, applications such as WordPerfect are supplied with a learning diskette. The files on this diskette can be placed in a subdirectory under the WordPerfect subdirectory. Then, if it is later decided that the learning material is no longer needed, it is a simple matter to delete the subdirectory. This is easier than trying to determine which programs are associated with the learning diskette in one large WordPerfect directory. In addition to the learning material, you may also wish to have a subdirectory for WordPerfect text documents, macros, .SET files, and graphics.

As you create directories and subdirectories, avoid creating an excessive number of levels. Normally, it is hard to manage more than three or four levels of subdirectories. Once you know what software is to be installed, develop a chart or tree diagram to document the directory structure before you begin installation.

Besides APP, there are other viable names for the kinds of directories you are likely to create. Compilers may be installed under a COMPILER directory, and utilities may go under a directory called UTIL. A print server application is an example of software that may go into a subdirectory under the UTIL directory.

Many Novell LANs have a user directory or directories to enable users to store their personal files. This directory might be called USERS or USR. Within the directory, there can be home directories for each user.

Naming the File Server

Although your organization may start with only one file server, others may be added in the future. Additional file servers can be connected to an existing LAN, or you may decide to install a wide-area network backbone to which several LANs will be attached. Plan for this possibility by establishing naming conventions for each file server.

Naming conventions for LANs may focus on any of the following characteristics of the organization:

- The group that will use the file server, such as sales staff or secretarial services
- The building where the file server resides, such as Building A or Physical Plant
- The specific department or division that uses the file server, such as the engineering division or accounting department
- The function of the file server, such as research/development or word processing

For example, if one file server is used for engineering, it might be called ENG. If there are two file servers for different engineering groups, they might be called ENG1 and ENG2. Some organizations name file servers after area themes. A file server in a Western state might be named CORRAL or DEPUTY.

When naming a server, keep in mind the value of brevity. Short names are easier to type when establishing search drives and mappings. Another consideration is if the server will be part of a wide area network such as the Internet. In this instance, the Internet naming conventions should be followed.

Log-In ID Names

Log-in IDs work best when they reflect the user's name. They should also be designed so individuals can easily be reached by electronic mail. Nicknames, such as Dr_Byte or BigRed, are not particularly helpful in identifying the user. The simplest naming convention is to use the individual's first initial and last name. For example, Thomas Scott's log-in would be TSCOTT. If there are two Thomas Scotts, you might include the middle initials: TJSCOTT and TMSCOTT.

An alternate log-in ID convention might consist of user initials. In our previous example, Thomas J. Scott and Thomas M. Scott would have the user IDs TJS and TMS.

In some situations, there may be a workstation pod where a number of workstations are placed in a workroom or lab. These workstations are established for users who do not need to be identified by name. (A word-processing pod in a public library is an example of this kind of situation. Here, anyone from the community might come in to use word-processing facilities.) Log-in IDs would then reflect workstation names, rather than user names. If there are 15 workstations, there might be user IDs WS1 to WS15.

Group Names

Group names can be developed and used within the directory structure. In this way, the directory structure becomes a mirror of the organizational structure. User subdirectories can branch according to the group to which a particular user belongs. This makes it easier to establish a user on the network, to troubleshoot problems, and to ensure establishment of the correct group rights.

For example, accounting department users TSCOTT, JPERRY, and RPAGE would have subdirectories under the subdirectory ACCTING and in the USERS directory on the file server ACCT as follows:

```
ACCT/SYS:USERS/ACCTING/TSCOTT

ACCT/SYS:USERS/ACCTING/JPERRY

ACCT/SYS:USERS/ACCTING/RPAGE
```

Notice we have used the naming conventions discussed to this point, observing the principles of brevity and descriptiveness.

Having groups and directories set up in this fashion expedites maintenance on directories and maintenance in establishment of group rights. Users in the ACCTING group can easily be given file scan, read, write, and other rights to sensitive accounting data that they manage. All that is necessary is to create the ACCTING group, place the appropriate users in this group, and grant the necessary trustee rights. When new accounting users are hired, they can be added to the group.

Likewise, individuals in other selected groups can be prevented from modifying the data and even prevented from viewing it. Users in a management group might be granted rights to read the accounting or payroll data but not to update the database. Sales representatives might be prevented from having any access to the data through withholding trustee rights to this group.

Menus

To keep a low-maintenance networking environment, standardize the menuing system. No matter how many file servers can be accessed via a LAN, plan to standardize on one menuing system. The menuing system can be Novell's or one available through other sources, such as Saber Software. (The Saber menu system is offered with NetWare version 4.)

Network Utilities

Every network manager needs to be knowledgeable about utilities that can prevent and solve network problems. In the sections that follow, we will examine several popular utilities. Some of these utilities are obtained from Novell, while others are sold by third-party vendors.

Network Loadable Modules

Many NetWare utilities are offered as **NetWare Loadable Modules (NLMs)**. These programs are loaded at the file server console and run in the file server's memory. The NLM links with the operating system to provide added program features, such as printer server and back-up capabilities.

Make certain that all NLMs are certified by Novell before implementing them. Test each NLM with your server before moving it into daily production. Some NLMs can make the file server unreliable because they use too much server memory or because they do not return memory after use.

NLMs are loaded by using the following command at the file server console:

```
LOAD [PATH] nlm-name [Parameter]
```

The default path is the SYSTEM directory. The NLM program file can be loaded from DOS drive C: of the file server. For example, to load the INSTALL utility (used to configure NetWare) you would enter the following command from the file server colon prompt:

```
LOAD INSTALL
```

The sections that follow introduce several network utilities. The SBACKUP, MONITOR, RCONSOLE, and VREPAIR NLMs are utilities provided by Novell. ARCserve, Archivist, and SiteLock are sold by third-party vendors. ARCserve and Archivist are used for tape backup, and SiteLock is metering and virus control software.

System Back-Up and Disaster Recovery

Critical to any successful administration of a network is the formulation of a plan for **system back-up** and disaster recovery. This plan makes it possible to restore important files and system information if a problem or emergency develops. Possible problems include fire, water and flood damage, unstable power damage, and equipment failure. Of these, equipment failure, such as the failure of memory or a fixed disk, is the most likely to occur. Unstable power is another frequent enemy of a network.

In disaster recovery you need regular system back-ups. Although you can back up a file server with diskettes, you can do it better with a tape back-up system. Many tape back-up systems are available, the most reliable being those that are Novell-compatible and Novell-certified. Some examples of back-up systems are Novell's SBACKUP, Cheyenne Software's ARCserve, and Palindrome's Archivist. All are NLMs, which means the back-ups are performed at the file server. Palindrome has an option to load .EXE programs instead of an NLM so back-ups can be performed from a workstation connected to the file server.

Most back-up systems use cassette, digital audio tape (DAT), or digital linear tape (DLT) tape technologies. Some will back up 60 MB of data on one tape. Others, such as DLT, will back up several gigabytes of data. For example, Cipher makes DLT tape drives that back up 5 GB per tape.

Most tape subsystems perform error checking to verify the data on the tape as it is written. This is typically done by quickly reading the data just after it is written and comparing what is on tape with the data on the file server. Tape subsystems also come with tape verification utilities that enable the tape to be checked for parity errors after the data are fully on the tape.

Tape subsystems generally comprise a tape drive and software used to manage the tape back-up and restore activities. The tape drive is physically connected to the file server or to a workstation on the LAN. Depending on the manufacturer, the software may be accessed from the file server or from a physical drive on the workstation. It is also possible to connect more than one tape drive in tandem, for large-capacity LANs. The tape drives come in internal and external models. Internal drives, like disk drives, are installed in the file server or workstation cabinet. External tape drives come in a standalone case, along with a controller board that is installed in the computer. Most tape drive controller boards are SCSI adapters.

Tape subsystem software often comes with **file-by-file** or **binary** (or image) back-up. As a rule, the best option is to back up the system file-by-file. This gives you the option of restoring only one file, one subdirectory, one directory, or any combination of files and directories, as well as the entire system.

A binary restore requires restoring all of the files at one time. Also, it is necessary to have the same fixed-disk configuration for the restore as was present for the binary save. Thus, if the original file server had a 1.2 GB fixed disk, it must be replaced with another computer that has the same 1.2 GB fixed disk.

When backing up the file server onto tape, the network manager needs to establish a regular schedule for back-ups. For instance, if users have the authority to create or change data files stored on the file server, back-ups should be performed daily. If only application software is stored on the file server, then back-ups are necessary any time new software or new users are added.

A system for making and rotating the tapes needs to be developed and recorded into a notebook. For instance, if back-ups are performed on a daily basis, the network manager is likely to have one or more tapes for each day of the week. Thus there will be a Monday tape, a Tuesday tape, and so on. In this way, if something goes wrong with Thursday's back-up tape and a restore becomes necessary, there is always Wednesday's tape available, even though it may not be as current as Thursday's tape. Wednesday's tape can still be used for the restore, and only one day's worth of work is lost instead of two, three, four, or more.

For a daily back-up procedure, some network managers prefer to have four or five weeks' worth of tapes. This means that some tapes are not recycled for up to five weeks. Thus in case there is a need, data that existed in a file two or three weeks ago can be viewed at any time.

If data on the file server are critical to the organization, off-site storage of selected tapes is necessary. For example, once a week a tape might be taken to a safe-deposit box in a bank. Then there will be a way to restore the file server in the event of fire or some other disaster.

An important drawback of some tape back-up subsystems is their inability to save trustee-rights data. When you purchase a tape back-up subsystem, make certain it can restore trustee rights to all volumes and directories on your file server(s). Fully test the back-up subsystem before moving it to production.

Besides tape back-up, there are other ways to provide for disaster recovery. One is to maintain a back-up file server. The back-up file server might run on a standalone basis or be connected to the network, in which case it must have a server name that is different from the main server and a separate NetWare license. The back-up file server can be restored with tape back-up to ensure that a system is back on-line as soon as possible. If the main server has a fatal hardware error, such as in the main CPU board, the back-up server can be restored, and users will be back on-line in a short time.

For even quicker restoration, the back-up file server can be attached to the LAN with its own licensed software. Programs designed to "shadow" data can be run so changes that occur on the main server are also copied onto the back-up server at regular intervals. The back-up server is then made accessible to users only when the main server can no longer function.

Another form of back-up is to enable disk mirroring through the Novell software. If two disk drives are present in the file server, data on the main server drive can be mirrored to another drive. Should the main drive fail, the second drive takes its place. This option works well in the event of a disk drive failure, but it does not provide for immediate operations if the CPU board or another critical part fails.

As back-up alternatives are considered, it is important to adhere to software licensing requirements for both the Novell operating system and the application software on the file server. You must develop back-up procedures that honor all licensing constraints.

SBACKUP

SBACKUP, Novell's backup utility, is used to back up all files on one or more file servers connected to the same network. The files are backed up to a tape drive or an optical drive attached to the server.

Prior to using SBACKUP, appropriate drivers for the tape or optical drive must be installed. The drivers should be installed on the file server by following the instructions provided by the equipment vendor. For example, if the device is connected to an Adaptec SCSI controller, the ADAPTEC.NLM driver is loaded before loading SBACKUP.

The file server must have a minimum of 2 MB of memory to run SBACKUP. Before SBACKUP is started, it is necessary to load the TSA.NLM utility.

SBACKUP displays a menu that asks for the target device for the backup or restore. For example, the target device might be volume USERS:. The file server to be backed up or restored is also specified on the menu.

ARCSERVE

ARCserve is a full-featured back-up utility that offers management capabilities beyond those in SBACKUP. Figure 10.2 shows the main menu and submenus of ARCserve.

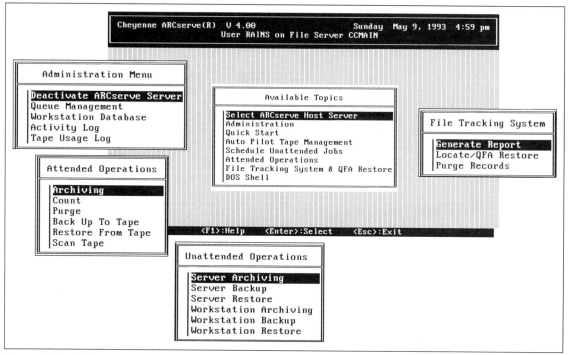

Figure 10.2 *ARCserve Main Menu Displaying the Available Functions*

As with SBACKUP, it is necessary to install a controller card, driver, and tape drive on the file server. ARCserve works with several types of tape drives, such as DAT and DLT.

ARCserve can back up one or more file servers on the same network. It can also back up network workstations. Figure 10.3 shows the ARCserve menu used to select workstations and file servers for backups.

ARCserve runs in attended or unattended modes. The attended mode relies on input and tape mount activity from an operator. The unattended mode completes backups without intervention.

ARCserve can be instructed to purge files after they are backed up. Old, temporary, or duplicate files are managed in this way so valuable server disk space is regained. Files are purged based on the file name, date of creation, and last access date.

Information about backed-up files is stored in a file tracking database. If a file or directory must be restored, the database is used to quickly locate the file on tape and perform a restore.

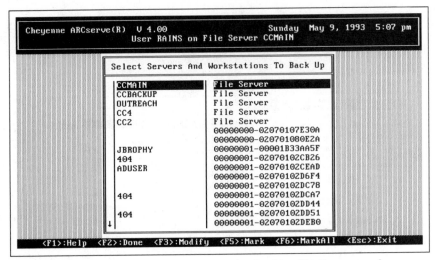

Figure 10.3 *ARCserve Quick Start Option for Backing Up Servers and Workstations*

ARCHIVIST

Palindrome's Archivist is a full-featured system with the ability to run back-ups from a workstation or from a file server. The advantage to using a workstation is that the back-ups can be performed from any network location.

Archivist allows you to specify a daily or weekly back-up rotation of tapes. Also it has automated on-site and off-site tape vaulting procedures. Archivist builds a tape and file history database as does ARCserve. A separate database is built for each file server and each volume designated for back-up. Database restore procedures are available in the event a portion of the database is corrupted.

Archivist has a utility for unscheduled backups that are not part of the normal tape rotation. For example, you may perform regular back-ups beginning at midnight each day. You may also wish to back up critical payroll information every Monday and Thursday at noon. Archivist makes this easy by designating the noon backup tape as "foreign," so this special tape is kept separate from the regular backup scheme.

As with ARCserve, Archivist can be configured for attended or unattended service. Many computer centers are stressing unattended or "lights out" capabilities as a means of reducing the staff needed to manage computer equipment.

Bindery Maintenance

NetWare maintains security information on users, groups, and files in a database called the **bindery**. The bindery controls access and protects NetWare security for objects, properties, and property data sets.

An **object** is a user, group, file server, print server, or any other named entity on the file server. When an object is created, NetWare assigns a unique ID number to the object.

A bindery object has one or more properties associated with it. A property can be password information, account restrictions, account balances, group membership, and network addresses.

The property data sets are values assigned to the bindery object's properties. The values for the user names and passwords are property data sets.

The bindery consists of three files that reside in the SYS:SYSTEM directory. These files are NET$OBJ.SYS (for objects), NET$PROP.SYS (for properties), and NET$VAL.SYS (for property set values).

The bindery is accessed each time a user logs into the file server. For example, when MARY logs into the file server, she types LOGIN MARY. The LOGIN program checks in NET$OBJ.SYS for the object name MARY to verify she is a valid user. If there is an object name of MARY, LOGIN checks the NET$PROP.SYS file for the properties associated with the object MARY, such as a password. When a password is entered from the workstation, it is compared with the password value in NET$VAL.SYS. A match results in successful access to the account. The person using account MARY is able to access files, directories, and other resources as determined by the security data in the bindery.

BINDFIX and BINDREST

Data in the three bindery files can get out of synchronization as users are added or deleted. BINDFIX is a NetWare .EXE utility for repairing the bindery files. Use BINDFIX when a user name cannot be deleted, a password cannot be changed, rights cannot be modified, the "unknown server" error occurs during spooling, or errors referring to the bindery are displayed on the console.

BINDFIX should also be run when users or groups are added and deleted, because the bindery is not purged of the deleted user and group information until BINDFIX is run. Mail directories linked to the bindery are also not removed when a user is deleted. Running BINDFIX once a month will ensure a properly maintained bindery.

BINDFIX is in the SYS:SYSTEM directory, and it can be run by the supervisor by entering BINDFIX. The file server must be up and running. All users other than supervisor must be logged off.

```
F:\SYSTEM>BINDFIX
Rebuilding Bindery.  Please Wait.
Checking object's property list.
Checking properties to see if they are in an object property list.
Checking objects for back-link property.
Checking set consistency and compacting set.
Checking Properties for proper order.
Checking user objects for standard properties.
Checking group objects for standard properties.
Checking links between users and groups for consistency.
Delete mail directories of users that no longer exist? (y/n): Y
Checking for mail directories of users that no longer exist.
Checking for users that do not have mail directories.
Adding mail directory for user CHEY_ARCHSUR.
Delete trustee rights for users that no longer exist? (y/n): Y
Checking volume SYS:  Please wait.
Checking volume USR:  Please wait.

Bindery check successfully completed.
Please delete the files NET$OBJ.OLD, NET$PROP.OLD, and NET$VAL.OLD after you
have verified the reconstructed bindery.
```

Figure 10.4 *The BINDFIX.EXE Utility Being Run to Rebuild the Bindery Files*

Before the bindery files are rebuilt, the existing bindery files are closed and backed up with the extension .OLD. This procedure protects the existing bindery information from being destroyed in case the rebuilding is not successful. BINDFIX will then scan the current bindery files, looking for inconsistencies. If the program finds an inconsistency, it displays a prompt asking whether or not to proceed. A completed bindery check is shown in Figure 10.4.

After BINDFIX is run, you should down the file server. Type DOWN at the file server console. Next reboot the server. This causes the updated bindery files to be loaded into memory on the file server. Should a problem occur after running BINDFIX, the original bindery files can be restored by running BINDREST from the SYSTEM directory.

Monitoring the Server

The network manager is responsible for monitoring functions on the file server. The monitoring gives early warning about developing problems, such as memory or disk problems. Awareness of connection problems is also made possible through regular monitoring.

The MONITOR NLM is for viewing information about the file server and locking the file server console. The network manager can view connection information, disk information, server statistics, server configuration information, information on file locking, and information about how server resources are being used. Figure 10.5 shows the MONITOR menu and information screens.

One important statistic provided by MONITOR is *File Server Up Time:*. This shows how many days the server has been running without

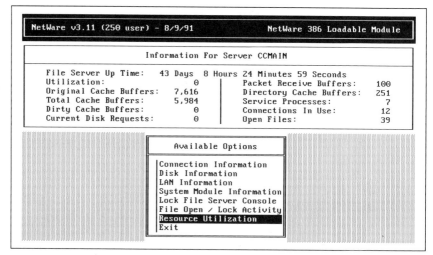

Figure 10.5 *MONITOR.NLM Utility's Main Menu and Information Screen*

interruption. Another useful statistic is *Utilization*. In Figure 10.5 the file server utilization is 0 percent. This means that only 0 percent of the server's CPU is currently being used. A consistent utilization above 75 percent signals that the file server CPU is heavily used and a CPU upgrade or adding another server may be necessary.

Read the NetWare documentation on MONITOR. This tool will help you see warning signs—for example, that a disk is about to fail or that the server does not have enough memory. It is also used to log-off a user and to broadcast messages to users. Plan to use MONITOR each day to check on the server.

Remote Management

As the network manager, you may find it most convenient to access the file server console from your office. The Remote Console utility makes this possible. With Remote Console you can do the following:

- Execute console commands
- Edit the DOS and NetWare files on the file server
- Transfer files to the file server from the workstation
- Install NetWare on a remote file server
- Reboot the file server from the remote console

Remote Console can be used through an access server for long-distance network management, such as from another city.

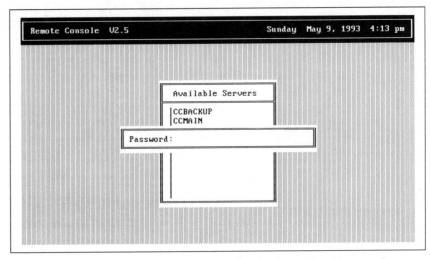

Figure 10.6 *RCONSOLE Utility Prompting for the Supervisor Password*

Remote Console requires loading two NLMs: REMOTE.NLM and RSPX.NLM. REMOTE.NLM handles the remote access to the server's hardware and file system. RSPX.NLM is the communication driver that provides for data transfer between the file server and the remote console. Load these utilities from the AUTOEXEC.NCF file if you plan to use Remote Console frequently.

To start Remote Console at the workstation, log onto an account with supervisor privilege and enter *RCONSOLE*. A menu is displayed showing a list of file servers. You must enter the Remote Console password to access a server. Figure 10.6 shows the RCONSOLE menu prompting for a password.

When you select a file server, the console screen is displayed at your workstation. Figure 10.7 shows an example console screen where the VREPAIR utility has been exited and the console prompt is displayed.

```
:VOLUME
Mounted Volumes          Name Spaces
   SYS                      DOS
   USR                      DOS

:DISMOUNT USR
Dismounting volume USR
Volume USR has been dismounted
:LOAD VREPAIR
Loading module VREPAIR.NLM
   NetWare 386 Volume Repair Utility
   Version 2.17  February 7, 1991
   Copyright 1991 Novell, Inc.  All rights reserved.
```

Figure 10.7 *The File Server Monitor Being Displayed on the Remote Console*

Salvaging Files

NetWare retains deleted files until the file server needs the space for new files. The deleted files are hidden from DIR or NDIR. To determine the space used by these deleted files, use the CHKVOL utility. The CHKVOL utility displays the following for Volume USR: on file server CCMAIN:

Statistics for fixed volume CCMAIN/USR (in K Bytes)

Total volume space	586,956
Space used by files	126,996
Space in use by deleted files	204,100
Space available from deleted files	204,100
Space remaining on volume	459,960
Space available to SUPERVISOR	459,960

In this example, the space occupied by deleted files is 204 MB, which is about a third of the total volume space (587 MB).

The SALVAGE utility permits the supervisor or the owner of a deleted file to recover that file. Figure 10.8 shows the SALVAGE menu. SALVAGE allows the user to recover files from deleted directories or from the current directory. The *Salvage From Deleted Directories* option is used to recover files in deleted directories.

If the user is not in the directory containing the deleted files, SALVAGE enables him or her to switch to the directory by using the *Select Current*

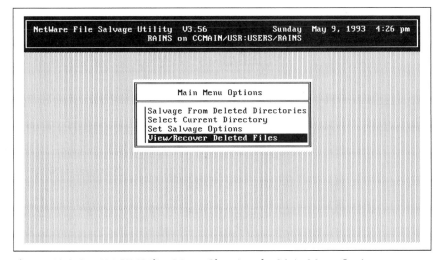

Figure 10.8 *SALVAGE Utility Menu Showing the Main Menu Options*

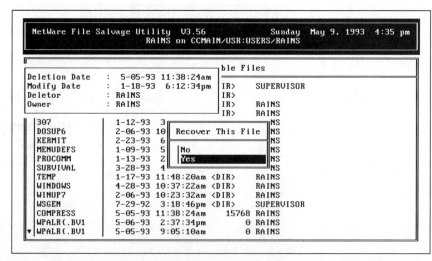

```
NetWare File Salvage Utility   V3.56              Sunday  May 9, 1993  4:30 pm
                      RAINS on CCMAIN/USR:USERS/RAINS

                           9 Salvageable Files

   ..                  7-01-92 12:03:06pm <DIR>     SUPERVISOR
   /                   0-00-80 12:00:00am <DIR>
   123                 1-14-93  2:28:58pm <DIR>     RAINS
   125                 1-14-93  3:12:50pm <DIR>     RAINS
   307                 1-12-93  3:39:02pm <DIR>     RAINS
   DOSUP6              2-06-93 10:24:20am <DIR>     RAINS
   KERMIT              2-23-93  6:57:44pm <DIR>     RAINS
   MENUDEFS            1-09-93  5:05:10pm <DIR>     RAINS
   PROCOMM             1-13-93  2:27:04pm <DIR>     RAINS
   SURVIVAL            3-28-93  4:25:30pm <DIR>     RAINS
   TEMP                1-17-93 11:48:20am <DIR>     RAINS
   WINDOWS             4-28-93 10:37:22am <DIR>     RAINS
   WINUP7              2-06-93 10:23:32am <DIR>     RAINS
   WSGEN               7-29-92  3:18:46pm <DIR>     SUPERVISOR
   COMPRESS            5-05-93 11:38:24am   15768   RAINS
   WPALR{.BV1          5-06-93  2:37:34pm       0   RAINS
 ▼ WPALR{.BV1          5-05-93  9:05:10am       0   RAINS
```

Figure 10.9 *The SALVAGE Utility Showing the Deleted Files That Can Be Salvaged*

Directory option. Once the directory is selected, the user can view or recover deleted files with the *View/Recover Deleted Files* option. In our example, the current directory is USERS/RAINS. Figure 10.9 shows the deleted files that can be salvaged.

When a file is selected for recovery, a screen is displayed (see Figure 10.10) that shows the deletion date, modify date, deletor, and owner of the file. A box appears with the option to continue with the recover process.

```
NetWare File Salvage Utility   V3.56              Sunday  May 9, 1993  4:35 pm
                      RAINS on CCMAIN/USR:USERS/RAINS
┌─────────────────────────────────────────┐ble Files
│ Deletion Date  :  5-05-93 11:38:24am     │
│ Modify Date    :  1-18-93  6:12:34pm │IR>   SUPERVISOR
│ Deletor        :  RAINS              │IR>
│ Owner          :  RAINS              │IR>   RAINS
└──────────────────────────────────────┘IR>   RAINS
   │ 307               1-12-93  3┌──────────────────┐NS
   │ DOSUP6            2-06-93 10│ Recover This File│NS
   │ KERMIT            2-23-93  6│                  │NS
   │ MENUDEFS          1-09-93  5│┌────┐            │NS
   │ PROCOMM           1-13-93  2││ No │            │NS
   │ SURVIVAL          3-28-93  4││Yes │            │NS
   │ TEMP              1-17-93 11:48:20am <DIR>     RAINS
   │ WINDOWS           4-28-93 10:37:22am <DIR>     RAINS
   │ WINUP7            2-06-93 10:23:32am <DIR>     RAINS
   │ WSGEN             7-29-92  3:18:46pm <DIR>     SUPERVISOR
   │ COMPRESS          5-05-93 11:38:24am   15768   RAINS
   │ WPALR{.BV1        5-06-93  2:37:34pm       0   RAINS
 ▼ │ WPALR{.BV1        5-05-93  9:05:10am       0   RAINS
```

Figure 10.10 *The SALVAGE Utility Prompting to Recover a Deleted File*

Security

SECURITY is a utility that scans the file server for potential security holes. It checks for users without passwords, users with supervisor rights, users without login scripts, and other areas of concern. Figure 10.11 shows an example of the security warnings provided for accounts ADMIN, TESTWS, SON, ALL_EMAIL_USERS, and AD3.

SECURITY is a program in the SYS:SYSTEM directory. To run the program, log onto an account with supervisor privilege and enter SECURITY. You can redirect the security information from the screen to a file called PROBLEM.TXT by using the following command:

```
SECURITY > PROBLEM.TXT
```

TRACK ON

There are times when it is necessary to view network traffic—for example, when there is a workstation with a failing NIC or a file server sending bad packets. TRACK ON is a network monitoring utility available from the file server console (or from the remote console). The command turns the screen into a display of packets sent or received on the network. Figure 10.12 reproduces the TRACK ON display and shows that there is normal communication on the network. You will know that a workstation or file server has problems when you see excessive packets from the workstation or server. This might be hundreds of packets sent within one or two minutes. Notice in this figure that the information is formatted as *IN* (receiving a packet) or *OUT* (sending a packet). For example, the first two lines of the figure show the following:

```
IN [00000AAA:000000000001] 10:56:52am CCMAIN          1
IN [00000001:00001B33A956] 10:56:52am 0000000A 1/2
```

```
SECURITY EVALUATION UTILITY, Version 2.23

User ADMIN
   Does not require a password
   No Full Name specified

User TESTWS (Full Name: TESTING A WORKSTATION)
   Does not require a password

User SON (Full Name: Paul Son)
   Account has not been used for more than 3 weeks
     Last Login: Tuesday  June 1, 1993  8:15 am
   Is not required to change passwords periodically

Group ALL_EMAIL_USERS
   No Full Name specified

User AD3
   Account has not been used for more than 3 weeks
     Last Login: Monday  May 24, 1993  9:00 am
   Does not require a password
   No Full Name specified
```

Figure 10.11 *The SECURITY Utility Showing Potential Security Holes*

```
Router Tracking Screen
IN  [00000AAA:000000000001] 10:56:52am  CCMAIN       1
IN  [00000001:00001B33A956] 10:56:52am  000000A   1/2
OUT [00000AAA:FFFFFFFFFFFF] 10:56:52am  0000001   1/2     0000002  1/2
    0000000A   2/3
OUT [00000001:FFFFFFFFFFFF] 10:56:52am  0000002   1/2     00000AAA 1/2
OUT [00000002:FFFFFFFFFFFF] 10:56:52am  0000001   1/2     0000000A 2/3
    00000AAA   1/2
IN  [00000AAA:000000000001] 10:57:19am  CCMAIN       1
IN  [00000001:00001B33A956] 10:57:22am  CC4          1  CC4            2
OUT [00000AAA:FFFFFFFFFFFF] 10:57:22am  CC2          2  CC4            2
    CC4        3    CCMAIN       1  CCMAIN       2
OUT [00000001:FFFFFFFFFFFF] 10:57:22am  CCMAIN       1  CCMAIN         2
OUT [00000002:FFFFFFFFFFFF] 10:57:22am  CC2          2  CC4            2
    CC4        3    CCMAIN       1  CCMAIN       2

<Use ALT-ESC or CTRL-ESC to switch screens, or any other key to pause>
```

Figure 10.12 *Using the File Server TRACK ON Utility to Display Routing Packets*

The *IN* means the message is incoming. The *00000AAA* is the network number of the file server sending the packet. This value is created when NetWare is installed and is the file server's internal address. The address is loaded with the AUTOEXEC.NCF file.

The 000000000001 is the node address of the file server sending the packet. Following the node address, there is either server or network information. A network address is assigned to each network cable segment at the time the file server operating system is installed. For example, a file server with two NICs has an address for the server and an address for each NIC. Traffic on one segment, such as an Ethernet segment, might have a network address of 1 and the other segment, such as ARCNET, might have a network address of 2. Every segment has a unique network or segment address. This allows the server to direct traffic to the appropriate network segment.

The information about the server in line 1 of Figure 10.12 is the following:

- CCMAIN   The name of a file server.
- 1   The number of hops from the sending file server to this file server. Hops refers to the number of network devices a packet travels through to get to its destination.

The network information in line 2 is as follows:

- 0000000A   The network number of a network known by the sending file server.
- 1/   The number of hops from the sending file server to this network.

- 2   The number of ticks that a packet takes to reach this network from the sending file server. A tick is 1/18 of a second. Communication protocols are very time sensitive.

How do you interpret the big picture? This network has four network segments (AAA, A, 2, and 1) and three file servers (CCMAIN, CC4, and CC2). That makes seven entities broadcasting their presence on the network. The broadcasting helps to keep the lines open for traffic.

With the first *IN*, the file server CCMAIN is receiving a packet from its internal router or traffic cop. The sending and receiving file servers are the same, and the hop count is one. CCMAIN is directly connected to network 00000AAA.

The second *IN* is a network segment with an address of 0000001. It is broadcasting that it knows of segment 000000A and that 000000A is 1 hop and 2 ticks from the sending file server.

The format for outgoing packets is the following:

```
OUT [00000AAA:FFFFFFFFFFFF] 10:56:52am 0000001 1/2 0000002 1/2
```

Each portion of the outgoing packet is described as follows:

- OUT   Indicates that this packet is outbound.
- 00000AAA   The network number of the file server sending the packet.
- FFFFFFFFFFFF   Indicates that this packet is for every node.

File server or network information follows the address. In the example OUT message the file server on network AAA knows about networks 1 and 2 and their number of hops and ticks away from the file server.

Plan to run TRACK ON once a day to monitor network traffic. Turn the utility off by entering TRACK OFF at the file server console when you are finished monitoring the traffic.

Volume Repair

Sometimes file servers go down unexpectedly—for example, during a hardware or power failure. Upon boot-up, one or more volumes may show there are **file allocation table (FAT)** mismatches (the table that tracks the location of files on disk). The VREPAIR NLM is used to fix the mismatches.

```
                    NetWare 386 Volume Repair Utility

             Options:

                   1. Repair A Volume

                   2. Set Vrepair Options

                   0. Enter your choice:
```

Figure 10.13 *VREPAIR.NLM's Main Menu*

There are different versions of VREPAIR for different versions of NetWare. Only use the version of VREPAIR that came with your operating system disk from Novell. In most cases, VREPAIR is run when the file server cannot mount a volume or when there are FAT or directory mismatches.

VREPAIR is loaded from a floppy disk on the file server or from the DOS C: drive. The server should be downed and the console at the DOS prompt. Figure 10.13 shows the menu displayed after loading VREPAIR.

Figure 10.14 shows the default configuration and the options to change the defaults. Options 2 and 3 achieve the same result. The difference is in how the updates are made to disk. Option 3 writes the changes immediately to disk as they are found; option 2 caches the changes and writes them to disk after all changes are complete. The option selected depends on whether there is enough server memory to cache the changes before updating the disk.

If VREPAIR encounters a large number of FAT or directory errors, it may stop with a message that the volume is not usable. If this happens, run the utility again. VREPAIR may need to be run several times to completely fix the volume errors.

```
     Current Vrepair Configuration:

         Quit If A Required VRepair Name Space Support NLM Is Not Loaded

         Write Only Changed Directory And FAT Entries Out To Disk

         Keep Changes In Memory For Later Update

     Options:

         1. Remove Name Space support from the volume

         2. Write All Directory And FAT Entries Out To Disk

         3. Write Changes Immediately To Disk

         0. Return To Main Menu

         Enter you choice:
```

Figure 10.14 *VREPAIR.NLM'S Options Menu*

```
Total errors: 0
Current settings:
  Pause after each error
  Do not log errors to a file
Press F1 to change settings

Start 11:38:33am
Checking volume USR

FAT blocks>................................................<
Counting directory blocks and checking directory FAT entries
Mirror mismatches>.........................................<
Directories>...............................................<
Files>.....................................................<
Trustees>..................................................<
Deleted Files>.............................................<
Free blocks>...............................................<

Done checking volume
Total Time 0:00:58
<Press any key to continue>
```

Figure 10.15 *VREPAIR.NLM Status Screen Showing the Repair in Process*

As VREPAIR works, a status screen is displayed on the file server monitor. Figure 10.15 shows an example status screen. Sometimes there is too much damage to the FAT and directory tables. The only alternative in these instances is to perform a restore of the volume from tape back-up.

Virus Checking and Metering

The network manager is charged with the responsibility to honor licensing restrictions imposed by applications vendors. Metering software is available from several vendors for this purpose. Brightwork Development offers a popular **metering** product called SiteLock.

SiteLock restricts the number of users of a software application to the number of licenses purchased. During the metering process data are gathered for reports on application use. The reports contain information on when an application is used, the number of simultaneous users, and how often access was denied because the license limit was reached. SiteLock metering allows managers to determine how many licenses to purchase based on actual use statistics.

Sitelock also permits the network manager to check for **viruses**. A virus might damage program files or the FAT. Sitelock virus checking tests an application before it is executed. If the application appears to have been altered by a virus, Sitelock keeps it from running.

SiteLock is an NLM that will be loaded whenever the server is running. Because it is always used, the *LOAD SITELOCK* command should be placed in the AUTOEXEC.NCF file. Figure 10.16 shows SiteLock's main menu with the *Status* option selected.

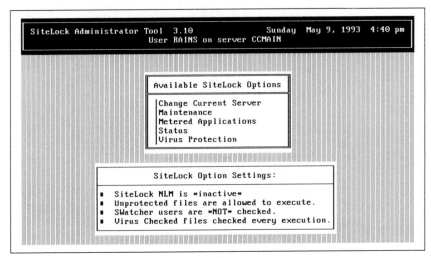

Figure 10.16 *SiteLock Main Menu and the Current Status of Options*

SiteLock requires that the SWATCHER.COM program be run on each workstation. (It is run from the SYS:LOGIN directory prior to running LOGIN.) SWATCHER is a TSR utility that stays resident in the workstation's memory. The TSR uses 4 KB of memory. SiteLock will automatically log off any workstation that is not running SWATCHER.

User Training

The key to effective use of a LAN is in training the users. LANs offer a host of options that make them very powerful user tools. The more that users know about the network, the more productive they become.

Once users become sophisticated in how to use the network, the network manager can be relieved of solving small problems, such as how to delete a print job. This provides the network manager the opportunity to spend more time on preventive maintenance, installing and testing new software, and planning for future growth of the network.

There are several ways to offer training. One is to hold classes periodically in a lab or environment where users can access workstations to practice what they are learning. Classes taught in this manner are most effective if they are small, from 5 to 12 students. This enables both direct interaction with the instructor and the opportunity to try out what is learned on the network. Creating practice accounts for this type of training is also helpful.

One way to make training sessions even more effective is to supply handouts that summarize what is covered and a list of relevant user commands or actions. The results of the training are not likely to be long-lasting unless those who have attended are required to practice what they have learned in the days just after the training. This kind of practice is best if the trainee is isolated from interruptions during the practice.

Another way to offer training is through computer-aided instruction (CAI). A brief tutorial comes with most applications that can be put in Folio (see the next section) or in a training account.

A third way is to create a training videotape that can be used in conjunction with hands-on practice. By using a videotape or CAI, or both, training can occur nearly any time without a scheduled class. And the training can be offered on an individualized basis.

Common topics to include in network training include the following:

- Booting the workstation
- Logging onto the network
- Using related DOS commands
- Accessing and exiting specific application software
- Printing on the network
- Deleting or manipulating printouts
- Logging out from the network
- Reporting problems
- Performing basic maintenance on printers, such as loading paper
- Taking care of a workstation

Folio

Folio, developed by the Folio Corporation, makes it easy to provide on-line documentation and training to users. The NetWare manuals, tutorials, software bulletins, and technical information can be placed in Folio. Documentation for software applications can also be put in Folio for easy access by users. Folio is an executable (.EXE) program that comes with NetWare in the SYS:PUBLIC directory. Figure 10.17 shows the opening Folio menu.

The Folio menu can be customized to offer specific topics. The *!NETWARE* topic provides information on the NetWare operating system. When this topic is selected, the *NetWare Help* menu shown in Figure 10.18 is displayed. This menu provides access to information about NetWare commands, an index to the NetWare manuals, information about NetWare installation and setup, an explanation of NetWare concepts, and NetWare administration information.

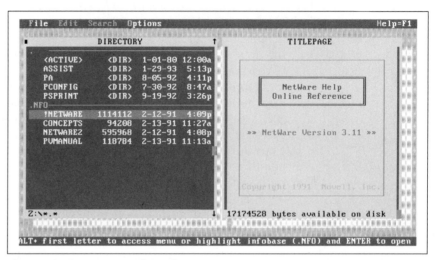

Figure 10.17 *NetWare Help Utility Menu*

Reporting LAN Problems

LAN problems may range from printer malfunctions to events that cause fatal error messages displayed at the file server console. Some problems are caused by users, such as placing too many files in their home directory so that the allotted space is used up (and applications will not run).

```
 File  Edit  Search  Options                              Help=F1
■NetWare Help Utility                                      1/2766




                    NetWare Help v3.11 Main Menu

              ▼Commands and Utilities A - J
              ▼Commands and Utilities L - R
              ▼Commands and Utilities S - X
              ▼Index to Printed NetWare Manuals
              ▼Installation, Setup
              ▼Network Concepts
              ▼Administration, Maintenance, Troubleshooting, etc.

              ▼How to use NetWare Help v3.11 (NFOLIO)
              ▼License Agreement, Disclaimer, Other Information




       Tab to a link (▼), then press <Enter>. Press <Escape> to exit

1:NetWare v3.11:                                              ↓
```

Figure 10.18 *The Help Utility's Main Menu*

Most problems have simple solutions, such as deleting unneeded files from the home directory. Other problems are more severe, such as file-server disk errors.

The key to solving problems quickly is to train users to resolve simple problems and to report the more serious ones. Some users will work around even serious problems without informing the network manager. Others will report every small problem as it occurs. Training can help create a body of informed users who develop basic skills in addressing small problems. Likewise, users can be trained to record any serious error messages, along with LAN activities associated with the messages. This information can then be passed along to the network manager for appropriate action.

Some network managers use a problem reporting form. Such forms show the date, time, and location of the problem, as well as a brief description of it.

Equipment for Resolving Problems

Cable troubleshooting devices can be extremely useful in diagnosing many LAN problems. For example, an electrical short might develop in the LAN cable or in a connector to a workstation; or a length of cable might be added to the LAN, making the total length of a segment too long; or different brands of cable may cause incompatibilities; or a terminator may be defective. These situations may cause the LAN to behave in unpredictable ways or to fail entirely.

One device used to diagnose cable problems is called a Time Domain Reflectometer (TDR). This device detects breaks and shorts in the cable. It also measures the cable length. (Every LAN has a maximum effective length.) TDRs typically produce a printout of the results showing the cable length, impedance, pulse width, line noise, and other diagnostic information.

Cable-scanning devices (see Figure 10.19) are usually less expensive than a TDR, and they yield information about breaks, shorts, and cable length. Many of these do not have a printout of information; instead they display the results on a small one- or two-line display. These results are often displayed briefly, such as "short at 100 feet." Most of these scanning devices work with different types of cable. Some cable scanning devices can be connected to an oscilloscope for more detailed information. Connections to printers are also possible. Some generate an analysis of LAN traffic.

When the LAN is down or not functioning properly, these cable diagnostic tools can prove essential to resuming service as soon as possible. They can also save money by reducing system downtime.

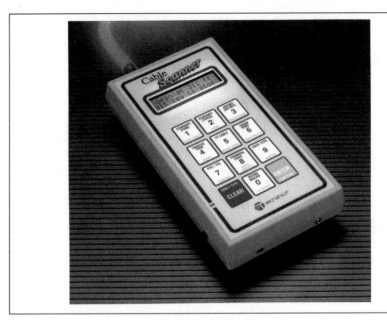

Figure 10.19 *Cable Scanner (Courtesy of Microtest)*

LAN Growth and Modifications

Implementation of a LAN is an evolving process. As users become proficient with what they have, they will soon find new applications they want to have on the LAN. Requests for new printers and more LAN capabilities will emerge. Simultaneously, users are likely to want customization of menus or applications. Some users will want to upgrade their workstations. Growth is a constant in the LAN environment.

Network managers can prove their worth by accommodating this growth. They can represent both management and users in finding ways to expand the LAN services and to control costs.

The key to successful growth involves realistic needs analyses, accompanied by timely implementation plans. Each needs analysis should deal with these matters:

- What facilities are currently available
- The capacity left on current LANs
- What facilities are needed to increase user productivity
- A cost/benefit rationale for increasing facilities
- An analysis of extra personnel required to make LAN additions function

Implementation of additions to the LAN should include:

- Appropriate drawings of building layouts and cable runs
- Well-defined responsibilities of vendors and of organizational resource persons, such as the network manager
- A realistic timeline for installation of cable, workstations, printers, application software, and modifications to user menus
- A plan for training users
- A plan for bringing users on-line

An important ingredient in this overall process is time to make the whole process work. No matter how well each step is planned, factors intervene to make the process take longer than expected. For example, portions of a building may need to be modified unexpectedly; the vendor may send the wrong kind of cable; several workstations may not work on arrival; or application software may take longer to install than anticipated. If the new installation is brought up before everything is working and tested, problems are likely to occur, and users will initially lose confidence in the installation.

Summary

This chapter begins by stressing the importance of formulating a plan for network administration. Such a plan provides for the selection of a network manager, implementing backups and disaster recovery, implementing network utilities, ensuring network security, and so on.

The duties of the network manager include loading the operating system, creating user accounts, designing the directory structure, administering security, monitoring server functions, and providing for server backups.

Each network manager must also install and run utilities that help manage the file servers. Several utilities are presented in this chapter, such as MONITOR and Folio. MONITOR is an NLM for tracking file server resource use; Folio is a .EXE program for on-line documentation. Backup subsystems such as SBACKUP, ARCserve, and Archivist enable deleted or corrupted files to be restored from tape. They also make possible restoration of entire volumes or file servers when disaster strikes.

BINDFIX and VREPAIR are two other important utilities. BINDFIX is run to correct problems with a file server's data on users, groups, and print servers. VREPAIR is used to fix damaged FAT or directory tables on a file server volume.

Last, user training and planning for LAN growth are discussed. Both are interrelated, since well-informed users tend to feed the growth cycle of a LAN environment. Growth brings the need to plan new LAN additions as a means for ensuring further success of these implementations.

Key Terms

Binary Backup   Also known as image backup, this type of backup takes a picture or image of a volume or disk. Data can only be restored in its entirety. Individual files cannot be restored.

Bindery   NetWare's database of information about users, groups, and printers that have been defined by the supervisor. Each record of information is called an object.

File Allocation Table (FAT)   A table containing pointer information showing where a file is located on a disk.

File-by-File Backup   A type of backup that writes individual files to the backup medium, keeping the directory structure in place. Any file or combination of files can be restored as needed.

Metering   A monitor that records the number of simultaneous users of specific software so that software licensing requirements are met.

Network Manager   The person responsible for all network and file server administration. The network manager loads the operating system, creates and maintains user accounts, provides for server backups, monitors the server and server software, fixes problems, and implements security.

NLM (NetWare Loadable Module)   A software program designed to be loaded at the file server console and linked in with the NetWare operating system.

Object   In the file server bindery, a separate entity or object known to the file server, such as user account name, group name, and print server information.

Request for Proposal (RFP)   A detailed description of a proposed installation of equipment, such as a LAN, that is submitted to vendors. Interested vendors respond with a written statement of the cost and how they would fulfill the RFP requirements.

System Back-up A back-up subsystem that consists of software and hardware used to copy file server files to tape or some other medium. The subsystem enables file server files, directories, and volumes to be restored.

Virus A program hidden within an .EXE or .COM file that works to corrupt programs, data, files, directories, the FAT, and other key microcomputer resources.

Questions and Exercises

1. Summarize the typical duties of the network manager.
2. What is an RFP for a LAN? What elements should go into the writing of an RFP?
3. Develop a list of standards that would apply to establishing directories on a file server you manage.
4. Outline standards you would apply to establishing user IDs and file server names.
5. Explain how NLMs are loaded and run. For your discussion use the NLM called BACKUP. What additional NLMs might need to be loaded for BACKUP to function?
6. You are assigned the responsibility of backing up two file servers. One file server has important accounting and payroll information that are updated daily. The other file server has sales statistics and other information that is updated every Monday and Thursday. Develop a back-up plan for both file servers.
7. You have purchased a tape back-up system for your LAN, and you perform back-ups on a regular schedule. One day the disk drive on a file server will no longer function and you replace it. You install a new disk drive and restore the server files with your tape back-up system. When users log-on, they discover they can no longer access the files and programs once available to them. You log-on as supervisor and verify that the files and programs have been restored to the server. What would you do to diagnose this problem? What steps should you take to fix it? How could you have prevented the problem?

8. Use the Folio utility to display information on the NDIR command. What are the commands before and after NDIR? Print the opening screen of information about NDIR. Besides providing on-line NetWare manuals, what other uses of Folio can you suggest?

9. Back-up solutions are either workstation or file-server based. Discuss the advantages and disadvantages of both solutions. Which one would you recommend and why?

10. What is the file server bindery? What files make up the bindery? Explain why it is necessary to rebuild the bindery.

11. Explain the purpose of cache buffers. How is the size of cache buffers determined? What makes the size smaller and what makes it larger?

12. How is the remote console loaded and what are the benefits of having a remote console utility?

13. One morning you find that the file server will not mount a volume. What steps should you take to get the volume mounted? Your answer should be complete enough so that if you were explaining the process over the phone someone could follow your instructions. What would you do if your efforts failed to mount the volume?

14. A network manager has the choice of using a NetWare backup utility (SBACKUP) or purchasing a third-party utility. How would you evaluate which backup system to use? What are three of the most important functions each system must be able to perform?

Enterprise Networking: LANs and Beyond

Chapter Objectives

The objectives of this chapter are the following:

- To provide an introduction to enterprise networking.
- To explain bridge and routing technology.
- To explain how LANs are connected to host gateways.
- To present LAN-to-LAN communication technologies.

Introduction

Local area networks are effective for distributing computing, applications, and disk space to a small geographic area of an organization. The full benefits of networking are achieved, however, when the total enterprise is networked. In most situations the enterprise is "geographically dispersed," which means it encompasses offices and buildings outside of what could be connected with LAN technology. Enterprises also have mini and mainframe computers, which must be included in the enterprise's network. If users are to dial into a network, an organization must provide the following networking solutions before achieving total enterprise networking:

- Networked remote and local LANs
- LANs networked to mini and mainframe hosts
- Remote workstations networked to LANs

Bridges and Routers

One way to connect LANs is by bridging. A **bridge** consists of hardware and software configured to allow packets to move among LANs. The bridge connects different LANs, permitting communication among devices on the separate LANs. For example, a bridge might connect an Ethernet LAN to an ARCNET LAN. A network bridge connects LANs having different topologies and protocols. There are two kinds of bridges: **internal** and **external bridges**. An internal bridge resides within the file server. Two or more file server NICs are the hardware, and the NetWare operating system provides the software. An external bridge, outside of the file server, is a workstation or other communication device configured to connect LANs together.

A **router** also connects LANs but is more sophisticated than a bridge. Routers have the following advantages over bridges:

- Routers are able to determine the "best" route to send packets across a network—the best being, for example, the fastest or cheapest route.
- Routers have the ability to adapt to different packet sizes.
- Routers can detect and circumvent loops in the network. Such loops cause packets to go in circles, resulting in traffic jams on the network.
- Routers can be connected to devices called CSU/DSUs that transmit digital signals over digital lines.

Routers also have the following disadvantages when compared to bridges:

- Bridges can process and pass along packets faster than routers (since they are not concerned about the best route).
- Routers are normally protocol-dependent, meaning they only manage one type of packet, such as IPX. Bridges process several different protocols.

Enterprise networks require the use of bridges and routers. Bridges are needed on portions of the network that require speed and that handle more than one protocol. Routers are needed for greater control of how packets are sent over the networks. Bridges and routers can be used to isolate portions of a wide area network for security. They can be set up so that only specified packets can travel through the bridge or router. For example, on a college campus, they can be used to prevent students in a lab area from reaching the administrative computers that process registration and the campus payroll.

Bridge and router technology is undergoing extensive research to combine the best qualities of both in one device.

Internal and External Network Bridges

Internal bridges can do one or more of the following: increase the performance of a large LAN; allow different kinds of media to be used; and extend the cable distance. Installing a bridge in a large, heavily used network can increase performance because the bridge isolates the network traffic. Packets that are local to one LAN are kept local. They do not cross the bridge. Only packets destined for a remote node on another LAN cross the bridge.

Another feature of the internal bridge is that it extends cable distance by adding the cable distance of one LAN to that of another LAN. Figure 11.1 illustrates an internal bridge connecting an Ethernet segment and an ARCNET segment.

The internal bridge hardware consists of Ethernet and ARCNET NICs installed in the file server. NetWare is configured to provide the software

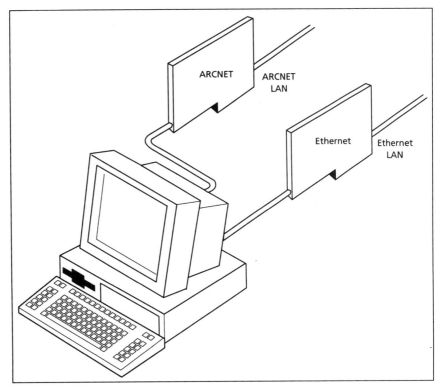

Figure 11.1 *Internal Bridge Connecting an ARCNET and Ethernet*

portion of the bridge. NetWare can be configured with four NICs to bridge four network segments.

An external bridge serves the same function as an internal bridge. However, the external bridge resides on a node other than the file server. The node can be a workstation or a special device that functions as a bridge only. External bridges connect to the network by using an NIC or a port on the bridge.

Remote Bridges

NetWare remote bridges enable users to transparently connect to distant or remote local area networks. For example, a network in Denver might connect to one in Chicago. If more traffic control is needed, a router can be used instead of the bridge.

Remote bridges are external bridges connected to communication equipment such as a modem. NetWare supports several remote bridging/routing products. The appropriate bridge solution depends on the application to be supported and the cost of the bridge. These bridge/router solutions are as follows:

• Asynchronous
• X.25
• High-speed 64 Kbps and T1

ASYNCHRONOUS REMOTE BRIDGES

A bridge that is **asynchronous** uses modems and RS-232 serial connections. Asynchronous communication is a low-cost way to transmit data over unlimited distances.

On each LAN, or from a computer at home, an asynchronous modem is connected to the bridge, and a communication line is connected to the modem. This is the same procedure used for connecting a modem to the telephone jack. Data are transmitted at speeds from 2,400 bps to 9,600 bps. Transfer rates can be up to 115.2 Kbps with conditioned lines and high-speed modems.

Using a modem to dial into a LAN or putting a modem on a LAN workstation to dial out of the LAN is very popular. Because the speed is slow, the primary use for asynchronous connections is to check mail and the status of the network. Running applications software and downloading data are cumbersome.

The components needed for an asynchronous bridge include the following:

- NetWare asynchronous software or other third-party software that provides remote dial-in access
- One or more Novell WNIM+ adapters or COM1/COM2 ports on the bridge
- Asynchronous modems

Wide Area Network Interface Module+ (WNIM+) provides four asynchronous ports. Two WNIM+ adapters can be installed in one bridge.

X.25 BRIDGES

X.25 is a protocol used by Public Data Networks, such as Telenet and Tymnet. Both of these networks provide connections through local telephone lines. Subscribers are charged a fee for their use of the network. Public Data Networks span international borders, with the X.25 protocol especially popular in Europe. X.25 networks are accessed through voice and dedicated leased communication lines. Figure 11.2 represents an X.25 wide area network.

X.25 bridges can operate at speeds of up to 56 Kbps. A workstation with access to an X.25 service like Tymnet can access a remote LAN. For example, people from all over the world can access a LAN in Denver.

The bridge can run as dedicated or nondedicated (which combines a bridge and workstation into one computer). The requirements for an X.25 bridge are as follows:

- X.25 software
- X.25 adapter board in a bridge workstation
- Full duplex synchronous modems

HIGH-SPEED BRIDGES

The fastest wide area networking connections use NetWare Link/64 or NetWare Link/T1. Both solutions can be installed on a workstation or the file server. The file server uses an NLM.

An enterprise may have several LANs with databases located in several cities. With NetWare Link/64 or NetWare Link/T1, the user can execute a database application that will query all the databases at once. These two wide area networking products offer great flexibility in designing applications requiring significant transmission throughput.

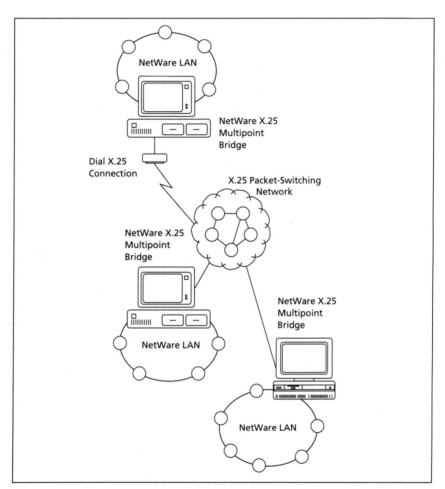

Figure 11.2 *A LAN Configured to Use an X.25 Network Protocol*

NetWare Link/64 offers a maximum data transmission rate of 64 Kbps. NetWare Link/T1 supports data transmission rates up to 1.544 Mbps. Users often use only part of the bandwidth of a T1 line, so they purchase a portion of the line, which is called a fractional T1. A fraction can be 9,600 Bps or a multiple of 9,600. These products support electronic mail, file transfer, and host access (mainframe and minicomputers). Figure 11.3 represents remote LANs connected with high-speed data links. The following are needed to configure a Link/64 or Link/T1 bridge:

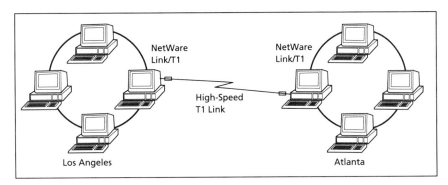

Figure 11.3 *LANs Networked with High-Speed Data Links*

- NetWare Link/64 or NetWare Link/T1 software
- Synchronous adapters with cabling
- Customer Service Unit (CSU), Data Service Unit (DSU), or combinations of CSU, DSU, and modems
- For external bridges, a workstation

CSU and DSU are expensive high-performance modems. Average modems transmit at 2,400 Bps or 9,600 Bps. CSU and DSU modems operate at up to 1.544 Mbps. Telephone companies charge a proportionately higher price for CSU/DSU installations.

Networking LANs with Host Gateways

Enterprises have used mini and mainframe computers for many years to provide multiuser applications. These computers are also required for large accounting and manufacturing applications and for on-line transaction processing. Also, there are substantial investments in mini and mainframe systems. This prevents a short-term conversion to LANs. Enterprise connectivity, therefore, requires connecting LANs to mini and mainframe host computers. We will discuss two computing environments: IBM and asynchronous.

IBM Gateways

Connecting LANs to an IBM host requires a **gateway**. Gateways are translators between networks that use different protocols. For example, a gateway permits a workstation using IPX/SPX to communicate with another device using the SNA protocol. Just as a human speaker might translate French into English, the gateway translates SNA protocol to IPX/SPX and vice versa. **Systems Network Architecture (SNA)** is the protocol used by IBM mainframes to communicate with terminals and other IBM computers.

Connecting a NetWare LAN to an IBM host requires converting NetWare packets to SNA packets. IBM host computers require a connected workstation or LAN to emulate an IBM-type terminal. There are 3270- and 5250-type terminal emulators.

NetWare's SNA gateway requires the following:

• NetWare SNA Gateway software
• An adapter installed in the gateway server
• NetWare 3270 LAN workstation software

The SNA Gateway software is installed on a workstation attached to the LAN. Any workstations with the NetWare 3270 emulation software are able to go through the gateway to attach to the IBM host.

An SNA Gateway allows different topologies and protocols to access an IBM host. The Gateway supports Ethernet, ARCNET, and token ring. (See Figure 11.4, which shows a ring and bus topology connected to a host computer.)

Remote SNA connection is provided with synchronous data-link control (SDLC) connections. SDLC is a communication protocol. Connecting a LAN via a synchronous connection requires a synchronous modem.

NetWare 5250 Gateway products are another solution that allows LANs to be connected to host IBM minicomputers, such as the AS/400. The NetWare 5250 Gateway allows NetWare workstations to emulate IBM 5250 and other IBM terminals. The following is a list of requirements for 5250 host connections:

• NetWare 5250 Gateway software
• An adapter installed in the gateway server
• NetWare 5250 LAN workstation software
• Synchronous modems

Figure 11.5 illustrates a LAN-to-IBM minicomputer network configuration. Each workstation uses the NetWare 5250 emulation software to communicate with the minicomputer.

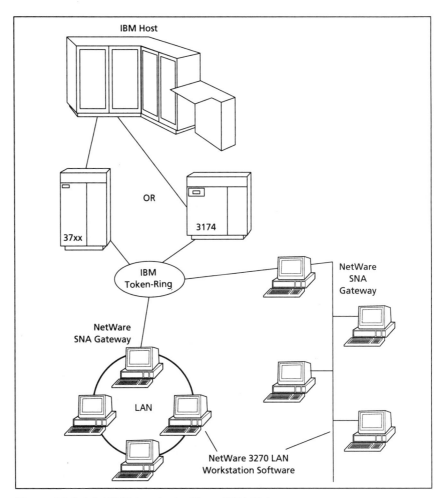

Figure 11.4 *A LAN Networked with an SNA Gateway*

ASYNCHRONOUS GATEWAYS

Many non-IBM computers use asynchronous communication protocols. For instance, asynchronous communication is used by Digital Equipment, SUN, and Hewlett-Packard. To realize enterprise connectivity, asynchronous computers must be connected to NetWare LANs.

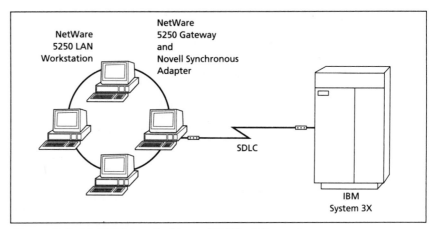

Figure 11.5 *A LAN Networked to an IBM Host Computer*

Two NetWare approaches to connecting to an asynchronous host are NetWare Asynchronous Communications Server (NACS) and NetWare Access Server.

NACS software allows any workstation on a LAN to communicate with any asynchronous device. Up to 32 users can share a pool of modems, minicomputer connections, and X.25 services from anywhere on the network. NACS is an NLM that runs on the file server.

Asynchronous communication allows users access to a modem to connect to such services as CompuServe. Since modems are pooled on the network, 100 users can share, for example, eight modems. A NACS configuration includes the following:

- NACS NLM software
- One or more Novell WNIM+ adapters or compatible adapters installed in the file server
- Asynchronous modems

Once the file server loads the NACS NLM and has the appropriate hardware installed and configured, workstations load **terminal emulation** software to access a minicomputer host. PROCOMM PLUS/LAN is one example of software that provides terminal emulation. Some of the popular terminals are VT100, VT220, Tektronix, Televideo, and WYSE. XMODEM, Kermit, ASCII, and other file transfer protocols are supported. NACS provides its asynchronous communications using voice-grade telephone lines.

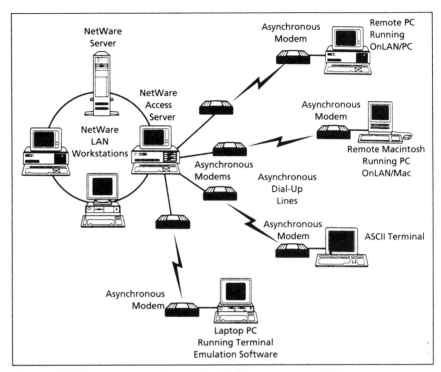

Figure 11.6 *Remote Access Server for Dial-In Access to a LAN*

An asynchronous solution similar to NACS is NetWare Access Server. NetWare Access Server (NAS) enables up to 16 remote users of DOS, Macintosh, and ASCII workstations to dial into a NetWare LAN. An 80386 or 80486 workstation can be configured to run up to 16 virtual DOS applications, depending on the amount of memory. A virtual machine is one that uses a 640 KB segment of memory but shares common hardware with the other virtual machines.

Each asynchronous connection requires a port or connection to a telephone line. The WNIM+ or compatible adapter will provide ports as well as X.25 adapters. Figure 11.6 illustrates an asynchronous network. This figure is very similar to one for a NACS solution except the connection would be to the file server and not the NetWare Access Server.

TCP GATEWAY

Transmission Control Protocol (TCP) is software that bundles data into packets and also unbundles it. TCP was developed for the Department of Defense to provide reliable communications under demanding conditions. It is implemented on LANs, minicomputers, and mainframes and is used extensively on education networks.

A TCP gateway allows a NetWare LAN to communicate with a network that uses TCP. TCP offers File Transfer Protocol (FTP) for sending and receiving files. FTP allows either the sending or receiving computer to act as the host.

TCP is a layer of software that allows a NetWare LAN to communicate with TCP host computers and NetWare nodes. TCP is used primarily with Ethernet networks using **TCP/IP** software. The **IP**, or Internet Protocol, was also developed for the Department of Defense to enable different computer systems to communicate using a common communication protocol. IP software keeps track of the addresses of nodes to guarantee a packet reaches the right node.

There are several companies that offer TCP solutions, including Novell. Some of the solutions use DOS only, while others use Windows. Novell's product, LAN WorkPlace for DOS, requires Windows version 3.

LAN WorkPlace for DOS, OS/2, and Macintosh implement a mouse interface so the user can access Unix systems, DEC VAXs, IBM hosts, or other systems using the TCP/IP protocol. These systems can be accessed without having to use a NetWare file server.

Under Windows, LAN WorkPlace for DOS offers three TCP/IP applications. One is terminal emulation or Host Presenter, which provides up to ten simultaneous **Telnet** (communication software) sessions. Users can access hosts and perform data transfers using the Windows Clipboard.

The second application is file transfer. This is File Express, which provides a typical Windows graphical interface for the FTP (File Transfer Protocol). Windows makes file transfers as easy as clicking on the appropriate icons.

The third application is an FTP server that runs in the background. It waits for an FTP user to establish a connection with the workstation and initiate a file transfer to or from local disk drives or NetWare volumes. For example, user JSMITH might use this application to allow MBLACK to establish an FTP session to copy files between workstations or NetWare volumes.

LAN WorkPlace for DOS requires that the workstation use Open Data-Link Interface (ODI) drivers. These drivers support Ethernet, token ring, and ARCNET LANs. Because NetWare can function as an IP router, LAN WorkPlace for DOS can be used to connect ARCNET, token ring, and Ethernet to a TCP/IP host.

Since LAN WorkPlace for DOS requires Windows, the minimum recommended workstation is an 80386 (see Chapter 9 for Windows hardware requirements).

Summary

NetWare offers a variety of alternatives providing enterprise-wide connectivity. Performance requirements, existing equipment, and cost constraints narrow these alternatives. To connect a NetWare LAN to an IBM host computer, it is necessary to use either 3270 or 5250 terminal emulation and the appropriate gateway hardware and software. Connecting a NetWare LAN to non-IBM hosts requires a NetWare Asynchronous Communications Server. This solution also requires a LAN workstation to emulate a terminal. The last connectivity product discussed was recommended for remote users dialing into the LAN. The remote user accesses a workstation on the LAN and the software transfers only the key strokes and screen information back and forth. These networking alternatives provide solutions for obtaining enterprise-wide connectivity.

Key Terms

Asynchronous   A communication method that places data in a discrete block. The block is surrounded by framing bits. Thus there are framing bits at the beginning and end of the block. These bits show where the block begins and where it ends.

Bridge   A device that allows a node on one LAN to communicate with a node on another LAN. Bridges connect LANs with different topologies and protocols, and they also isolate network traffic by keeping packets from being transmitted to segments where they are not needed.

External Bridge   A node configured with bridging software that is attached to a network to connect LAN segments. The primary function is to isolate traffic to either one side or the other of the bridge.

Gateway   A device that acts as a translator between networks that use different protocols. The gateway permits a workstation using one protocol, such as SNA, to communicate with a workstation using a different protocol, such as IPX/SPX.

Internal Bridge   A NIC in a NetWare file server that connects one NetWare LAN topology to another.

Internet Protocol (IP)   Software developed through contracts for the Department of Defense to ensure that data are routed to the correct node.

Repeater   A device that regenerates an electrical signal that effectively increases the length of a LAN segment.

Router   A device that connects two networks, controls the movement of network traffic, and determines the best route for sending traffic.

Systems Network Architecture (SNA)   A protocol used by IBM mainframe computers for connecting to terminals, printers, and other network devices.

TCP/IP   A combination of the TCP and IP protocols that is used to achieve common communications between many different LANs, mini, and mainframe computers. This protocol is used on national defense and education networks and on the Internet.

Telnet   A TCP/IP utility that provides terminal emulation such as VT100 or VT220.

Terminal Emulation   Software that makes a personal computer function like a terminal connected to a host computer.

Transmission Control Protocol (TCP)   Software developed for the Department of Defense that performs extensive error checking to ensure the integrity of transmitted data.

X.25   A communication protocol for accessing Public Data Networks such as Telenet.

Questions and
Exercises

1. Describe the functions of a repeater, bridge, and gateway. Under what conditions would each be used? Identify the protocols used, whether there are host computers, the number of workstations, distances of the cable, if the network is a LAN or WAN, and any other pertinent issues that would affect the selection process.

2. How does NetWare support internal and external bridging? What are they? Describe a LAN that uses internal bridging and one that uses external bridging.

3. You have two NetWare LANs, an Ethernet and an ARCNET. Both are in the same building, but on different floors. Also, you have a DEC minicomputer and you want to connect to the Internet (WAN using TCP/IP). How would you design a solution to connect both LANs and the DEC minicomputer to the Internet? Provide a drawing and sufficient narrative to explain your rationale.

12

Looking Ahead: New Directions and Technologies

Chapter Objectives

The objectives of this chapter are the following:

- To examine the issues involved in downsizing.

- To explore emerging technologies that affect LANs and NetWare.

- To explain new features offered in NetWare 4.

Introduction LANs and LAN applications are at the center of evolving computer technologies. Organizations are finding that LANs offer a cost-effective alternative to mini and mainframe computers. In many instances a LAN with Novell file servers can be installed at the same cost as yearly maintenance on a mini or mainframe computer. Once a LAN is implemented, new options for connectivity emerge, as discussed in Chapter 11.

The emphasis on connectivity along with the trend away from "big iron" is called downsizing. The trend is toward growing enterprise networks, with global educational, business, and research and development networks reaching into local schools, businesses, libraries, and homes.

Local schools are connecting to university networks so that students can work with their peers thousands of miles away on projects in social studies, biology, math, chemistry, music, and so on. Libraries share holdings with libraries in other states by networking book databases. A researcher in Colorado can work with researchers in North Carolina and Massachusetts by communicating through a network. Business persons are tapping into networks with portable computers for access to electronic mail, business information, and travel reservation systems.

To meet the demand, networking and computer technology are constantly moving forward. Portable and notebook computers are commonplace and some models come with a network interface card. FAX and CD-ROM access is growing on networks. New applications require greater network bandwidth to support full-motion video and document imaging.

Downsizing for network versatility is bringing challenges to information technology managers. People need training in networking, large systems need to be converted to networked systems, and equipment and software need to be purchased to match each organization's mode of business.

Downsizing

Downsizing means that LANs of all sizes will be the computing platform of the future. Personal computers with parallel processors and powerful workstations are doing the same work as mainframes. Manufacturers already build disk storage units that rival the size of mainframe disk storage at a fraction of the cost. GUI technology in the network and workstation domain are making everyday computing easier for users.

Today mainframes play an important role in the banking, airline, insurance, utilities, government, and education industries. Management information systems personnel in each of these areas are working on downsizing issues.

One issue is the need to manage information around-the-clock 365 days a year, with no system downtime. To go from a mainframe to file servers means incorporating redundant disks and CPUs. The computer and networking equipment must be protected from power and other environmental problems.

Novell is working on file server redundancy and reliability. Mirroring disks is one solution. Another is Novell's **System Fault Tolerant III (SFTIII)**. SFTIII consists of two file servers connected by a high-speed link. One server is active while the other is its mirror image. If the active server fails, the other takes over without interruption to the users.

On-line maintenance without interruption is possible with SFTIII. One file server can be shut down for maintenance, upgrade activity, or replacement. When the server is back up, the mirroring process continues.

SFTIII file servers do not have to be at the same location. If one location experiences power, water, or fire problems, the server in the other location continues unaffected. Since the servers can be at different locations, SFTIII helps address security and disaster recovery issues.

Another issue in downsizing is the need to handle large volumes of transactions. This is particularly true for banks and airlines. Some bank mainframes process several hundred transactions per second. Network software companies are working to improve high-volume transaction processing. This software is in its infancy and needs more development before downsizing is complete.

Database processing is another area that needs further development on the network side. There are many good database products available for NetWare, but more development is required for these databases to handle comparable data on mainframes.

Downsizing from host computers to LANs requires planning to meet existing needs with new technology. The rewards are cost savings, better interfaces for users, and better connectivity to local and distant computing resources.

Another advantage of the LAN is modularity. New segments and workstations can be added as needed. A new file server can be attached without having to be located in a machine room. Remote printers are quickly added using the print server software and equipment such as the Network Printer Interface.

Emerging Applications and Technologies

LANs face new demands as more applications become available. For example, some organizations are scanning documents onto CD-ROMS and want to make the CD-ROMS accessible from a network. Others want to transmit full-motion video images and sound across the network. There is also the need to use FAX technology from a LAN. Network managers must continue to stay current on technology to provide these services.

Each new technology has its costs. For example, scanned images and sound files are large and require extensive disk space. These files increase network traffic, causing transmission delays.

ATM

Technology is being developed to support applications that require high-speed data transmission on a network. **Asynchronous Transfer Mode (ATM)** is an emerging technology that supports speeds of 45 or 155 Mbps.

The speed is achieved between two nodes on a network. ATM uses a switching scheme to create a dedicated logical link between the nodes. This technology is used for LANs and WANs. It is media independent and supports text, images, voice, and graphics data transfers.

ATM converts packets of data into cells of data. Current cell designs hold 53 bytes per cell. Because all cells are the same length, they can be put into a packet and shipped to another node. An analogy is that of a freight train. Each car is a cell and the complete train is a packet.

ATM is a solution for networks with very high levels of traffic. Since this technology is expensive, early implementations will be restricted to large institutions such as the government and the military, universities, and large businesses (such as telephone companies).

ATM is not an established standard and will continue to evolve as standards bodies such as CCITT and ANSI work to complete definition of the technology.

Wireless Media

Wireless networks are in operation and growing in popularity. For example, some stores use wireless hand-held devices to enter inventory data. The operator keys in information and the hand-held device transmits it to a receiving device.

Persoft manufactures wireless bridges that have a range of three miles. These bridges are used with Ethernet and token-ring LANs. They are a cost-effective alternative to running cable between buildings, such as in an industrial park or on a college campus. Data are transmitted at a rate of 2 Mbps.

Notebook computers are a current target for wireless technology. Proxim offers a credit card size wireless LAN adapter for portable and notebook computers. It is called the RangeLAN/PCMCIA and comes with drivers for NetWare. The adapter card works with another wireless adapter that is installed in the file server. The range of the card is several hundred feet. This product makes notebook computers even more portable and convenient than they are now.

Soon notebook computer users are likely to have as much long distance freedom as cellular telephone users do currently. Several companies are working to deliver cellular technology to computers. IBM, along with a consortium of cellular carriers, is developing this kind of cellular system. The consortium is proposing a cellular packet technology called **Cellular Digital Packet Technology (CDPT)**.

There are important issues to be addressed with cellular networks. For example, it is relatively easy to intercept signals from a cellular transmission. Hardware and software will have to be developed to encrypt the transmissions. Another issue is speed. Cellular networks will have to work at speeds acceptable for the applications that users will need. Currently 19.2 Kbps is used in this technology with predicted improvement to 56 Kbps. These speeds are appropriate for electronic mail, but may not be adequate for transmission of sound and image files.

Multimedia

Multimedia will play a major roll in information processing and how computing technology is used. As the technology advances, it is easy to envision applications such as full-motion video training films distributed over the network to a desktop. Television programs also could be made available to a network workstation.

A multimedia workstation configured with a camera and sound could transmit live images of people along with the sound of their voices (telephone systems already have this capability).

A multimedia workstation on a LAN would require large bandwidth, such as that provided by ATM. This workstation also would have a variety of devices attached to it running from Windows. Some of the devices would include CD-ROM drives, speakers, cameras, and video disk players.

Multimedia applications are likely to be popular because of their entertainment quality. They can combine video, animation, sound, and text in captivating ways. For example, physicians can now learn about performing operations using multimedia computer applications. Similarly, chemistry students can interactively perform dangerous experiments from the safety of their computer keyboard.

Automated Software Upgrades

Some networks have thousands of workstations with DOS, Windows, and other applications that need to be upgraded on an annual basis. Imagine the work involved to upgrade the network shell for 500 users. Upgrades on large networks can be a time-consuming project.

Several vendors are currently working on the problem of automating software upgrades. New NLMs will be introduced in the future to provide help with upgrades.

These NLMs can be programmed to find outdated applications and perform upgrades without assistance from the user or network manager.

NetWare 4

NetWare 4 is an emerging technology that is designed to take NetWare users into the future. It is particularly suited to organizations with large networks and accompanying network management problems.

Large networks, such as those with ten or more file servers, need a global naming or directory facility. **NetWare 4** is designed to provide this feature. Without it, users experience difficulty in determining which users and printers are associated with each file server.

NetWare 4 has improved the tracking of network objects such as file servers, users, groups, printers, and communication devices. This version of NetWare has a database to keep track of these network objects. Each time an object is added, changed, or deleted, the database is updated. Redundant copies of the database exist on the network so that the data can be accessed when the main database server is down.

NetWare 4 also improves security and makes network access easier. Instead of logging into a file server, the users logs into the network. The log-in process validates users for the objects they have authorization to access. For example, a user on a network with eight file servers and 20 remote printers might have authorization to use three of the servers and three of the remote printers. NetWare 4 makes it easier to administer the authorization. It is also easier for the user to access the resources.

Another feature of NetWare 4 is time synchronization. There may be 10 or 20 or more file servers on a large network. Some of the servers may be in different time zones. Imagine resetting the time on these servers for daylight savings time. NetWare 4 eliminates the problem by automatically setting the time on each server.

NetWare 4 is a welcome addition that adds awareness of multiple file server needs to network management.

Summary

LANs have become the mode of choice for the present and for growth into the future. The shift of focus from mainframe to LAN solutions is further evidence of what the future holds. Many organizations are in the process of downsizing or have downsized to LAN technology.

Downsizing raises several important issues that need resolution. One issue is the need for around-the-clock processing every day of the year. A related issue is the need to build in redundancy and reliability of software and hardware. Novell has worked to address these issues with SFTIII.

As we move into the future, new technologies are emerging. ATM is an important new data transmission mode that provides high-speed communications. The introduction of wireless networking equipment will give users added independence and convenience.

Multimedia applications are another emerging technology. Network equipment will need to evolve to accommodate voice, video, and data applications made possible by multimedia software. Multimedia hardware will provide a challenge as well as excitement for network personnel. In the future, the network manager may have to be handy with a camera as well as with computers.

The last emerging technology discussed in this chapter is NetWare 4. This addition to Novell's product line helps to make managing large networks easier. It improves security and it makes downsizing from a mainframe even more viable.

Key Terms

Asynchronous Transfer Mode (ATM)   A new technology that provides very high-speed switching and transport of data over LANs and WANs.

Cellular Digital Packet Technology (CDPT)   An emerging technology to transmit digital information over a cellular communication system. This system will make connecting to a network easier.

Multimedia   A combination of computer hardware and software that provides animation, full-motion video, and sound to the desktop.

NetWare 4   A version of Novell's operating system offering global naming services and improved security management.

System Fault Tolerant Level III (SFTIII)   A system that offers file server mirroring. Mirroring provides the platform for downsizing mainframe applications to LANs.

Questions and
Exercises

1. Compose a list of the hardware and software configuration necessary for a multimedia system. (Refer to a current publication or visit a local computer vendor for the information.) The primary function of the system is to train elementary school teachers on interactive software. Specify the computer and hardware configuration, operating system, applications, and auxiliary equipment.

2. You are evaluating a utility to automate upgrading of software on workstations. Based on your experience or on what you have read, what specific files could be updated automatically? How might this utility be installed? Would it be an NLM? Why or why not?

3. Downsizing is a common process for host installations. But it is not an easy process. What is downsizing? Identify some of the issues involved in the process of downsizing. Identify one application or host system that is not a good candidate for downsizing.

Hardware Diagnostics

Microsoft supplies a diagnostic utility with Windows 3.1, MSD.EXE.
Running this program provides the following information.

```
     Microsoft Diagnostics version 2.00    1/18/93    4:26pm    Page   1
     ========================================================================
     ----------------------- Customer Information ------------------------

                                  Name: Rains

     ----------------------- Summary Information -------------------------

                      Computer: American Megatrend, 80386
                        Memory: 640K, 3328K Ext, 2056K XMS
                         Video: VGA, Oak
                       Network: Novell, Shell 3.22.00
                    OS Version: MS-DOS Version 5.00
                         Mouse: Logitech Serial Mouse,  5.00
                Other Adapters: Game Adapter
                   Disk Drives: A: B: C: F: H: M: O: Q:
                     LPT Ports: 3
                     COM Ports: 2

     ----------------------------- Computer ------------------------------

            Computer Name: American Megatrends
        BIOS Manufacturer: American Megatrends
             BIOS Version: OPTI 386 EXTENDED SETUP PROGRAM Ver - 2.0B,(C)1994
            BIOS Category: IBM PC/AT
            BIOS ID Bytes: FC 01 00
                BIOS Date: 08/30/90
                Processor: 80386
```

```
Math Coprocessor: None
        Keyboard: Enhanced
        Bus Type: ISA/AT/Classic Bus
  DMA Controller: Yes
   Cascaded IRQ2: Yes
BIOS Data Segment: None


     Microsoft Diagnostics version 2.00    1/18/93    4:26pm    Page  2
==============================================================================
------------------------------ Memory ------------------------------

Legend:  Available "  "  RAM "##"  ROM "RR"  Possibly Available ".."
   EMS Page Frame "PP"  Used UMBs "UU"  Free UMBs "FF"
1024K FC00 RRRRRRRRRRRRRRRR FFFF  Conventional Memory
      F800 RRRRRRRRRRRRRRRR FBFF                 Total: 640K
      F400 RRRRRRRRRRRRRRRR F7FF             Available: 538K
 960K F000 RRRRRRRRRRRRRRRR F3FF                      550912 bytes
      EC00                  EFFF
      E800                  EBFF  Extended Memory
      E400                  E7FF                 Total: 3328K
 896K E000                  E3FF
      DC00 FFFFFFFFFFFFFFFF DFFF  MS-DOS Upper Memory Blocks
      D800 UUUUUUUFFFFFFFFF DBFF            Total UMBs: 76K
      D400 UUUUUUUUUUUUUUUU D7FF         Total Free UMBs: 36K
 832K D000 UUUUUUUUUUUUUUUU D3FF       Largest Free Block: 24K
      CC00 ################ CFFF
      C800 ##FFFFFFFFFFFFF# CBFF  XMS Information
      C400 RRRRRRRRRRRRRRRR C7FF            XMS Version: 3.00
 768K C000 RRRRRRRRRRRRRRRR C3FF         Driver Version: 3.07
      BC00 ################ BFFF       A20 Address Line: Enabled
      B800 ################ BBFF       High Memory Area: In use
      B400                  B7FF              Available: 2056K
 704K B000                  B3FF  Largest Free Block: 2056K
      AC00                  AFFF       Available SXMS: 2056K
      A800                  ABFF   Largest Free SXMS: 2056K
      A400                  A7FF
 640K A000                  A3FF

------------------------------ Video ------------------------------

   Video Adapter Type: VGA
          Manufacturer: Oak
                 Model:
          Display Type: VGA Color
            Video Mode: 3
     Number of Columns: 80
        Number of Rows: 25
```

```
        Video BIOS Version: Copyright 1990, Oak Technology VGA BIOS
Dv2.17v-352
           Video BIOS Date:
    VESA Support Installed: No
         Secondary Adapter: None



     Microsoft Diagnostics version 2.00    1/18/93    4:26pm    Page  3
    =======================================================================


    ---------------------------- Network -----------------------------

                 Network Detected: Yes
                     Network Name: Novell
       MS-DOS Network Functions: Not Supported
                  NetBIOS Present: No
                    Shell Version: 3.22.00
                        Shell OS: MS-DOS
                 Shell OS Version: V5.00
                    Hardware Type: IBM_PC
                   Station Number: 2
         Physical Station Number: 0207:0108:0EED
                   IPX Installed: Yes
                   SPX Installed: Yes
               ODI/LSL Installed: No


    ------------------------- OS Version -----------------------------

                  Operating System: MS-DOS 5.00
                  Internal Revision: 00
                  OEM Serial Number: FFH
                 User Serial Number: 000000H
                OEM Version String: MS-DOS Version 5.00
                    DOS Located in: HMA
                        Boot Drive: C:
                   Path to Program: C:\WINDOWS\MSD.EXE


                       Environment Strings
         --------------------------------------------
    TEMP=C:\WINDOWS\TEMP
    NU=C:\NU
    DRIVE=B:
    COMSPEC=Y:COMMAND.COM
    PROMPT=$P$G
    PATH=Z:.;Y:.;X:.;W:.;V:.;U:.;T:.;S:.;R:.;Q:.
```

```
Microsoft Diagnostics version 2.00    1/18/93    4:26pm    Page  4
=============================================================================

----------------------------- Mouse -----------------------------------

               Mouse Hardware: Logitech Serial Mouse
          Driver Manufacturer: Logitech
              DOS Driver Type: Serial Mouse
             Driver File Type: .COM File
           DOS Driver Version: 5.00
     Microsoft Driver Version: 6.25
                    Mouse IRQ: 4
               Mouse COM Port: COM1:
       Mouse COM Port Address: 03F8H
       Number of Mouse Buttons: 3
        Horizontal Sensitivity: 50
         Mouse to Cursor Ratio: 1 : 1
          Vertical Sensitivity: 50
         Mouse to Cursor Ratio: 1 : 1
               Threshold Speed: 53
               Mouse Language: English

--------------------------- Other Adapters ----------------------------

                Game Adapter: Detected
           Joystick A - X: 0
                        Y: 0
                   Button 1: On
                   Button 2: On
           Joystick B - X: 2
                        Y: 2
                   Button 1: On
                   Button 2: On



Microsoft Diagnostics version 2.00    1/18/93    4:26pm    Page  5
=============================================================================

--------------------------- Disk Drives ------------------------------

    Drive  Type                                    Free Space  Total Size
    -----  ------------------------------------    ----------  ----------
     A:    Floppy Drive, 5.25" 1.2M
              80 Cylinders, 2 Heads
              512 Bytes/Sector, 15 Sectors/Track
     B:    Floppy Drive, 3.5" 1.44M
              80 Cylinders, 2 Heads
              512 Bytes/Sector, 18 Sectors/Track
```

```
C:    Fixed Disk, CMOS Type 47                29M        81M
      979 Cylinders, 10 Heads
      512 Bytes/Sector, 17 Sectors/Track
F:    Remote Drive                            29M        50M
      512 Bytes/Sector
H:    Remote Drive                           308M       511M
      512 Bytes/Sector
M:    Remote Drive                           308M       511M
      512 Bytes/Sector
O:    Remote Drive                           308M       511M
      512 Bytes/Sector
Q:    Remote Drive                           308M       511M
      512 Bytes/Sector
R:    Remote Drive                           308M       511M
      512 Bytes/Sector
S:    Remote Drive                           308M       511M
      512 Bytes/Sector
T:    Remote Drive                           308M       511M
      512 Bytes/Sector
U:    Remote Drive                           308M       511M
      512 Bytes/Sector
V:    Remote Drive                           308M       511M
      512 Bytes/Sector
W:    Remote Drive                           308M       511M
      512 Bytes/Sector
X:    Remote Drive                           308M       511M
      512 Bytes/Sector
Y:    Remote Drive                           308M       511M
      512 Bytes/Sector
Z:    Remote Drive                            29M        50M
      512 Bytes/Sector
LASTDRIVE=`:
```

```
Microsoft Diagnostics version 2.00    1/18/93    4:26pm    Page  6
=========================================================================
```

```
---------------------------- LPT Ports ----------------------------------

           Port    On     Paper    I/O    Time
   Port   Address  Line   Out      Error  Out     Busy    ACK
   -----  -------  ----   -----    -----  ----    ----    ---
   LPT1:  0378H    Yes    No       No     No      No      No
   LPT2:  03BCH    No     No       No     Yes     Yes     No
   LPT3:  03BCH    No     No       No     Yes     Yes     No
```

```
------------------------------- COM Ports ----------------------------------

                            COM1:      COM2:      COM3:      COM4:
                            -----      -----      -----      -----
        Port Address        03F8H      02F8H      N/A        N/A
        Baud Rate           2400       2400
        Parity              Odd        None
        Data Bits           8          8
        Stop Bits           2          1
        Carrier Detect (CD) No         No
        Ring Indicator (RI) No         Yes
        Data Set Ready (DSR) Yes       Yes
        Clear To Send (CTS) Yes        Yes
        UART Chip Used      8250       8250


----------------------------- IRQ Status -----------------------------------

IRQ  Address    Description     Detected              Handled By
---  --------   ------------    --------              ----------
  0  07C1:051B  Timer Click     Yes                   IPXPAC.COM
  1  D012:16E8  Keyboard        Yes                   Block Device
  2  046D:0057  Second 8259A    Yes                   Default Handlers
  3  046D:006F  COM2: COM4:     COM2:                 Default Handlers
  4  D68C:31BD  COM1: COM3:     COM1: Logitech SeriaMOUSE.COM
  5  071B:05AB  LPT2:           Yes                   LOGIN.EXE
  6  046D:00B7  Floppy Disk     Yes                   Default Handlers
  7  0070:06F4  LPT1:           Yes                   System Area
  8  046D:0052  Real-Time Clock Yes                   Default Handlers
  9  F000:EEC7  Redirected IRQ2 Yes                   BIOS
 10  046D:00CF  (Reserved)                            Default Handlers
 11  046D:00E7  (Reserved)                            Default Handlers
 12  046D:00FF  (Reserved)                            Default Handlers
 13  F000:EED0  Math Coprocessor No                   BIOS
 14  046D:0117  Fixed Disk      Yes                   Default Handlers
 15  F000:FF53  (Reserved)                            BIOS


     Microsoft Diagnostics version 2.00    1/18/93    4:26pm    Page   7
============================================================================


----------------------------- TSR Programs ---------------------------------

Program Name         Address   Size   Command Line Parameters
------------------   -------   ------  -------------------------------
System Data          0253      11600
   HIMEM             0255      1072    XMSXXXX0
   EMM386            0299      3232    $MMXXXX0
   File Handles      0364      2960
   FCBS              041E      256
   BUFFERS           042F      512
   Directories       0450      448
   Default Handlers  046D      3008
```

```
System Code            0529      64
COMMAND.COM            052E    2368
Free Memory            05C3      64
COMMAND.COM            05C8    1024
Free Memory            0609     128
LOGIN.EXE              0612    4128
Free Memory            0715      64
LOGIN.EXE              071A    2640    -N 96 5 816 52224
IPXPAC.COM             07C0   15824
NETX.COM               0B9E   42880
Free Memory            1617      48
LOGIN.EXE              161B   13712
MSD.EXE                1975     144
MSD.EXE                197F  316576
MSD.EXE                66CA    8192
MSD.EXE                68CB   10032
Free Memory            6B3F     544
Free Memory            6B62  215488
Excluded UMB Area      9FFF  167488
MOUSE.COM              C8E4     128    SER 1
IPXPAC.COM             C8ED     128
Free Memory            C8F6     128
Free Memory            C8FF   12256
Excluded UMB Area      CBFE   16416
MOUSE.COM              D001   26768
MOUSE.COM              D68B   13744    SER 1
Free Memory            D9E7   24960
```

```
        Microsoft Diagnostics version 2.00   1/18/93   4:26pm   Page  8
===========================================================================


------------------------- Device Drivers -------------------------

        Device     Filename  Units  Header      Attributes
        ---------- --------  -----  ---------   ----------------
        NUL                         0116:0048   1...........1..
        Block Device         3      D012:1ED2   ....1...11....1.
        $MMXXXX0   EMM386           0299:0000   11.............
        XMSXXXX0   HIMEM            0255:0000   1.1............
        CON                         0070:0023   1.........1..11
        AUX                         0070:0035   1..............
        PRN                         0B9F:658A   1...1..........
        CLOCK$                      0070:0059   1..........1...
        Block Device         3      0070:006B   ....1...11....1.
        COM1                        0070:007B   1..............
        LPT1                        0B9F:659C   1...1..........
        LPT2                        0B9F:65AE   1...1..........
        LPT3                        0B9F:65C0   1...1..........
        COM2                        0070:00CA   1..............
        COM3                        0070:00DC   1..............
        COM4                        0070:00EE   1..............
```

```
    Microsoft Diagnostics version 2.00    1/18/93    4:26pm    Page  9
===========================================================================

---------------- ROM BIOS            F000    65536 ------------------

F000:73ED System Configuration (C) Copyright 1985-1989, American
Megatrends Inc,.

F000:D5E3 CMOS SETUP (C) Copyright 1985-1990, American Megatrends
Inc., Date (mn/date/year):

F000:000A 08/21/90 SETUP PROGRAM FOR OPTI 386 CHIPSET(C)1989, American
Megatrends Inc.All rights reserved.1346 Oakbrook Drive, Suite-120,
Norcross GA.-30093, Phone-(404)-263-8181.

F000:10AC OPTI 386 EXTENDED SETUP PROGRAM Ver - 2.0B,
(C)1990, American Megatrends Inc.    Prev/Next Window -

F000:8000 XXXX88886666----0123AAAAMMMMIIII Date:-06/13/90
(C)1985-1990, American Megatrends Inc. All Rights Reserved.

F000:E0CA R(C)1985-1990, American Megatrends Inc.,All Rights Reserved.
1346 Oakbrook Drive, Suite-120, Norcross, GA-30093. Phone-(404)-263-8181.

F000:E2D0 0000000000000000(C)1990 American Megatrends Inc.386-BIOS
(C)1989 American Megatrends Inc

F000:E00E IBM COMPATIBLE IBM IS A TRADEMARK OF INTERNATIONAL BUSINESS
MACHINES CORP.

F000:7504 ROM-BIOS Date      :
F000:D560 ROM-BIOS CHECKSUM ERROR CHECK ROM (27256)?
F000:D70D Hard disk D: type  :
          Primary display    :
          Keyboard           :
          Video BIOS shadow  :
          Scratch RAM option :
F000:D73B Keyboard           :
          Video BIOS shadow  :
          Scratch RAM option :
          Main BIOS shadow   :
          Relocate option    :
F000:DB4E If required, BIOS will use 256 bytes of RAM
          (1) : Using BIOS stack area at 0030:0000
          (2) : Reducing base memory size by 1KB
F000:F5AF 128KB BIOS SHADOW RAM ENABLED
F000:FF59 (C)1990AMI,404-263-8181
```

```
      Microsoft Diagnostics version 2.00    1/18/93    4:26pm    Page 10

---------------- Video ROM BIOS        C000    32768 ------------------

     C000:0154 Wed Jul 10 17:20:04 1991

               COPYRIGHT 1990, OAK TECHNOLOGY VGA BIOS
     C000:054C Copyright 1990, Oak Technology VGA BIOS Dv2.17v-352
     C000:0007 FOAK VGA BIOS, not for IBMPQRVW

------------------------- C:\AUTOEXEC.BAT ----------------------------

C:\SMARTDRV.EXE
@ECHO OFF
Prompt $p$g
PATH C:\BATCH;C:\DOS;C:\;C:\NET;C:\NU
SET TEMP=C:\WINDOWS\TEMP



      Microsoft Diagnostics version 2.00    1/18/93    4:26pm    Page 11


DOSKEY
rem **************** MouseWare 5.0 Setup *****************
LOADHIGH C:\MOUSE\MOUSE SER 1
SET NU=C:\NU
IMAGE



------------------------- C:\CONFIG.SYS -----------------------------

FILES=55
BUFFERS=30
SHELL=C:\DOS\COMMAND.COM /E:1024 /p
DEVICE=C:\HIMEM.SYS /M:11
DOS=HIGH,UMB
DEVICE=C:\EMM386.EXE NOEMS
STACKS=9,256



------------------------- C:\WIN31\SYSTEM.INI -----------------------

[boot]
shell=progman.exe
mouse.drv=lmouse.drv
network.drv=netware.drv
language.dll=
sound.drv=mmsound.drv
```

```
comm.drv=comm.drv
keyboard.drv=keyboard.drv
system.drv=system.drv
386grabber=vga.3gr
oemfonts.fon=vgaoem.fon
286grabber=vgacolor.2gr
fixedfon.fon=vgafix.fon
fonts.fon=vgasys.fon
display.drv=vga.drv
drivers=mmsystem.dll

[keyboard]
subtype=
type=4
keyboard.dll=
oemansi.bin=
```

```
         Microsoft Diagnostics version 2.00    1/18/93    4:26pm    Page 12
===============================================================================
```

```
[boot.description]
keyboard.typ=Enhanced 101 or 102 key US and Non US keyboards
mouse.drv=Logitech
network.drv=Novell NetWare (shell versions 3.21 and above)
language.dll=English (American)
system.drv=MS-DOS System
codepage=437
woafont.fon=English (437)
aspect=100,96,96
display.drv=VGA

[386Enh]
32BitDiskAccess=OFF
device=*int13
device=*wdctrl
mouse=lvmd.386
OverlappedIO=off
network=*vnetbios,vnetware.386,vipx.386
ebios=*ebios
woafont=dosapp.fon
display=*vddvga
EGA80WOA.FON=EGA80WOA.FON
EGA40WOA.FON=EGA40WOA.FON
CGA80WOA.FON=CGA80WOA.FON
CGA40WOA.FON=CGA40WOA.FON
keyboard=*vkd
device=vtdapi.386
device=*vpicd
device=*vtd
device=*reboot
```

```
device=*vdmad
device=*vsd
device=*v86mmgr
device=*pageswap
device=*dosmgr
device=*vmpoll
device=*wshell
device=*BLOCKDEV
device=*PAGEFILE
device=*vfd
device=*parity
device=*biosxlat
device=*vcd
device=*vmcpd
device=*combuff
device=*cdpscsi
local=CON
FileSysChange=off


      Microsoft Diagnostics version 2.00    1/18/93    4:26pm    Page 13
=======================================================================

    PagingFile=C:\WIN31\WIN386.SWP
    MaxPagingFileSize=12288
    MinTimeslice=20
    WinTimeslice=100,50
    WinExclusive=0
    Com1AutoAssign=2
    Com2AutoAssign=2

    [standard]

    [NonWindowsApp]
    localtsrs=dosedit,ced
    CommandEnvSize=1024

    [mci]
    WaveAudio=mciwave.drv
    Sequencer=mciseq.drv
    CDAudio=mcicda.drv

    [drivers]
    timer=timer.drv
    midimapper=midimap.drv

    [LogiMouse]
    Type=Serial
    Model=C_Series
    Port=1
    DragLock=None
    Orientation=1
```

```
---------------------- C:\WINDOWS\SYSTEM.INI ------------------------

[boot]
shell=progman.exe
mouse.drv=LMOUSE.DRV
network.drv=netware.drv
language.dll=
sound.drv=mmsound.drv
comm.drv=comm.drv
keyboard.drv=keyboard.drv
system.drv=system.drv
386grabber=vga.3gr
oemfonts.fon=vgaoem.fon
286grabber=vgacolor.2gr
fixedfon.fon=vgafix.fon
fonts.fon=vgasys.fon
display.drv=vga.drv
drivers=mmsystem.dll



         Microsoft Diagnostics version 2.00    1/18/93    4:26pm    Page 14
========================================================================
[keyboard]
subtype=
type=4
keyboard.dll=
oemansi.bin=

[boot.description]
keyboard.typ=Enhanced 101 or 102 key US and Non US keyboards
mouse.drv=Logitech
network.drv=Novell NetWare (shell versions 3.21 and above)
language.dll=English (American)
system.drv=MS-DOS System
codepage=437
woafont.fon=English (437)


aspect=100,96,96
display.drv=VGA

[386Enh]
32BitDiskAccess=OFF
device=*int13
device=*wdctrl
mouse=LVMD.386
OverlappedIO=off
network=*vnetbios,vnetware.386,vipx.386
ebios=*ebios
```

```
woafont=dosapp.fon
display=*vddvga
EGA80WOA.FON=EGA80WOA.FON
EGA40WOA.FON=EGA40WOA.FON
CGA80WOA.FON=CGA80WOA.FON
CGA40WOA.FON=CGA40WOA.FON
keyboard=*vkd
device=vtdapi.386
device=*vpicd
device=*vtd
device=*reboot
device=*vdmad
device=*vsd
device=*v86mmgr
device=*pageswap
device=*dosmgr
device=*vmpoll
device=*wshell
device=*BLOCKDEV
device=*PAGEFILE
device=*vfd
device=*parity
device=*biosxlat
device=*vcd
```

```
Microsoft Diagnostics version 2.00    1/18/93    4:26pm    Page 15
========================================================================
```

```
device=*vmcpd
device=*combuff
device=*cdpscsi
local=CON
FileSysChange=off
PagingFile=C:\WINDOWS\WIN386.SWP
MaxPagingFileSize=12288
COM2Irq=3
COM2Base=02F8
MinTimeslice=20
WinTimeslice=100,50
WinExclusive=0
Com1AutoAssign=2
Com2AutoAssign=-1
COM1Irq=4
COM1Base=03F8

[standard]

[NonWindowsApp]
localtsrs=dosedit,ced
CommandEnvSize=1024
```

```
[mci]
WaveAudio=mciwave.drv
Sequencer=mciseq.drv
CDAudio=mcicda.drv

[drivers]
timer=timer.drv
midimapper=midimap.drv

[LogiMouse]
Type=2
Port=1
Buttons=3
Orientation=1
```

Microsoft Diagnostics version 2.00   1/18/93   4:26pm   Page 16
==

----------------------- C:\WINDOWS\WIN.INI ----------------------------

```
[windows]
spooler=yes
load=nwpopup.exe
run=
Beep=yes
NullPort=None
BorderWidth=3
CursorBlinkRate=530
DoubleClickSpeed=452Programs=com exe bat pif
Documents=
DeviceNotSelectedTimeout=15
TransmissionRetryTimeout=45
KeyboardDelay=2
KeyboardSpeed=31
ScreenSaveActive=0
ScreenSaveTimeOut=120
NetWarn=1
MouseThreshold1=2
MouseThreshold2=0
MouseSpeed=1
device=WINFAX,WINFAX,COM2:

[Desktop]
Pattern=(None)
Wallpaper=(None)
GridGranularity=0
```

```
[Extensions]
cal=calendar.exe ^.cal
crd=cardfile.exe ^.crd
trm=terminal.exe ^.trm
txt=notepad.exe ^.txt
ini=notepad.exe ^.ini
pcx=pbrush.exe ^.pcx
bmp=pbrush.exe ^.bmp
wri=write.exe ^.wri
rec=recorder.exe ^.rec
hlp=winhelp.exe ^.hlp

[intl]
sLanguage=enu
sCountry=United States
iCountry=1
iDate=0
iTime=0
iTLZero=0
```

Microsoft Diagnostics version 2.00   1/18/93   4:26pm   Page 17
===

```
iCurrency=0
iCurrDigits=2
iNegCurr=0
iLzero=1
iDigits=2
iMeasure=1
s1159=AM
s2359=PM
sCurrency=$
sThousand=,
sDecimal=.
sDate=/
sTime=:
sList=,
sShortDate=M/d/yy
sLongDate=dddd, MMMM dd, yyyy
[ports]
; A line with [filename].PRN followed by an equal sign causes
; [filename] to appear in the Control Panel's Printer Configuration
  dialog
; box. A printer connected to [filename] directs its output into this
  file.
LPT1:=
LPT2:=
LPT3:=
```

```
COM1:=9600,n,8,1,x
COM2:=2400,n,8,1,x
COM3:=9600,n,8,1,x
COM4:=9600,n,8,1,x
EPT:=
FILE:=
LPT1.DOS=
LPT2.DOS=

[FontSubstitutes]
Helv=MS Sans Serif
Tms Rmn=MS Serif
Times=Times New Roman
Helvetica=Arial

[TrueType]

[Sounds]
SystemDefault=ding.wav, Default Beep
SystemExclamation=chord.wav, Exclamation
SystemStart=tada.wav, Windows Start
SystemExit=chimes.wav, Windows Exit
SystemHand=chord.wav, Critical Stop
SystemQuestion=chord.wav, Question


     Microsoft Diagnostics version 2.00    1/18/93    4:26pm    Page 18
=========================================================================
SystemAsterisk=chord.wav, Asterisk

[mci extensions]
wav=waveaudio
mid=sequencer
rmi=sequencer

[Compatibility]
NOTSHELL=0x0001
WPWINFIL=0x0006
CCMAIL=0x0008
AMIPRO=0x0010
REM=0x8022
PIXIE=0x0040
CP=0x0040
JW=0x42080
TME=0x0100
VB=0x0200
WIN2WRS=0x1210
PACKRAT=0x0800
VISION=0x0040
MCOURIER=0x0800      _BNOTES=0x24000
```

```
MILESV3=0x1000
PM4=0x2000
DESIGNER=0x2000
PLANNER=0x2000
DRAW=0x2000
WINSIM=0x2000
CHARISMA=0x2000
PR2=0x2000
PLUS=0x1000
ED=0x00010000
APORIA=0x0100
EXCEL=0x1000
GUIDE=0x1000
NETSET2=0x0100
W4GL=0x4000
W4GLR=0x4000
TURBOTAX=0x00080000


[Microsoft Word 2.0]
HPDSKJET=+1


[fonts]
Arial (TrueType)=ARIAL.FOT
Arial Bold (TrueType)=ARIALBD.FOT
Arial Bold Italic (TrueType)=ARIALBI.FOT
Arial Italic (TrueType)=ARIALI.FOT
Courier New (TrueType)=COUR.FOT
```

```
      Microsoft Diagnostics version 2.00    1/18/93    4:26pm    Page 19
===========================================================================
Courier New Bold (TrueType)=COURBD.FOT
Courier New Italic (TrueType)=COURI.FOT
Times New Roman (TrueType)=TIMES.FOT
Times New Roman Bold (TrueType)=TIMESBD.FOT
Times New Roman Bold Italic (TrueType)=TIMESBI.FOT
Times New Roman Italic (TrueType)=TIMESI.FOT
Courier New Bold Italic (TrueType)=COURBI.FOT
WingDings (TrueType)=WINGDING.FOT
MS Sans Serif 8,10,12,14,18,24 (VGA res)=SSERIFE.FON
Courier 10,12,15 (VGA res)=COURE.FON
MS Serif 8,10,12,14,18,24 (VGA res)=SERIFE.FON
Symbol 8,10,12,14,18,24 (VGA res)=SYMBOLE.FON
Roman (Plotter)=ROMAN.FON
Script (Plotter)=SCRIPT.FON
Modern (Plotter)=MODERN.FON
Small Fonts (VGA res)=SMALLE.FON
Symbol (TrueType)=SYMBOL.FOT
```

```
[embedding]
SoundRec=Sound,Sound,SoundRec.exe,picture
Package=Package,Package,packager.exe,picture
PBrush=Paintbrush Picture,Paintbrush Picture,pbrush.exe,picture

[Windows Help]
H_WindowPosition=[213,160,213,160,0]

[spooler]    window=110 110 526 298

[HPPCL5A,LPT1]
FontSummary=C:\WINDOWS\FS5LPT1.PCL

[PrinterPorts]
HP LaserJet III=hppcl5a,LPT1:,15,45
WINFAX=WINFAX,COM2:,15,45

[devices]
HP LaserJet III=hppcl5a,LPT1:
WINFAX=WINFAX,COM2:

[WINFAX]
Fax Path=C:\WINDOWS\winfax\
Fax Device=Class2
Paper Format=Letter (8.5 x 11 inches)
Orientation=Portrait
Dial Prefix=
Resolution=Standard
Retries=0
Call Progress=Yes
CSID=268.2416
Sender=Janet Ahlquist


    Microsoft Diagnostics version 2.00    1/18/93    4:26pm    Page 20
==========================================================================

    Header Left=Date: $D  Time:  $T
    Header Center=FAX from  $S
    Header Right=Page  $P  of   $N
    modem=
    Max Tx Rate=9600
    Retry Time=60
    Dial Control=None
    Volume=Low
    Speaker Mode=Off
    Dial Mode=Tone
    Partial Match=Yes
```

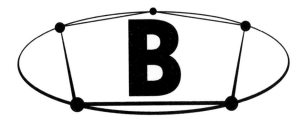

Login Scripts, NET.CFG, and Shell Command Parameters

Login Scripts

Login scripts set up the user's network environment. The system login script is run for every user. The commands set global values for all users.

User login scripts are specific to individual users. When there is no user login script a default user login script is run. These commands are in LOGIN.EXE and cannot be edited. This is the same login script the supervisor uses when he or she logs in for the first time.

The default user login script is:

```
WRITE "Good %GREETING_TIME, %LOGIN_NAME."

MAP DISPLAY OFF

MAP ERRORS OFF

Rem: Set 1st drive to most appropriate directory.

MAP *1:=SYS:;*1:=SYS:%LOGIN_NAME

If "%1"="SUPERVISOR" THEN MAP *1:=SYS:SYSTEM

Rem: Set search drives (S2 machine_OS dependent).

MAP INS S1:=SYS:PUBLIC

MAP INS S2:=S1:%MACHINE/%OS/%OS_VERSION

Rem: Now display all the current drive settings

MAP DISPLAY ON

MAP
```

System Login Script   This login script is an ASCII file, NET$LOG.DAT, which is in the PUBLIC directory. The system login script is created using SYSCON. The user must be supervisor or equivalent to access the system login script.

```
map display off
pccompatible
map ROOT h:=usr:users/%login_name
drive h:
map root s1:=sys:public
map root s2:=usr:appl/%os/%os_version
map s4:=usr:appl
map s5:=usr:appl
map s6:=usr:appl
map s7:=usr:appl
map root s8:=usr:winapps
comspec=s2:command.com
dos set prompt="$P$G"
```

User Login Script   This login script is an ASCII file residing in the user's MAIL directory. It is created and changed using SYSCON. The variables created are used in the menu. Each user who logs into the network must set similar variables that are used to inform the application about the hardware configuration and printing. In this example, the user has a Hercules monitor that has to be configured for Lotus.

```
dos set video="herclj"
dos set room="ad6a"
#capture j=ad6
exit "ad.bat"
```

Login Script Commands

The login script commands are the following:

ATTACH	BREAK	COMSPEC
DISPLAY	DOS BREAK	DOS SET
DOS VERIFY	DRIVE	EXIT
FDISPLAY	FIRE PHASERS	GOTO
IF..THEN..ELSE	INCLUDE	MACHINE
MAP	PAUSE	PCCOMPATIBLE
REMARK	SHIFT	WRITE

Variables Used with Login Script Commands

Variable	Function
CONDITIONAL	
ACCESS_SERVER	Returns TRUE if Access Server is functional else FALSE
ERROR_LEVEL	An Error Number, 0 if no errors
MEMBER OF "group"	TRUE if member else FALSE
DATE	
DAY	Number 01 – 31
DAY_OF_WEEK	Monday, Tuesday, etc.
MONTH	Number 01 – 12
MONTH_NAME	January, February, etc.
NDAY_OF_WEEK	Number 1 –7 with Sunday being day 1
SHORT_YEAR	90, 91, 92, etc.
YEAR	1990, 1991, 1992, etc.
DOS ENVIRONMENT	
< >	DOS environment variable
NETWORK	
NETWORK_ADDRESS	Number of network cable (8 hex digits)
FILE_SERVER	Name of file server

(continued)

Variable	Function
TIME	
AM_PM	Day or night (am or pm)
GREETING_TIME	Morning, afternoon, evening
HOUR	Number 1 – 12
HOUR24	Number 00 – 23 midnight is 00
MINUTE	Number 00 – 59
SECOND	Number 00 – 59
USER	
FULL_NAME	User's full name entered with SYSCON
LOGIN_NAME	User's login name
USER_ID	Number assigned to users at login
WORKSTATION	
MACHINE	The workstation the network shell identifies (IBMPC)
OS	The workstation's operating system
OS_VERSION	The version of DOS
P_STATION	Node address in 12 hex digits
SHELL_TYPE	The workstation's shell version
SMACHINE	Short workstation name (IBM)
STATION	Connection number

Rules that Apply to Login Script Commands

- Commands are limited to 150 characters.
- Long commands must wrap; do not use the Return Key.
- One command per line.
- Command can be in uppercase or lowercase.
- Variables enclosed in quotations must be preceded by a % and entered in uppercase.
- * or ; in the first column are treated as comments.
- Use conditional variables only with IF..THEN.

The external execution command is #. A DOS or NetWare command can be executed with the #.

```
#[path] filename parameters

#CAPTURE J=123
```

The login script is held in memory until the external command execution is complete.

Login Script Command Syntax	### ATTACH

ATTACH

```
ATTACH [fileserver[/username[;password]]]
```

```
ATTACH TEST/SUPERVISOR
```

The supervisor is attached to the file server TEST and also stays logged into the current server. In this situation, the supervisor would be prompted to enter a password. A user can attach up to 8 file servers.

BREAK

```
BREAK ON¦OFF
```

With BREAK ON, the user can use the CTRL-C or CTRL-BREAK keys to abort the login script execution. BREAK OFF is the default.

COMSPEC

```
COMSPEC=[path] filename
```

The COMSPEC command is used to specify the directory that loads COMMAND.COM.

DISPLAY

```
DISPLAY [directory] filename
```

This command displays the contents of the file during login (for example, DISPLAY SYS:PUBLIC/NEWS/MONDAY.TXT).

DOS BREAK

```
DOS BREAK [ON ¦ OFF]
```

DOS BREAK is used to control the ability of DOS to recognize the CTRL-BREAK keys. The default is DOS BREAK OFF.

DOS SET

```
[option] [DOS] SET name = "value"
```

This option can be replaced with LOCAL, TEMP, or TEMPORARY. Setting these variables does not affect the PC environment. This command is similar to the DOS SET command.

DOS VERIFY

```
DOS VERIFY [ON ¦ OFF]
```

This command verifies that data copied to a local drive can be read. The default is OFF.

DRIVE

```
DRIVE [d: ¦ *n:]
```

d is replaced with a local or network drive letter. n is replaced with a drive number. This command is used to set the default drive.

EXIT

```
EXIT ["filename"]
```

EXIT terminates the login script execution. When a filename with an extension of .COM, .EXE., or BAT is used the login script executes the command.

FDISPLAY

```
FDISPLAY [directory/]filename
```

FDISPLAY will display a file on a monitor. For example, to display a message for a specific group during log-on the command would be:

```
IF MEMBER OF "STAFF" THEN FDISPLAY SYS:PUBLIC/NEWS/SALES.TXT
```

FIRE PHASERS n TIMES

This command causes the computer to make a phaser-like sound to alert the user that something has happened. Phasers can go off every time a user logs in or they may be set to a specific situation—for example, when the day of the week is Friday.

GOTO label

The GOTO command is used to branch to specific login script commands. This command functions much like a GOTO statement does using DOS or a programming language.

IF...THEN...ELSE

```
IF condition(s) [AND|OR|NOR] conditional(s)
THEN command ELSE command END
```

This command can be very complex with many login script commands or only one line. An example of each is:

```
IF LOGIN_NAME="SUPERVISOR" THEN EXIT


IF DAY_OF_WEEK="Friday" THEN
FDISPLAY SYS:PUBLIC/NEWS/FRIDAY.TXT
ELSE
WRITE "Keep at it!"
END
```

There are many variables that can be used in the IF...THEN...ELSE statements. The following table lists the NetWare variables and their function. DOS variables can also be used but are enclosed in angle brackets.

Variable	Function
Conditional	
ACCESS_SERVER	TRUE if Access Server is functional else FALSE
ERROR_LEVEL	An Error Number, 0 indicates no errors
	This is like the DOS errorlevel function
MEMBER OF "group"	TRUE or FALSE
Date	
DAY	number 01 – 31
DAY_OF_WEEK	Monday, etc.
MONTH	number 01 – 12
MONTH_NAME	January, etc.
NDAY_OF_WEEK	1 – 7 where Sunday is 1
SHORT_YEAR	92, 93, etc.
YEAR	1992, 1993, etc.
DOS Environment	
< >	Any DOS environment variable
Network	
NETWORK_ADDRESS	Number of network cable (8 hex digits)
FILE_SERVER	File server name

(continued)

Variable	Function
Time	
AM_PM	Day or night
GREETING_TIME	Morning, afternoon, evening
HOUR	Number 1 - 12
HOUR24	Number 00 - 23 where 00 is midnight
MINUTE	Number 00 - 59
SECOND	Number 00 - 59
User	
FULL_NAME	Full name of user from SYSCON
LOGIN_NAME	Login name from SYSCON
USER_ID	Number assigned to users
Workstation	
MACHINE	The computer type, e.g. IBMPC
OS	Version of computer's operating system, e.g. MSDOS
OS_VERSION	Version of DOS
P_STATION	The node address in 12 hex digits (for Ethernet it is the Ethernet address)
SHELL_TYPE	Version of computer's shell program
SMACHINE	Short machine name, e.g. IBM
STATION	Connection number such as 01, 02, etc which is assigned at log in

Notes: Variables have relationships to values in an IF...THEN...ELSE statement. These relationships are: equal to, not equal to, greater than, less than, greater than or equal to, and less than or equal to. Some notations for these conditions are: IS, IS NOT, =, <>, and EQUALS. Some example commands are:

IF P_STATION="000000000011" THEN
WRITE "Report any network problems to the lab assistant"
END

IF "%ERROR_LEVEL"="0" THEN
MAP SYS:DATA/ACCTG
ELSE
MAP SYS:DATA/SALES
END

INCLUDE

```
INCLUDE [path]filename
```

This command allows for subscripts to be executed during the login process. The filename has login script commands that are executed. An example command is:

```
IF MEMBER OF "STAFF" THEN
INCLUDE SYS:STAFF/STAFF.LOG
END
```

This would preclude the need to have individual login scripts for the staff.

MACHINE

```
MACHINE = "name"
```

The default name for IBM compatibles is IBM_PC. Some software such as NETBIOS may require this variable.

MAP

```
MAP [option][drive:= [path[:,.,][variable]
```

```
Option can be replaced with
DISPLAY ON/OFF
ROOT
ERRORS ON/OFF
INS
DEL
```

Drive can be any valid network or local drive. The path is replaced with a valid DOS drive letter or NetWare path that includes volume name. Variable can be replaced with the following:

```
OS
OS_VERSION
MACHINE
SMACHINE
```

OS and OS_VERSION are determined by the operating system. MACHINE or SMACHINE is assigned in NET.CFG which is discussed later in this Appendix. Some example commands using MAP include the following:

```
MAP drive:=directory
```

This maps a logical drive letter to a directory.

```
MAP drive:=drive
```

This maps two drive letters to the same directory.

```
MAP INS search drive:=directory
```

Search drives function the way the DOS PATH does. Search drives begin with the letter "Z" and go through the alphabet. When a command is executed and unless specified, the default directory is searched and then the search drives beginning with "Z".

```
MAP ROOT drive:=directory
```

A fake root directory is created at this directory level. This shortens the path and prevents access to higher levels of the directory. For example, MAP ROOT H:=USR:/USERS, would make USERS the root. A user would not be able to access the real root.

```
MAP DISPLAY OFF
```

This prevents displaying the mapping as the commands are executed. Setting it to ON would display the mapping.

```
MAP ERRORS OFF
```

This prevents the displaying of any error messages when a map command is executed. Using ON would allow the errors to be displayed.

PAUSE OR WAIT

This command pauses the login process to allow a message to be read without it being passed by. The message, "Strike a key when ready..." is displayed.

[PC]COMPATIBLE

This command is useful when using more than one version of DOS. A TANDY computer may boot with TANDY DOS but once logged on the network use MSDOS.

REM[ARK] [TEXT] OR * OR ;

There are three ways to enter comment statements in a login script.

SHIFT

```
SHIFT [n]
```

Command line arguments such as %0, %1, %2, up to %9 can be used with commands such as LOGIN. The SHIFT command permits you to enter these arguments in any order. An example of SHIFT and the command parameters is:

```
LOGIN SERVER1/JSMITH WP
```

```
SERVER1 is %0
JSMITH  is %1
WP      is %2
```

A partial login script might have:

```
IF "%2"= "WP" THEN MAP P:=USR:/APPL/WP
```

The SHIFT command allows this same command to work with the following login command which does not have the file server name.

```
LOGIN JSMITH WP
```

With the SHIFT command WP is the %2 parameter.

WRITE

```
WRITE "text"
```

The WRITE command is used to write information to the screen. Text must be in double quotes. The following characters have the functions as described:

\r	is a carriage return
\n	move the cursor to a new line
\"	used to embed quotations
\7	sounds a beep
;	concatenates text
*/%	multiply, divide, modulo
+-	add, subtract
>><<	Truncate left or right — for example, "12345">>2 becomes "123"

Variable can be used in the text when preceded with the percent "%" or within the brackets <>. Some examples are:

```
WRITE "Path is %<path>"


WRITE "Good %GREETING_TIME, %LOGIN_NAME"
```

Configuring a Workstation with NET.CFG

NET.CFG

NET.CFG is an ASCII file that changes the default setting of workstation shells. It functions much like CONFIG.SYS. NET.CFG may also be required by some applications such as databases, electronic mail, or NETBIOS. NET.CFG, if used, must be accessible when the workstation executes the shells. Using a NET.CFG file implies that the default settings for NETX.COM, LSL.COM, IPXODI.COM, and NETBIOS will be changed. This should only be performed with a great deal of care. For the purpose of discussion, a table of NET.CFG options is provided with default settings. The LAN driver information refers to the network interface card settings and the software.

LAN Driver

Settings	Default Value
LINK DRIVER drivername	
DMA [#1 ¦ #2] channel_number	
INT [#1 ¦ #2] interrupt_request_number	
MEM [#1 ¦ #2] hex_starting_address [hex_length]	
PORT [#1 ¦ #2] hex_starting_address [hex_number_of_ports]	
NODE ADDRESS hex_address	
SLOT number	
FRAME frame_type	
PROTOCOL name hex_protocol_ID frame_type	
SAPS number	
LINK STATIONS number	
ALTERNATE	
MAX FRAME SIZE number	
CONNECTOR DIX	

(continued)

Settings	Default Value

Link Support Layer

LINK SUPPORT
    BUFFERS communication_number[size]
    MEMPOOL number [k]
    MAX BOARDS number [size]
    MAX STACKS number

Protocol

PROTOCOL protocol_name
    BIND #board_number

NETBIOS.EXE

NETBIOS ABORT TIMEOUT= n	540 (30 seconds)
NETBIOS BROADCAST COUNT=n	2
NETBIOS BROADCAST DELAY=n	18 (1 second)
NETBIOS COMMANDS=n	ON
NETBIOS INTERNET=on/off	ON
NETBIOS LISTEN TIMEOUT=n	108 (6 seconds)
NETBIOS RECEIVE BUFFERS=n	6
NETBIOS RETRY COUNT=n	10 (1 second)
NETBIOS RETRY DELAY=n	10 (1 second)
NETBIOS SEND BUFFERS=n	6
NETBIOS SESSION=n	32
NETBIOS VERIFY TIMEOUT=n	54 (3 seconds)
NPATCH=byte offset,value	

NETX.COM

ALL SERVERS=on/off	OFF
CACHE BUFFERS=n	5 blocks
DOS NAME=name	DRDOS
ENVIRONMENT PAD=n	17
EOJ=on/off	ON
FILE HANDLES=n	40 open files

(continued)

Settings	Default Value
GET LOCAL TARGET STACKS=n	1
HOLD=on/off	OFF
LOCAL PRINTERS=n	# of ports
LOCK DELAY=n	1
LOCK RETRIES=n	3
LONG MACHINE TYPE=name	IBM_PC
MAX CUR DIR LENGTH=n	64
MAX PATH LENGTH=n	255
MAX TASKS=n	31
PATCH=byte offset, value	
PB BUFFERS=n	
PREFERRED SERVER=name	
PRINT HEADER=n	64 bytes
PRINT TAIL=n	16 bytes
READ ONLY COMPATIBILITY=on/off	OFF
SEARCH MODE=n	1
SET STATION TIME=on/off	ON
SHARE=on/off	ON
SHORT MACHINE TYPE=name	IBM
SHOW DOTS=on/off	OFF
SPECIAL UPPERCASE=on/off	OFF
TASK MODE=n	2

IPXODI.COM

CONFIG OPTION=n	
INT64=on/off	ON
INT7A=on/off	ON
IPATCH=byte offset, value	
IPX PACKET SIZE LIMIT=n	4160 or set by LAN driver
IPX RETRY COUNT=n	20
IPX SOCKETS=n	20
SPX ABORT TIMEOUT=n	540 (30 seconds)
SPX CONNECTIONS=n	15
SPX LISTEN TIMEOUT=n	108 (6 seconds)
SPX VERIFY TIMEOUT=n	54 (3 seconds)

Shell Command Parameters

Workstation shells have parameters that can be used with NETX, IPX, LSL, and NETBIOS. The following list shows the file and parameter and the result of using the parameter.

```
NETX/C=[path\]filename
```

The /C parameter specifies the NET.CFG file to use. This parameter also works with IPXODI and LSL.

```
NETX/F
```

This forcibly unloads the shell NETX. This works only with NETX.

```
NETX/I
```

The /I displays the shell version information and works with the other shells.

```
NETX/PS=
```

The parameter selects the file server and works only with NETX.

```
NETX/U
```

Unloads the shell if no other terminate-and-stay resident programs are loaded above the shell. This works with all shells except IPX.

```
NETX/?
```

Displays information and works for all shells except NETBIOS.

```
IPX/O#
```

The /O# loads the shell with the specified hardware option #. This works only with IPX.

A Sample NET.CFG File

```
#
# Sample NET.CFG file:
#   Please modify to match your hardware and software environment.
#


#
# Protocol Stack Section:
#
Protocol Stack IPX
    Bind NI5210
```

```
#
# Link Driver Section: Remove the '#' sign where appropriate
#    Required fields: Port, Int, Mem.
#
Link Driver NI5210
     Port 330
     Int 5
     Mem CC000 400
#    Node Address XXXXXXXXXXX
     Protocol IPX 0 Ethernet_802.3
     Frame Ethernet_802.3
#
spx connections=60
```

DOS Batch File Menus, DOS Text Screens, and the GETNUM Utility

The GETNUM utility is a DOS batch file that is used as a menu for a network of 200 computers. The computers are monochrome 8088, VGA 80286, and VGA 80386. Some computers have floppy and hard drives while others have one floppy drive only. All computers log onto the network from disk, so no boot PROMs are used.

This menu is used by all computers on the network. The menu requires that DOS variables be used and menu options created that provide the user the ability to select the floppy drive.

The general operation of the menu is that a text file is displayed from which the user selects an option by entering a number between 0 – 9. GETNUM translates the number into a DOS ERRORLEVEL code and the menu then branches to the location associated with that ERRORLEVEL.

Each workstation sets DOS environment variables through AUTOEXEC.BAT, which are then used by the menu.

The advantage of using DOS commands is that most system administrators can create this type of menu and maintain it. It is a no-cost menu solution. The limitation is that the DOS commands are limited to the lowest DOS version used on the network. While DOS 5 has useful commands, they do not all work on a machine with DOS 3.1. DOS commands are limited whereas commercial menu systems have many commands that use network functions. For example, some commercial menus can determine the network shells loaded and make calls directly to the network operating system.

```
========================================================================
ECHO OFF
REM ;   THIS IS THE MENUING SYSTEM FOR FILE SERVER CC
REM ;
REM ;                       FILE NAME   AD.BAT
REM ;
REM ;
REM ;   VIRSTOP.EXE is a virus checking program.

VIRSTOP

REM ;   SWATCHER.EXE is a TSR loaded to track the use of application
REM ;   software.  This is a BrightWorks product.

F:SWATCHER

CLS
PROMPT $p$g
REM ;   NEWS1 is a text file which is displayed when a user first
REM ;   logs onto the network.  It informs users of items like lab
REM ;   hours and general information about the network.
TYPE X:NEWS1
PAUSE > NUL

REM ;   This section determines the floppy drive which the user
REM ;   will be using.

:DRIVE
    CLS
        CAPTURE J=%ROOM% TI=5 > NUL
        TYPE X:DRIVES.TXT

REM ;   GETNUM.COM is a program to monitor the keyboard for a
REM ;   numeric which corresponds to a menu option.  For example,
REM ;   49 corresponds to menu option 1.

GETNUM
IF ERRORLEVEL 57 GOTO EXIT
IF ERRORLEVEL 56 GOTO EXIT
IF ERRORLEVEL 55 GOTO EXIT
IF ERRORLEVEL 54 GOTO EXIT
IF ERRORLEVEL 53 GOTO EXIT
IF ERRORLEVEL 52 GOTO EXIT
IF ERRORLEVEL 51 GOTO EXIT
IF ERRORLEVEL 50 GOTO DRIVEB
IF ERRORLEVEL 49 GOTO DRIVEA
IF ERRORLEVEL 48 GOTO EXIT
:DRIVEA
    SET DRIVE=A:
    GOTO TOP
```

```
:DRIVEB
    SET DRIVE=B:

REM ;  This section displays the first list of menu options.

:TOP
    CLS
        TYPE X:MAIN.TXT
GETNUM
IF ERRORLEVEL 57 GOTO DOS
IF ERRORLEVEL 56 GOTO NETWORK
IF ERRORLEVEL 55 GOTO MISC
IF ERRORLEVEL 54 GOTO TYPING
IF ERRORLEVEL 53 GOTO CS
IF ERRORLEVEL 52 GOTO ACCT
IF ERRORLEVEL 51 GOTO DBASE
IF ERRORLEVEL 50 GOTO SS
IF ERRORLEVEL 49 GOTO WP
IF ERRORLEVEL 48 GOTO EXIT
GOTO DRIVE

REM ;  This is the word processing section of the menu.

:WP
    CLS
        TYPE X:WORD.TXT
GETNUM
IF ERRORLEVEL 57 GOTO DRIVE
IF ERRORLEVEL 56 GOTO DRIVE
IF ERRORLEVEL 55 GOTO DRIVE
IF ERRORLEVEL 54 GOTO DRIVE
IF ERRORLEVEL 53 GOTO WS6
IF ERRORLEVEL 52 GOTO WS4
IF ERRORLEVEL 51 GOTO WORKS
IF ERRORLEVEL 50 GOTO WORD
IF ERRORLEVEL 49 GOTO WP51
IF ERRORLEVEL 48 GOTO DRIVE

REM ;  WordPerfect

:WP51
    CLS
    ECHO LOADING WP51......      INSERT YOUR DATA DISK in %DRIVE%
    PAUSE
    CD V:\APPL\WP51
    %DRIVE%
    WP/NC/NT=1/U-%ROOM%/D-%DRIVE%
    CD V:\APPL
    H:
    GOTO DRIVE

REM ;  MS-Word Word requires that the graphics driver be determined
REM ;   and that is the function of GRPHXCRD
```

```
:WORD
    CLS
    ECHO LOADING  WORD 5.5 ....   INSERT YOUR DATA DISK IN %DRIVE%
    PAUSE
    CD V:\APPL\WORD
    SET MSWNET55=%DRIVE%
    GRPHXCRD
    IF ERRORLEVEL 10 GOTO ENDWORD
    IF ERRORLEVEL  9 GOTO WORDVGA
    IF ERRORLEVEL  8 GOTO ENDWORD
    IF ERRORLEVEL  7 GOTO WORDHGC
    IF ERRORLEVEL  6 GOTO ENDWORD
    IF ERRORLEVEL  5 GOTO ENDWORD
    IF ERRORLEVEL  4 GOTO ENDWORD
    IF ERRORLEVEL  3 GOTO ENDWORD
    IF ERRORLEVEL  2 GOTO ENDWORD
    IF ERRORLEVEL  1 GOTO ENDWORD
    GOTO ENDWORD
:WORDVGA
    CLS
    NCOPY V:VGA.VID   H:SCREEN.VID  > NUL
    NCOPY V:MW.INI    H:            > NUL
    WORD/N
    GOTO ENDWORD


:WORDHGC
    NCOPY V:HERCLJ.VID   H:SCREEN.VID  > NUL
    NCOPY V:MONO.INI   H:MW.INI      > NUL
    V:WORD/N
    GOTO ENDWORD



:ENDWORD
    CD V:\APPL
    H:
    DEL H:*.INI  > NUL
    DEL H:*.VID  > NUL
    GOTO DRIVE

REM ;  MS-Works

:WORKS
    CLS
    ECHO LOADING WORKS......    PLACE YOUR DATA DISK IN %DRIVE%
    CD V:\APPL\MSWORKS
    WORKS/N %DRIVE% /G %VIDEO%.VID
    CD V:\APPL
    H:
    GOTO DRIVE
```

```
REM ;   WordStar 4

:WS4
    CLS
    ECHO LOADING WORDSTAR 4.....  PLACE YOUR DATA DISK IN %DRIVE%
    PAUSE
    CD V:\APPL\WS4
    WS
    CD V:\APPL
    H:
    GOTO DRIVE

REM ;   WordStar 6

:WS6
    CLS
    ECHO LOADING WORDSTAR 6......  PLACE YOUR DATA DISK IN %DRIVE%
    PAUSE
    CD V:\APPL\WS6
    CD U:\APPL\WS6\PREVIEW
    WS /=MONO.CFG
    CD U:\APPL
    CD V:\APPL
    H:
    GOTO DRIVE
:WSVGA
    T:RDB
    GOTO ENDWS

:ENDWS
    MAP DEL S5:  > NUL
    MAP DEL S4:  > NUL
    MAP DEL S3:  > NUL
    GOTO DRIVE
;************************************************************
;*              end wordprocessing                         *
;************************************************************
;*              begin spreadsheets                         *
;************************************************************
:SS
    CLS
        TYPE X:SS.TXT
GETNUM
IF ERRORLEVEL 57 GOTO DRIVE
IF ERRORLEVEL 56 GOTO DRIVE
IF ERRORLEVEL 55 GOTO DRIVE
IF ERRORLEVEL 54 GOTO DRIVE
IF ERRORLEVEL 53 GOTO DRIVE
IF ERRORLEVEL 52 GOTO ALLWAYS
```

```
IF ERRORLEVEL 51 GOTO SSWORKS
IF ERRORLEVEL 50 GOTO PGRAPH
IF ERRORLEVEL 49 GOTO LOTUS
IF ERRORLEVEL 48 GOTO DRIVE

REM ;  Lotus 1-2-3 r2

:LOTUS
    CLS
    ECHO LOADING LOTUS......    PLACE YOUR DATA DISK IN %DRIVE%
    PAUSE
    MAP S7:=USR:LOTSHARE/123.V22 > NUL
    CD V:\APPL\L123R22
    CD U:\APPL\L123R22\ALLWAYS
    %DRIVE%
    V:123 %VIDEO%
    CD V:\APPL
    CD U:\APPL
    MAP DEL S7:  > NUL
    H:
    GOTO DRIVE

REM ;  Note that the time out parameter is increased because it
REM ;  takes longer to print graphics.

:PGRAPH
    CLS
    ECHO LOADING PGRAPH ......    INSERT YOUR DATA DISK.
    CD V:\APPL\L123R22
    CAPTURE J=%ROOM% TI=40 > NUL
    PGRAPH %VIDEO%
    CD V:\APPL
    H:
    CAPTURE J=%ROOM% TI=5  > NUL
    GOTO DRIVE

REM ;  This option calls Works from the word processing section.

:SSWORKS
    GOTO WORKS

REM ;  This is Allways for Lotus 1-2-3 v2

:ALLWAYS
    CLS
    ECHO LOADING LOTUS......    PLACE YOUR DATA DISK IN %DRIVE%
    PAUSE
    CAPTURE J=%ROOM% TI=40  > NUL
    MAP S7:=USR:LOTSHARE/123.V22 > NUL
```

```
CD V:\APPL\L123R22
CD U:\APPL\L123R22\ALLWAYS
%DRIVE%
V:123 %VIDEO%
CD V:\APPL
CD U:\APPL
MAP DEL S7:  > NUL
H:
CAPTURE J=%ROOM% TI=5  > NUL
GOTO DRIVE


;*****************************************************************
;*                  END SPREADSHEETS
;*****************************************************************
;*                  BEGIN DBASE
;*****************************************************************

REM ;  This section on dBASE IV seems a bit confusing but
REM ;  illustrates a typical work-around.  The issue is
REM ;  that computers in room 127 have 512 RAM and the version
REM ;  of dBASE which was used for other users would not load.

:DBASE
        IF %ROOM%.==. GOTO OLDDBASE
        IF %ROOM%==127 GOTO TEMPDB4
        GOTO GETCHOICE

:TEMPDB4
        CLS
        TYPE X:DBASE2.TXT
        GOTO GETCHOICE

:OLDDBASE
        CLS
        TYPE X:DBASE.TXT

:GETCHOICE
GETNUM
IF ERRORLEVEL 57 GOTO DRIVE
IF ERRORLEVEL 56 GOTO DRIVE
IF ERRORLEVEL 55 GOTO DRIVE
IF ERRORLEVEL 54 GOTO DRIVE
IF ERRORLEVEL 53 GOTO DRIVE
IF ERRORLEVEL 52 GOTO LOISDB4
IF ERRORLEVEL 51 GOTO DBSAMP
IF ERRORLEVEL 50 GOTO DBIII
IF ERRORLEVEL 49 GOTO DBIV
IF ERRORLEVEL 48 GOTO DRIVE
GOTO DRIVE
```

```
:LOISDB4
      CLS
    ECHO       INSERT YOUR DATA DISK
    ECHO .
    PAUSE
      SET DBTMP=C:
      SET DBHEAP=95
      CD V:\APPL\DBASE4\DBSAMPLE
    %DRIVE%
      V:DBASE -T
    CD V:\APPL
    H:
      SET DBHEAP=
    GOTO DRIVE

REM ;  This section could be removed but it is worthwhile to
REM ;  leave old statements in until the new statements are
REM ;  working.  Part of the reason this code does not work
REM ;  is that the room was reconfigured.  There were two printers
REM ;  and now there is one.  Also, the application (APPL)
REM ;  directory structure was changed.

:DBIV
    CLS
    ECHO  NOT READY AT THIS TIME
    ECHO.
    ECHO.
    PAUSE
    GOTO DRIVE
    ECHO LOADING DBASE......    PLACE YOUR DATA DISK IN DRIVE A.
    MAP INS S3:=SYS:APPL/CC/DBASE  > NUL
    MAP T:=S3:   > NUL
REM     MAP INS S4:=SYS:APPL/DBASE/SQLHOME  > NUL
REM     MAP INS S5:=SYS:APPL/DBASE/SAMPLES  > NUL
REM     MAP INS S6:=SYS:APPL/DBASE/DBTUTOR  > NUL
REM     CAPTURE Q=%QUEUE% NB TI=2  NFF > NUL

    IF %USER_NAME%==122 CAPTURE J=DBASE-HP122N
    IF %USER_NAME%==22N CAPTURE J=DBASE-HP122N
    T:DBASE /T
  REM     MAP DEL S6:  > NUL
  REM     MAP DEL S5:  > NUL
  REM     MAP DEL S4:  > NUL
    MAP DEL S3:  > NUL
    MAP DEL T:   > NUL

    GOTO DRIVE
```

```
REM :  dBASE III

:DBIII
    CLS
    ECHO        INSERT YOUR DATA DISK
    ECHO .
    PAUSE
    V:
    CD\APPL\DBASEIII
    DBASE
    CD\APPL
    H:
    GOTO DRIVE

REM :  This is the educational version of dBASE IV.

:DBSAMP
    CLS
    ECHO        INSERT YOUR DATA DISK
    ECHO .
    PAUSE
    SET DBHEAP=75
    CD V:\APPL\DBSAMPLR
    %DRIVE%
    V:DBASE -T
    CD V:\APPL
    H:
    SET DBHEAP=
    GOTO DRIVE

REM  :                      BEGIN ACCOUNTING

:ACCT
    CLS
    TYPE X:ACCT.TXT
GETNUM
IF ERRORLEVEL 57 GOTO DRIVE
IF ERRORLEVEL 56 GOTO DRIVE
IF ERRORLEVEL 55 GOTO DRIVE
IF ERRORLEVEL 54 GOTO ACCTSIM
IF ERRORLEVEL 53 GOTO SOUNDS
IF ERRORLEVEL 52 GOTO PEACH
IF ERRORLEVEL 51 GOTO GLAS
IF ERRORLEVEL 50 GOTO CBPI
IF ERRORLEVEL 49 GOTO ATB
IF ERRORLEVEL 48 GOTO DRIVE
GOTO DRIVE
```

```
REM ;  ATB is Accounts Trial Balance

:ATB
    CLS
    ECHO    LOADING   ATB.......  INSERT YOUR DATA DISK
    ECHO .
    PAUSE
    CD V:\APPL\ATB3
    CD U:\APPL\ATB3\ATB3_SYS
    MAP S8:=CCMAIN/USR:APPL\ATB3\CLIENTS  > NUL
    V:
    ATB3
    CD V:\APPL
    CD U:\APPL
    MAP DEL S8: > NUL
    H:
    GOTO DRIVE


:CBPI
    cls
    echo  not installed yet.
    pause > nul
    GOTO DRIVE
    MAP INS S3:=SYS:APPL/CC/CBPI  > NUL
    MAP T:=S3:  > NUL
    T:CBPI
    MAP REM S3:  > NUL
    MAP REM T:   > NUL
    GOTO DRIVE

:GLAS
    CLS
    ECHO Place your General Ledger disk # 1 in A: Space Key to go.
    ECHO.
    PAUSE > NUL
    A:
    GLAS
    H:
    GOTO DRIVE

:PEACH
    CLS
    ECHO .... Place your data disk in drive A: ...Space Key to go.
    PAUSE > NUL
    CD V:\APPL\NETPCIII
    CD U:\APPL\NETPCIII\PCDATA
    SET PC3ID=AA
    V:
```

```
        NETPEACH
        CD V:\APPL
        CD U:\APPL
        H:
        GOTO DRIVE

:SOUNDS
        CLS
        ECHO Place your data disk in drive A.... Space Key to go.
        PAUSE > NUL
            IF NOT EXIST A:BASICA.COM COPY X:BASICA.* A:
        A:
        BASICA CAS
        H:
        GOTO DRIVE

:ACCTSIM
        CLS
        ECHO .... Place your data disk in drive A.... Space Key to go.
        PAUSE  > NUL
        CD V:\APPL\ACCTSIM
        GWBASIC CONTROL
        CD V:\APPL
        H:
        GOTO DRIVE

REM :                        BEGIN COMPUTER SCIENCE
REM : These applications run differently than the others.
REM : A programming environment has been created where
REM : students access an editor and programming compilers.
REM : CSC is a program which puts the student in this
REM : environment.  Students have access to Pascal, Fortran,
REM : COBOL, and RPG.

:CS
        CLS
        ECHO -          YOU'RE ENTERING THE WORLD OF
        ECHO --              COMPUTER SCIENCE
        ECHO ---
        \APPL\COSCI\CSC
        GOTO DRIVE




REM :                        BEGIN KEYBOARDING
REM :

:TYPING
        CLS
        TYPE X:KEY.TXT
```

```
GETNUM
IF ERRORLEVEL 57 GOTO DRIVE
IF ERRORLEVEL 56 GOTO DRIVE
IF ERRORLEVEL 55 GOTO DRIVE
IF ERRORLEVEL 54 GOTO DRIVE
IF ERRORLEVEL 53 GOTO DRIVE
IF ERRORLEVEL 52 GOTO DRIVE
IF ERRORLEVEL 51 GOTO DRIVE
IF ERRORLEVEL 50 GOTO MKC
IF ERRORLEVEL 49 GOTO MKW
IF ERRORLEVEL 48 GOTO DRIVE

:MKW
    CLS
    ECHO LOADING MICROKEY......  PLACE YOUR DATA DISK IN DRIVE  A.
    PAUSE > NUL
    ECHO.
    ECHO  SPACE KEY TO CONTINUE
    CD V:\APPL\MKEYWORD > NUL
    V:MENUT40
    H:
    GOTO DRIVE


:MKC
    CLS
    ECHO LOADING  MICRO KEYBOARD .... PLACE YOUR DISK IN DRIVE A:.
    ECHO.
    ECHO.  SPACE KEY TO CONTINUE.
    PAUSE  > NUL
    A:
    MK
    H:
    GOTO DRIVE

REM ;                             BEGIN MISCELLANEOUS

:MISC
    CLS
    TYPE X:MISC.TXT

GETNUM
IF ERRORLEVEL 57 GOTO ENABLE45
IF ERRORLEVEL 56 GOTO KERMIT
IF ERRORLEVEL 55 GOTO MPP
IF ERRORLEVEL 54 GOTO GERMAN
IF ERRORLEVEL 53 GOTO PM
IF ERRORLEVEL 52 GOTO MINITAB
IF ERRORLEVEL 51 GOTO TKSOLVER
```

```
IF ERRORLEVEL 50 GOTO ENABLE
IF ERRORLEVEL 49 GOTO MC
IF ERRORLEVEL 48 GOTO DRIVE
GOTO DRIVE

:MC
     CLS
     U:
     CD\APPL\MICROCAL\DATA
     V:
     CD\APPL\MICROCAL
     TYPE X:MICRO.TXT

GETNUM
IF ERRORLEVEL 57 GOTO DRIVE
IF ERRORLEVEL 56 GOTO DRIVE
IF ERRORLEVEL 55 GOTO DRIVE
IF ERRORLEVEL 54 GOTO DRIVE
IF ERRORLEVEL 53 GOTO DRIVE
IF ERRORLEVEL 52 GOTO DRIVE
IF ERRORLEVEL 51 GOTO MCC
IF ERRORLEVEL 50 GOTO MCB
IF ERRORLEVEL 49 GOTO MCA
IF ERRORLEVEL 48 GOTO DRIVE
GOTO DRIVE

REM : Microcalc is a math application which has three parts
REM : A, B, and C.

:MCA
     MCA
     GOTO ENDMC

:MCB
     MCB
     GOTO ENDMC
:MCC
     MCC
     GOTO ENDMC

:ENDMC
     U:
     CD\APPL
     V:
     CD\APPL
     H:
     GOTO DRIVE
```

```
:MINITAB
     CLS
     CD V:\APPL\MINITAB
     CD U:\APPL\MINITAB\DATA
     V:MTB61_A %1 %2 %3 %4 %5 %6
     CD V:\APPL
     CD U:\APPL
     H:
     GOTO DRIVE

:ENABLE
     CLS
     ECHO  To save your work you must include the 'A:' or 'B:'
     ECHO  in your statement.  SAVE 'A:MYFILE' or  SAVE 'B:MYFILE'
     ECHO  This is also true for the  OUTFILE command.
     ECHO .
     PAUSE
     CD V:\APPL\ENABLE
     V:ENABLE (V:,V:,V:,V:,%DRIVE%),I=%ID%
     CD V:\APPL
     H:
     GOTO DRIVE

REM ;  This is an application used for math and physics students.

:TKSOLVER
     CLS
     CD V:\APPL\TKSOLVER
     V:TK
     CD V:\APPL
     H:
     GOTO DRIVE

REM ;  PageMaker 3  using a runtime version of Windows 2.
REM ;  The menu determines if the student is in room 123
REM ;  before running the program.

:PM
     CLS
     IF NOT %ROOM%==123 GOTO PMMSG
     CD V:\APPL\PMCLASS
     CD U:\APPL\PMCLASS\PCLFONTS
     MAP P:=USR:APPL/PMCLASS/VGA > NUL
     MAP L:=USR:APPL/PMCLASS/CLIPART > NUL
     MAP M:=USR:APPL/PMCLASS/PCLFONTS > NUL
     SET TEMP=C:\WINDOWS\TEMP
     CAPTURE J=123 TI=45  > NUL
     M:
     PM
     CAPTURE J=123 TI=5
     H:
```

```
        MAP DEL M: > NUL
        MAP DEL L: > NUL
        MAP DEL P: > NUL
        CD V:\APPL
        CD U:\APPL
        GOTO DRIVE


:GERMAN
        CLS
        ECHO    Place your data disk in drive A:
        ECHO.
        PAUSE  > NUL
        ECHO    Space key to continue.
        A:
        GO
        H:

REM :  This is a math application.

:MPP
        CLS
        ECHO Put your data disk (3 1/2") in drive B:
        ECHO.
        PAUSE > NUL
        ECHO Space key to continue.
        CAPTURE J=%ROOM% TI=30 > NUL
        CD V:\APPL\MPP
        CD U:\APPL\MPP\EXAMPLES
        V:MPP
        CD V:\APPL
        CD U:\APPL
        CAPTURE J=%ROOM% TI=5  > NUL
        H:
        GOTO DRIVE

:KERMIT
        CLS
        CD V:\APPL\KERMIT
        KERMIT
        CD V:\APPL
        H:
        GOTO DRIVE

:ENABLE45
        CLS
        CD V:\APPL\ENAB
        EN45DEMO
        CD V:\APPL
        H:
        GOTO DRIVE
```

```
REM ;                              BEGIN  NETWORK
REM ;  Provide menu access to NetWare utilities.

:NETWORK
     CLS
     TYPE X:NETWORK.TXT

GETNUM
IF ERRORLEVEL 57 GOTO DRIVE
IF ERRORLEVEL 56 GOTO DRIVE
IF ERRORLEVEL 55 GOTO DRIVE
IF ERRORLEVEL 54 GOTO DRIVE
IF ERRORLEVEL 53 GOTO DRIVE
IF ERRORLEVEL 52 GOTO DRIVE
IF ERRORLEVEL 51 GOTO GRAPHICS
IF ERRORLEVEL 50 GOTO ENDCAP
IF ERRORLEVEL 49 GOTO PCONSOLE
IF ERRORLEVEL 48 GOTO DRIVE
GOTO DRIVE

:PCONSOLE
     CLS
     PCONSOLE
     GOTO DRIVE

:ENDCAP
     CLS
     ENDCAP
     ECHO..... Begin local printing........
     ECHO.
     PAUSE
     GOTO DRIVE

:GRAPHICS
     CLS
     ECHO .... Graphics Printing takes longer, 30 - 60 seconds.
     ECHO.
     CAPTURE J=%ROOM% TI=30
     PAUSE
     GOTO DRIVE

REM ;                              BEGIN  DOS

:DOS
     CLS
     TYPE X:DOS.TXT

GETNUM
IF ERRORLEVEL 57 GOTO DRIVE
```

```
IF ERRORLEVEL 56 GOTO EXITTOC
IF ERRORLEVEL 55 GOTO EDIT
IF ERRORLEVEL 54 GOTO B14
IF ERRORLEVEL 53 GOTO B720
IF ERRORLEVEL 52 GOTO A144
IF ERRORLEVEL 51 GOTO A12
IF ERRORLEVEL 50 GOTO A720
IF ERRORLEVEL 49 GOTO A360
IF ERRORLEVEL 48 GOTO DRIVE
GOTO DRIVE


REM :  Formatting on a variety of computers requires numerous
REM :  format options.  On most computers the 3.5 drive is B: but
REM :  on some it is A:.

:A360
 .  CLS
    IF %ROOM%==AD6 GOTO 360
    IF %ROOM%==122 GOTO 360
    IF %ROOM%==127 GOTO 360
    FORMAT A: /N:9  /T:40 /V
    GOTO DRIVE

:360
    FORMAT A: /V
    GOTO DRIVE

:A720
    CLS
    FORMAT A: /T:80 /N:9 /V
    GOTO DRIVE

:A12
    CLS
    FORMAT A: /F:1.2 /V
    GOTO DRIVE

:A144
    CLS
    FORMAT A:  /V
    GOTO DRIVE

:B720
    CLS
    FORMAT B: /T:80 /N:9 /V
    GOTO DRIVE
:B14
    CLS
    FORMAT B:
    GOTO DRIVE
```

```
REM :  Students have access to WordPerfect Office editor.

:EDIT
    CLS
    %DRIVE%
    ED
    H:
    GOTO DRIVE


:===============================================================
:=                       THE END
:===============================================================
:EXIT
    cls
    f:logout  > nul
    cls

:PMMSG
    CLS
    ECHO    YOU MUST BE IN ROOM 123 TO RUN PAGEMAKER.
    PAUSE
    CLS
    GOTO DRIVE

:EXITTOC
    CLS
    ECHO.
    ECHO    You are able to run DOS commands and print.
    ECHO.
    ECHO    When finished please enter  AD
    ECHO    to return to the menu.
    ECHO.
    PAUSE
    CLS
    %DRIVE%
    PROMPT  Enter 'H: enter key  then AD'  to return to the
            menu.$_$P$G
```

Examples of
Text File Menus

```
           W E L C O M E   T O   T H E   N E T W O R K


***********  Place your data disk in the drive ***********


     Enter a "1" if you are using disk drive   A:


     Enter a "2" if you are using disk drive   B:


     Enter any other number to EXIT the network.




 >>>>>>>>  Report any problems to Brad @ 2481 <<<<<<<
 ........                        or Jay  @ 2363 .......




                    MAIN  MENU


          1.  Word Processing
          2.  Spreadsheets
          3.  Data Bases

          4.  Accounting
          5.  Computer Science
          6.  Keyboarding

          7.  Miscellaneous
          8.  Network Utilities  ====> Select for
              graphics
          9.  DOS  printing

          0.  EXIT

      Enter a number for your selection:


              ----->
```

```
W O R D   P R O C E S S I N G
        MENU


1.  WordPerfect  5.1

2.  MS-Word

3.  Works

4.  WordStar 4

5.  WordStar 6.0

0.  EXIT


Enter your selection

------>
```

```
S P R E A D S H E E T S
        MENU


1.  Lotus 2.2

2.  Pgraph

3.  Works

4.  Allways

0.  EXIT


Enter your selection


------>
```

```
D A T A   B A S E
     MENU


1.  dBASE IV  (Not Available)

2.  dBASE III

3.  dBASE IV  Educational Version

4.  dBASE IV Educational Version:
    Lois Davis Class


0.  EXIT
```

Enter your selection

```
        ----->
```


```
D A T A   B A S E
     MENU


1.  dBASE IV  (Not Available)

2.  dBASE III

3.  dBASE IV  Educational Version



0.  EXIT
```

Enter your selection

```
        ----->
```

```
A C C O U N T I N G
        MENU


1.  ATB

2.  CBPI

3.  General Ledger Applications

4.  PeachTree

5.  Sounds Abound

6.  Outfitters Electronics

0.  EXIT


Enter your selection

----->




K E Y B O R D I N G
        MENU


1.  MicroKey Word

2.  Microcomputer Keyboarding




0.  EXIT

Enter your selection

----->
```

```
M I S C E L L A N E O U S
        MENU

1.  Microcalc

2.  Enable
3.  TKSolver

4.  Minitab
5.  PageMaker

6.  German
7.  MPP

8.  Kermit
9.  Enable 4.5  Demo Version

0.  EXIT

 Enter your selection

   ------->


M I C R O C A L C
        MENU


  1.  A

  2.  B

  3.  C


  0.  EXIT


 Enter your selection

   ----->
```

```
             N E T W O R K   U T I L I T I E S
                          MENU


              1.  Pconsole

              2.  Start Local Printing

              3.  Start Graphics Printing


              0.  EXIT

              Enter your selection

              ----->


                      D O S
                       MENU


              1.   Format A:   360KB
              2.   Format A:   720KB
              3.   Format A:   1.2MB
              4.   Format A:   1.44MB

              5.   Format B:   720KB
              6.   Format B:   1.4MB

              7.   Editor
              8.   Exit to floppy drive.

              0.   EXIT


              Enter your selection

              ----->
```

GETNUM.COM

This utility is used throughout the DOS batch file to take a user's selection and then branch to the address and execute an application. The source of this program is the public domain. Use the DOS Debugger utility to create GETNUM.COM. The following lines are entered after the debug session is started. You should refer to a DOS manual for the use of Debugger.

```
E 100 B4 00 CD 16 3C 30 72 F8 3C 39 77 F4 B4 4C CD 21
N GETNUM.COM
RCX
10
```

IF ERRORLEVEL in DOS accepts only decimal values and Debug accepts only hexidecimal. GETNUM.COM accepts only a value between 0 and 9. When any other value is entered, it rejects it and waits for a correct value. The following table shows the correspondence of GETNUM.COM, ERRORLEVEL, and debug.

Digit	Decimal	Hex
0	48	30
1	49	31
2	50	32
3	51	33
4	52	34
5	53	35
6	54	36
7	55	37
8	56	38
9	57	39

The Capture Utility

CAPTURE directs output to a network print queue. Usually CAPTURE redirects print requests to the LPT1 port, but also it can redirect requests to LPT2 or LPT3. Print requests can be anything from DOS print screens to files created in applications such as WordPerfect or Lotus. The CAPTURE command must be configured depending on whether the output is text or graphic. The following information illustrates the variety of CAPTURE options. The options are followed with a letter in parentheses which can be used.

The general command is CAPTURE [options]

Show (SH) displays the current options. This parameter should not be used with any other parameters.

Timeout (TI) sets the amount of time in seconds that output waits before it is sent to the print queue. Graphics files that take up to several minutes to compose require more time than text files. For example, a Lotus graph might require TI=45. The TI should be increased if the output comes out on more than one page. The default timeout is TI=0, which indicates that timeout is disabled.

NoTabs (NT) instructs the printer to leave tabs or printer formatting to the application.

Tabs (T) sets the number of spaces between tabs. The limits are from 0 to 18 spaces. Most applications perform this function so the preferred option is NT.

NoAutoendcap (NA) prevents output from being sent to the print queue when an application is started or exited. The default is AUTOENDCAP enabled.

Autoendcap (A) closes the output file and sends it to the print queue when starting or exiting an application.

Keep (K) has the file server keeping the print files in case the workstation loses its connection. If a connection is lost during the CAPTURE process and before the printing is finished, the file server discards the print request.

NoFormFeed (NFF) has CAPTURE not send form feeds to the print queue.

FormFeed (FF) has CAPTURE send a form feed to the print queue. This is the default.

NoBanner (NB) suppresses the printing of a banner page. The default is to print a banner page.

Name (NAM) specifies the user name on the banner page. The default is the login name.

Banner (B) specifies a text string up to 12 characters to appear on the banner page.

Create (CR) indicates the directory path and name of the file to send the output. Just CR redirects the printing to the file in the default directory.

Form (F) indicates the form on which the output is designed to go. Forms are created with PRINTDEF. The form can be specified by number or name.

Job (J) indicates the job configuration that has been created using PRINTCON.

Copies (C) indicates the number of copies up to 255.

NoNotify (NNOTI) will not notify the user about the status of the printing. This is the default.

Notify (NOTI) notifies the user submitting the printout when it is complete.

Local (L) indicates the local printer port, such as LPT1. The default is LPT1. Up to three printer ports can be selected at the same time.

Queue (Q) indicates the print queue.

Server (S) indicates the file server that has the print queue to be used. The default is the default server.

Windows Initialization Files

In this example Windows files are in the user's home directory on the file server. After the installation of Windows and the applications, the files are flagged RO so that the user cannot change the settings. Where practical, the settings that are specific to running Windows on a network have been set in boldface and are followed by "*" and a comment. The "*" and comments have been added to the files.

WIN.INI

The WIN.INI file is organized into sections that contain related statements for configuring the workstation's hardware and software. This file is updated when hardware or software is changed. When the network manager or user makes changes, this file must be flagged to RW to make the changes permanent and then flagged back to RO so they cannot be altered.

```
[windows]
spooler=yes
load=nwpopup.exe            * Pops up a dialogue box for NetWare SEND
run=                          messages.
Beep=yes
NullPort=None
BorderWidth=3
CursorBlinkRate=530
DoubleClickSpeed=452
Programs=com exe bat pif
Documents=
DeviceNotSelectedTimeout=15
TransmissionRetryTimeout=45
KeyboardDelay=2
KeyboardSpeed=31
```

```
ScreenSaveActive=0
ScreenSaveTimeOut=120
device=HP LaserJet IIISi,hppcl5a,LPT1.DOS    * This LaserJet IIISi
                                               is a network printer
                                               and performs best if
                                               it prints directly
                                               to the LPT1 port and
                                               does not use Windows
                                               Print Manager.

[Desktop]
Pattern=(None)
Wallpaper=(None)
GridGranularity=0

[Extensions]
cal=calendar.exe ^.cal
crd=cardfile.exe ^.crd
trm=terminal.exe ^.trm
txt=notepad.exe ^.txt
ini=notepad.exe ^.ini
pcx=pbrush.exe ^.pcx
bmp=pbrush.exe ^.bmp
wri=write.exe ^.wri
rec=recorder.exe ^.rec
hlp=winhelp.exe ^.hlp
doc=S:\WINWORD\winword.exe ^.doc    * Notice that Excel and Word
dot=S:\WINWORD\winword.exe ^.dot      are set to look at drive
rtf=S:\WINWORD\winword.exe ^.rtf      S:.  The drive settings
xla=S:\WINEXCEL\EXCEL.EXE ^.xla       must be planned when an
xlb=S:\WINEXCEL\EXCEL.EXE ^.xlb       application is installed.
xlc=S:\WINEXCEL\EXCEL.EXE ^.xlc
xll=S:\WINEXCEL\EXCEL.EXE ^.xll
xlm=S:\WINEXCEL\EXCEL.EXE ^.xlm
xls=S:\WINEXCEL\EXCEL.EXE ^.xls
xlt=S:\WINEXCEL\EXCEL.EXE ^.xlt
xlw=S:\WINEXCEL\EXCEL.EXE ^.xlw

[intl]
sLanguage=enu
sCountry=United States
iCountry=1
iDate=0
iTime=0
iTLZero=0
iCurrency=0
iCurrDigits=2
iNegCurr=0
iLzero=1
```

```
iDigits=2
iMeasure=1
s1159=AM
s2359=PM
sCurrency=$
sThousand=,
sDecimal=.
sDate=/
sTime=:
sList=,
sShortDate=M/d/yy
sLongDate=dddd, MMMM dd, yyyy

[ports]
; A line with [filename].PRN followed by an equal sign causes
; [filename] to appear in the Control Panel's Printer Configuration dialogue
; box. A printer connected to [filename] directs its output into this file.
LPT1:=
LPT2:=
LPT3:=
COM1:=9600,n,8,1,x
COM2:=9600,n,8,1,x
COM3:=9600,n,8,1,x
COM4:=9600,n,8,1,x
EPT:=
FILE:=
LPT1.DOS=                    *  While these are not set, it is
LPT2.DOS=                       important to be aware of them and
                                how they function.
[FontSubstitutes]
Helv=MS Sans Serif
Tms Rmn=MS Serif
Times=Times New Roman
Helvetica=Arial

[TrueType]

[Sounds]
SystemDefault=ding.wav, Default Beep
SystemExclamation=chord.wav, Exclamation
SystemStart=tada.wav, Windows Start
SystemExit=chimes.wav, Windows Exit
SystemHand=chord.wav, Critical Stop
SystemQuestion=chord.wav, Question
SystemAsterisk=chord.wav, Asterisk

[mci extensions]
wav=waveaudio
mid=sequencer
rmi=sequencer
```

```
[Compatibility]
NOTSHELL=0x0001
WPWINFIL=0x0006
CCMAIL=0x0008
AMIPRO=0x0010
REM=0x8022
PIXIE=0x0040
CP=0x0040
JW=0x42080
TME=0x0100
VB=0x0200
WIN2WRS=0x1210
PACKRAT=0x0800
VISION=0x0040
MGOURIER=0x0800
_BNOTES=0x24000
MILESV3=0x1000
PM4=0x2000
DESIGNER=0x2000
PLANNER=0x2000
DRAW=0x2000
WINSIM=0x2000
CHARISMA=0x2000
PR2=0x2000
PLUS=0x1000
ED=0x00010000
APORIA=0x0100
EXCEL=0x1000
GUIDE=0x1000
NETSET2=0x0100
W4GL=0x4000
W4GLR=0x4000
TURBOTAX=0x00080000
```

```
[Microsoft Word 2.0]                  * This has not been bolded
HPDSKJET=+1                             but notice the reference
AUTOSAVE-path=H:\WINWORD                to H: and S:.
INI-path=H:\WINWORD
programdir=S:\WINWORD\
DOC-path=H:\WINWORD
Spelling 1033,0=S:\WINWORD\SPELL.DLL,S:\WINWORD\SP_AM.LEX
Hyphenate
1033,0=S:\WINWORD\HYPH.DLL,S:\WINWORD\HY_AM.LEX,S:\WINWORD\SP_AM.
LEX
Thesaurus 1033,0=S:\WINWORD\THES.DLL,S:\WINWORD\TH_AM.LEX
Grammar 1033,0=S:\WINWORD\GRAMMAR.DLL,S:\WINWORD\GR_AM.LEX
DOT-path=H:\WINWORD
```

```
[fonts]
Arial (TrueType)=ARIAL.FOT
Arial Bold (TrueType)=ARIALBD.FOT
Arial Bold Italic (TrueType)=ARIALBI.FOT
Arial Italic (TrueType)=ARIALI.FOT
Courier New (TrueType)=COUR.FOT
Courier New Bold (TrueType)=COURBD.FOT
Courier New Italic (TrueType)=COURI.FOT
Times New Roman (TrueType)=TIMES.FOT
Times New Roman Bold (TrueType)=TIMESBD.FOT
Times New Roman Bold Italic (TrueType)=TIMESBI.FOT
Times New Roman Italic (TrueType)=TIMESI.FOT
Courier New Bold Italic (TrueType)=COURBI.FOT
WingDings (TrueType)=WINGDING.FOT
MS Sans Serif 8,10,12,14,18,24 (VGA res)=SSERIFE.FON
Courier 10,12,15 (VGA res)=COURE.FON
MS Serif 8,10,12,14,18,24 (VGA res)=SERIFE.FON
Symbol 8,10,12,14,18,24 (VGA res)=SYMBOLE.FON
Roman (Plotter)=ROMAN.FON
Script (Plotter)=SCRIPT.FON
Modern (Plotter)=MODERN.FON
Small Fonts (VGA res)=SMALLE.FON
Symbol (TrueType)=SYMBOL.FOT
Fences (TrueType)=FENCES.FOT
MT Extra (TrueType)=MTEXTRA.FOT
MS LineDraw (All res)=WINLD.FON


[embedding]
SoundRec=Sound,Sound,SoundRec.exe,picture
Package=Package,Package,packager.exe,picture
PBrush=Paintbrush Picture,Paintbrush Picture,pbrush.exe,picture
WordDocument=Word Document,Word
Document,S:\WINWORD\winword.exe,picture
MSDraw=Microsoft Drawing,Microsoft
Drawing,S:\WINWORD\msdraw\msdraw.exe,picture
MSGraph=Microsoft Graph,Microsoft
Graph,S:\WINWORD\msgraph\graph.exe,picture
Equation=Equation,Equation,S:\WINWORD\equation\eqnedit.exe,picture
WordArt=MS WordArt,MS
WordArt,S:\WINWORD\wordart\wordart.exe,picture
ExcelMacrosheet=Microsoft Excel Macrosheet,Microsoft Excel
Macrosheet,S:\WINEXCEL\EXCEL.EXE,picture
ExcelWorksheet=Microsoft Excel Worksheet,Microsoft Excel
Worksheet,S:\WINEXCEL\EXCEL.EXE,picture
ExcelChart=Microsoft Excel Chart,Microsoft Excel
Chart,S:\WINEXCEL\EXCEL.EXE,picture
```

```
[PrinterPorts]
HP LaserJet IIISi=hppcl5a,LPT1.DOS,15,45     * Network printers set
                                               to LPT1.DOS.
[devices]
HP LaserJet IIISi=hppcl5a,LPT1.DOS

[MSWord Editable Sections]
DCAConv=yes
TextLytConv=yes
PCWordConv=yes
MacWordConv=yes
PCWorksConv=yes

[DCAConv]
AbsLineSpacing=no
StrikeThrough='-'
Tab=DecimalTab
TranslateBeta=German
Variant=DW42

[TextLytConv]
CharMaps=a,a
Width=80
PointSize=12

[PCWordConv]
ConvertMerge=yes
MirrorOriginal=no
NewSectForHdrFtr=yes
PCWordLayout=yes
StyleDialog=yes
TabsInHangInd=yes

[MacWordConv]
ConvertMerge=yes
FontDialog=yes
RetainInclude=yes

[PCWorksConv]

                                  * The following lines have many
                                    references to network drives.

[MSWord Text Converters]
DOS Text with Layout=DOS Text with Layout,
S:\WINWORD\TXTWLYT.CNV, asc
Text with Layout=Text with Layout, S:\WINWORD\TXTWLYT.CNV, ans
WrdPrfctDOS50=WordPerfect 5.0, S:\WINWORD\WPFT5.CNV, doc
WrdPrfctDOS=WordPerfect 5.1, S:\WINWORD\WPFT5.CNV, doc
```

```
MSWordWin=Word for Windows 1, S:\WINWORD\WORDWIN1.CNV, doc
MSWordDos=Word for DOS, S:\WINWORD\WORDDOS.CNV, doc
MSWordMac4=Word for Macintosh 4.0, S:\WINWORD\WORDMAC.CNV, mcw
MSWordMac=Word for Macintosh 5.0, S:\WINWORD\WORDMAC.CNV, mcw
RFTDCA=RFT-DCA, S:\WINWORD\RFTDCA.CNV, rft
MSBiff=Excel Worksheet, S:\WINWORD\XLBIFF.CNV, xls
ATdBase=Ashton-Tate dBASE, S:\WINWORD\DBASE.CNV, dbf
Lotus123=Lotus 1-2-3, S:\WINWORD\LOTUS123.CNV, wk1 wk3
WordStar 5.5=WordStar 5.5, S:\WINWORD\WORDSTAR.CNV, doc
WordStar 5.0=WordStar 5.0, S:\WINWORD\WORDSTAR.CNV, doc
WordStar 4.0=WordStar 4.0, S:\WINWORD\WORDSTAR.CNV, doc
WordStar 3.45=WordStar 3.45, S:\WINWORD\WORDSTAR.CNV, doc
WordStar 3.3=WordStar 3.3, S:\WINWORD\WORDSTAR.CNV, doc
Windows Write=Windows Write, S:\WINWORD\WRITWIN.CNV, wri

[MS Graphic Import Filters]
Windows Metafile(.WMF)=S:\WINWORD\GRPHFLT\wmfimp.flt,WMF
DrawPerfect(.WPG)=S:\WINWORD\grphflt\wpgimp.flt,WPG
Micrografx Designer/Draw(.DRW)=S:\WINWORD\grphflt\drwimp.flt,DRW
AutoCAD Format 2-D(.DXF)=S:\WINWORD\grphflt\dxfimp.flt,DXF
HP Graphic Language(.HGL)=S:\WINWORD\grphflt\hpglimp.flt,HGL
Computer Graphics
Metafile(.CGM)=S:\WINWORD\grphflt\cgmimp.flt,CGM
Encapsulated Postscript(.EPS)=S:\WINWORD\grphflt\epsimp.flt,EPS
Tagged Image Format(.TIF)=S:\WINWORD\grphflt\tiffimp.flt,TIF
PC Paintbrush(.PCX)=S:\WINWORD\grphflt\pcximp.flt,PCX
Lotus 1-2-3 Graphics(.PIC)=S:\WINWORD\grphflt\lotusimp.flt,PIC
AutoCAD Plot File(.PLT)=S:\WINWORD\grphflt\adimport.flt,PLT

[MS Graphic Export Filters]
DrawPerfect(.WPG)=S:\WINWORD\grphflt\wpgexp.flt,WPG

[HPPCL5A,LPT1]
FontSummary=H:\WINDOWS\FS5LPT1.PCL
prtcaps2=31

[MS Proofing Tools]
Spelling 1033,0=H:\WINDOWS\MSAPPS\PROOF\MSSPELL.DLL,H:\WINDOWS\MSAPPS\PROO
F\MSSP_AM.LEX

[spooler]
window=88 88 548 320

[HP LaserJet IIISi]
paper=1
prtindex=18
prtcaps=-4216
paperind=1
prtcaps2=31
```

SYSTEM.INI

The SYSTEM.INI file is created when Windows is installed and contains global system information that Windows uses when it starts.

```
[boot]
shell=progman.exe
mouse.drv=lmouse.drv
network.drv=netware.drv          * Netware.drv is added to this
language.dll=                      during installation.
sound.drv=mmsound.drv
comm.drv=comm.drv
keyboard.drv=keyboard.drv
system.drv=system.drv
386grabber=vga.3gr
oemfonts.fon=vgaoem.fon
286grabber=vgacolor.2gr
fixedfon.fon=vgafix.fon
fonts.fon=vgasys.fon
display.drv=vga.drv
drivers=mmsystem.dll

[keyboard]
subtype=
type=4
keyboard.dll=
oemansi.bin=

[boot.description]
keyboard.typ=Enhanced 101 or 102 key US and Non US keyboards
mouse.drv=Logitech
network.drv=Novell NetWare (shell versions 3.21 and above)
language.dll=English (American)
system.drv=MS-DOS System
codepage=437
woafont.fon=English (437)
aspect=100,96,96
display.drv=VGA

[386Enh]
32BitDiskAccess=OFF
device=*int13
device=*wdctrl
mouse=lvmd.386
OverlappedIO=off
network=*vnetbios,vnetware.386,vipx.386     * Used to support
                                              virtual IPX
                                              sessions.

ebios=*ebios
woafont=dosapp.fon
display=*vddvga
```

```
EGA80WOA.FON=EGA80WOA.FON
EGA40WOA.FON=EGA40WOA.FON
CGA80WOA.FON=CGA80WOA.FON
CGA40WOA.FON=CGA40WOA.FON
keyboard=*vkd
device=vtdapi.386
device=*vpicd
device=*vtd
device=*reboot
device=*vdmad
device=*vsd
device=*v86mmgr
device=*pageswap
device=*dosmgr
device=*vmpoll
device=*wshell
device=*BLOCKDEV
device=*PAGEFILE
device=*vfd
device=*parity
device=*biosxlat
device=*vcd
device=*vmcpd
device=*combuff
device=*cdpscsi
local=CON
FileSysChange=off
PagingFile=C:\WIN386.SWP
MaxPagingFileSize=12288

[standard]

[NonWindowsApp]
localtsrs=dosedit,ced
CommandEnvSize=1024

[mci]
WaveAudio=mciwave.drv
Sequencer=mciseq.drv
CDAudio=mcicda.drv

[drivers]
timer=timer.drv
midimapper=midimap.drv
[LogiMouse]
Type=Serial
Model=C_Series
Port=1
DragLock=None
```

PROGRAM.INI

The PROGMAN.INI file has entries that describe what should appear when Program Manager is run.

```
[Settings]
Window=68 48 580 384 1
display.drv=vga.drv
Order=1 5 4 2 3 6
SaveSettings=0
```

*   This will not save settings on exit.

*   The group information for each user is in the user's home directory.

```
[Groups]
Group1=H:\WINDOWS\MAIN.GRP
Group2=H:\WINDOWS\ACCESSOR.GRP
Group3=H:\WINDOWS\GAMES.GRP
Group4=H:\WINDOWS\APPLICAT.GRP
Group6=H:\WINDOWS\WORDPROC.GRP
Group5=H:\WINDOWS\MICROSOF.GRP
```

*   An important section can be added for network system administration. The [restrictions] can be added which provides additional controls over the Windows environment. The following section can have these entries:

```
[Restrictions]
NoRun=
NoClose=
NoSaveSettings=
NoFileMenu=
EditLevel=
```

Notes on these entries.

NoRun=   1 disables the Run command from the File menu. Applications can only be run by selecting an icon.

NoClose=   1 disables the Exit Windows command on the File menu. Users are not able to exit Windows even with the ALT-F4.

NoSaveSettings= 1 disables the ability to change settings.

NoFileMenu=   1 removes the File menu from Program Manager.
               Applications can only be started with icons.
               Users can exit Windows.

EditLevel=n   Sets restrictions for modifying Program Manager.
               The value 0 allows the user to modify anything.
               This is the default. Values 1, 2, 3, and 4 are
               each more restrictive in what the user can modify.

To change restrictions either delete the entry or use a value of
zero "0".

CONTROL.INI

The CONTROL.INI file specifies options set by selecting icons. The settings are not informative and are not presented.

WINFILE.INI

The WINFILE.INI specifies the options that can be set by choosing menu commands in File Manager.

[Settings]
Window=0,0,640,480, , ,1
dir1=0,0,515,294,-1,-1,1,0,201,1905,257,H:\WINDOWS*.*

Window=   Sets the size and position of the window and whether it
is maximized when opened.

dir1=   The current directory setting.

Index